Philosophy is a Human Mind Painting

Allen Schery

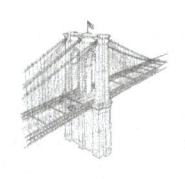

BROOKLYN BRIDGE BOOKS

Copyright © 2025 by Allen Schery

All rights reserved.

No portion of this book may be reproduced in any form without written permission from the publisher or author, except as permitted by U.S. copyright law.

Contents

Introduction	VI
1. The Canvas Awakens – From Survival to Sense-Making	1
2. The Sedentary Brush: Codification and the Birth of Philosophy	15
3. The Imperfect Transmission: Cultural Drift and the Fragmentation of Truth	26
4. The Situated and Distributed Canvas – Expanding the Boundaries of Mind Painting	42
5. The Divine Canvas: Medieval Philosophy and the Grand Design	55
6. The Humanist Bridge and Rationalist Foundations	70
7. The Enlightenment Social Revolution	86
8. The Logic and Language Canvas – Painting Reality Through Structure and Communication	101
9. The American Palette – Pragmatism and the Utility of Thought	121

10.	Beyond Homo Sapiens – Non-Human and Artificial Mind Paintings	148
11.	The Mind's Inner Canvas – Psychology, Neuroscience, and the Biased Brush	173
12.	Society's Canvas – Politics, Ideology, and the Power of Shared Paintings	221
13.	Contemporary Challenges and Digital Transformations	239
14.	Ecologies, Materiality, and the Cognitive Environment – The Contextual Canvas of Mind Painting	257
15.	The Embodied Canvas: Feeling, Living, and Being in the World	284
16.	Divergent Canvases: Eastern Philosophy and Alternative Orders	310
17.	The Scientific Canvas: Paradigms, Progress, and the Human Hand of Inquiry	332
18.	Shattered Frames and Digital Hues	362
19.	Situated and Distributed Cognition – Expanding the Mind Painting Framework	374
20.	Painting for Adaptive Futures	386
About the Author		389
Bibliography		395
Index		508

Endnotes

Introduction

Humans are natural storytellers, creators of meaning who have always sought to shape their experience into coherent narratives—what this book calls "mind paintings." This fundamental characteristic of human consciousness reflects not merely cultural preference but deep neurobiological architecture evolved over hundreds of thousands of years. Contemporary neuroscience reveals that our brains are literally wired for narrative construction: when we encounter stories, neural coupling occurs between storyteller and listener, creating synchronized brain activity across regions far beyond basic language processing areas. The default mode network—our brain's resting state—appears inherently structured for narrative thinking, suggesting that storytelling represents not an optional cultural embellishment but a core feature of human consciousness itself.

Throughout recorded history and across all known cultures, every human being has been born into stories—cosmologies, origin myths, social narratives, family histories, and cultural frameworks that provide templates for understanding reality, identity, and possibility. These inherited narratives exist in countless permutations and combinations, yet all remain fundamentally constrained and enabled by the evolutionary architecture of the human neo-cortex. From the earliest cave paintings at Lascaux and Altamira to contemporary digital media platforms, these mind paintings serve the primal human need to impose meaningful order on the apparent chaos of experience. They shape individual and collective identities, organize social structures, establish moral frameworks, and fundamentally influence our perceptions of truth, beauty, justice, and possibility.

Yet these meaning-making constructions are simultaneously robust and fragile, enduring and dynamic. They drift across generations through inevitable processes of cultural transmission and reinterpretation, fracture under the pressure of new experiences and challenges, adapt creatively to changing circumstances, and sometimes collapse entirely when confronted with overwhelming contradictions or environmental pressures. The archaeological record provides abundant evidence of civilizations whose entire worldviews disappeared, leaving only material traces of once-vibrant meaning systems that sustained millions of lives across centuries.

Before proceeding with this analysis, it is crucial to address the critical questions and potential objections that skeptics and scholars from multiple disciplines might legitimately raise. This book neither advocates naive cultural relativism—the position that all cultural constructions are equally valid or arbitrary—nor dismisses the profound and persistent human search for truth, knowledge, and understanding. It does not reduce rich cultural phenomena and sophisticated cognitive processes to mere illusions, oversimplified metaphors, or crude materialist determinism. Rather, it offers a nuanced, theoretically sophisticated framework grounded in rigorous interdisciplinary scholarship that acknowledges both the remarkable creative power and the biological, material, and social constraints inherent in human thought processes.

This framework recognizes the extraordinary complexity and diversity of cultural realities across human societies while identifying deep cognitive patterns, universal constraints, and shared evolutionary inheritances that bind humanity together across time, geography, and cultural difference. It seeks to avoid both the Scylla of reductive scientism—which would explain away cultural meaning as mere evolutionary byproduct—and the Charybdis of postmodern relativism—which would render impossible any systematic understanding of human meaning-making processes.

This work consciously embraces intellectual ambiguity and epistemological uncertainty not as failures of analysis or obstacles to knowledge but as vital sources of cognitive dynamism and cultural transformation. The recognition that human knowledge systems are provisional, contextual, and subject to continuous revision does not undermine their importance or effectiveness but rather illuminates the remarkable adaptive flexibility that has enabled human societies to survive and flourish across wildly diverse environmental and historical circumstances.

The "mind painting" metaphor is offered as an honest, empirically grounded, and theoretically robust analytical tool for understanding how humans construct, transmit, contest, and continuously revise systems of meaning—always operating within material, ecological, social, and cognitive constraints that shape but do not determine outcomes. Engaging seriously with this framework invites readers to become not passive recipients of inherited cultural narratives but active, reflective participants in the ongoing, often messy, sometimes conflicted, but absolutely necessary collective enterprise of making sense of human existence in an complex and frequently unpredictable world.

At the theoretical core of this interdisciplinary inquiry lies what this book terms the "Primate Principle"—the fundamental cognitive constraints and capacities imposed by human evolutionary history and the specific architecture of the human neo-cortex, extensively analyzed in my previous work of the same title. This principle reveals that human cognition represents a delicate evolutionary balancing act: we have evolved sophisticated pattern-recognition abilities and meaning-making capacities that enable us to build adaptive cultural frameworks for survival and flourishing (what might playfully be termed "banana acquisition" in reference to our fundamental drive to secure resources and reproductive success), yet our neurobiological limitations, cultural complexities, and environmental uncertainties ensure that these cognitive and cultural patterns remain necessarily provisional, contextual, and subject to continuous evolution through processes of "cultural drift" and historical reinterpretation.

The Primate Principle does not reduce human cultural achievement to simple biological determinism but rather illuminates the dynamic dialectical relationship between evolutionary constraints and cultural creativity. Our brains evolved specific capacities—for social cooperation, pattern recognition, temporal projection, symbolic thinking, and narrative construction—that enable the creation of sophisticated cultural systems. However, these same evolutionary inheritances also impose limits: cognitive biases, attentional constraints, memory limitations, and social psychological tendencies that influence how cultural systems develop, transmit, and transform across time and space.

This book represents a systematic attempt to integrate insights from anthropology, evolutionary biology, neuroscience, cognitive psychology, philosophy, history, sociology, and cultural studies into a comprehensive understanding of the mind painting process that characterizes human consciousness and culture. From the earliest evidence of human symbolic behavior in African archaeological sites through the flowering of complex philosophical and religious systems in ancient civilizations and into today's globally interconnected digital age, it traces how meaning is continuously produced, challenged, defended, modified, and sometimes abandoned by human communities navigating the permanent tension between inherited tradition and adaptive innovation.

This endeavor represents more than a purely descriptive academic project. It constitutes a call for enhanced metacognitive engagement—an invitation for readers to recognize, critically examine, and consciously participate in shaping the narratives they inherit, inhabit, and create. This invitation is grounded not in relativistic indifference to truth or uncritical celebration of diversity but in pragmatic, ethically informed responsibility to navigate cultural complexity with intellectual honesty, creative flexibility, and moral courage.

The philosophical position developed here avoids both crude objectivism—which would claim access to culture-independent truth—and self-defeating relativism—which would render impossible any critical evaluation of cultural claims. Instead, it articulates what might be termed "critical pragmatism": the position that while human knowledge is always culturally situated and historically contingent, some cultural frameworks prove more adaptive, more explanatorily powerful, more ethically defensible, or more practically effective than others in specific contexts for particular purposes.

The book's structure unfolds across four major parts, each addressing different dimensions of human meaning-making while maintaining focus on the central theme of mind painting as the fundamental process through which humans create, maintain, and transform cultural reality. Part One examines the evolutionary foundations of human sense-making, tracing the deep prehistorical origins of symbolic cognition and cultural transmission. Part Two explores major historical intellectual traditions—philosophical, religious, and scientific—as elaborate cultural mind paintings that emerged from specific social and material conditions while addressing universal human concerns about reality, morality, and meaning.

Part Three investigates the cognitive, psychological, and social mechanisms that enable and constrain human meaning-making, drawing on contemporary research in neuroscience, psychology, and sociology to illuminate how mind paintings operate at individual and collective levels. Part Four addresses contemporary global challenges and opportunities, including the implications of digital technology, ecological crisis, cultural globalization, artificial intelligence, and emerging forms of distributed cognition for human meaning-making processes.

Throughout, the analysis is supplemented by engagement with cutting-edge research in situated cognition, extended mind theory, enactive approaches to cognition, cross-species intelligence studies, ecological psychology, reflexive methodology, and practical applications of mind painting theory to education, therapy, organizational development, and social change initiatives.

This introduction serves as both welcome and warning: welcome to readers prepared to engage intellectually and emotionally with challenging questions about the nature of human consciousness, culture, and knowledge; warning that this journey requires abandoning simple answers and comfortable certainties in favor of nuanced thinking about complex phenomena that resist easy categorization or definitive resolution.

The invitation extended here is to embrace what might be called "the infinite canvas" of mind painting—the recognition that human meaning-making represents an ongoing, open-ended, creative process with no final completion or ultimate destination. This perspective does not lead to despair or nihilism but rather to appreciation of the remarkable human capacity for cultural creativity, adaptation, and moral growth within the constraints and possibilities provided by our evolutionary inheritance and material circumstances.

Let us begin this interdisciplinary journey of mind analysis with intellectual humility, methodological rigor, and openness to the possibility that understanding human meaning-making processes more clearly might contribute to more thoughtful, ethical, and effective participation in the collective human project of creating meaning, fostering cooperation, and navigating the challenges of existence in an uncertain but wonder-filled universe.

Chapter One
The Canvas Awakens – From Survival to Sense-Making

Humanity's cognitive and cultural story is rooted in the deep timetable of the hunter-gatherer epoch, spanning over 250,000 years and representing the primal soil from which all subsequent human sense-making has blossomed. This foundational era, stretching across the vast majority of human evolutionary history, was far more than a mere survivalist existence characterized by constant struggle against environmental threats. Rather, it constituted a prolonged and sophisticated crucible in which the key faculties of human cognition and symbolic culture—the earliest "mind paintings"—were systematically forged through relentless selective pressures and creative cultural adaptations. These cognitive constructs and symbolic narratives provided the essential frameworks for ordering an unpredictable and often hostile natural environment, securing social cohesion across diverse kinship networks, and transmitting accumulated knowledge across generations with remarkable fidelity and adaptive flexibility.

The neurological architecture that emerged during this extended period fundamentally shaped human consciousness in ways that continue to influence contemporary thought patterns. Archaeological evidence from sites across Africa, including Blombos Cave in South Africa and the Rift Valley sites of Kenya and Ethiopia, demonstrates that hunter-gatherer societies developed increasingly sophisticated cognitive tools for environmental navigation, social coordination, and symbolic expression. These developments were not gradual improvements on pre-existing capacities but represented qualitative leaps in cognitive organization that distinguish humans from all other species.

At the heart of this early cognitive landscape was what can aptly be described as sentinel awareness: a sharpened and sustained vigilance attuned to the minutiae of environmental variation and social dynamics. Unlike many species whose vigilance is transient, reactive, or narrowly focused on specific threat categories, early humans evolved remarkably sophisticated neurobiological architectures supporting near-constant environmental monitoring seamlessly blended with anticipatory cognition and complex social reasoning. This represents what neuroscientist Mark Whiten terms the "human socio-cognitive niche"—a unique evolutionary adaptation that allowed human groups to function as highly coordinated collective intelligence systems. It might also explain why a lack of focus is seen in human beings. Focus is important today but some 200,000 years ago it might have caused humans to be other animals' source of protein.

Neuroscientific research conducted by teams at Cambridge, Oxford, and Harvard Universities highlights the intricate interaction between subcortical limbic circuits—responsible for immediate emotional salience detection and rapid threat assessment—and the highly developed prefrontal cortex that governs executive functioning, mental simulation of future scenarios, and sophisticated social cognition involving theory of mind. This integrated network endowed humans not only with the capacity to detect present environmental threats and opportunities but, crucially, to project potential futures with remarkable accuracy, enabling anticipatory responses vital for both individual survival and complex group coordination across extended temporal horizons.

Contemporary neuroscience reveals that this sentinel awareness system operates through what researchers call "massively parallel pattern recognition," allowing the human brain to simultaneously process millions of environmental variables while maintaining focused attention on immediate tasks. Unlike artificial intelligence systems that process information sequentially, the human brain evolved to handle multiple cognitive demands simultaneously—monitoring for predators while tracking prey, maintaining social awareness while navigating terrain, and encoding spatial information while attending to immediate survival needs.

Ethnographic observations among extant hunter-gatherer peoples, meticulously documented by researchers such as Frank Marlowe among the Hadza of Tanzania and Richard Lee among the San Bushmen of southern Africa, illuminate the sophisticated nature of this distributed cognitive vigilance across social networks. Sentinel awareness emerges not as a solely individual attribute but as a socially extended enterprise involving complex information sharing protocols, collective risk assessment, and distributed decision-making processes. Observations of distant predator activity, vocal and gestural warning signals about environmental changes, and collective deliberation about resource exploitation circulate through hunting and gathering groups, effectively diffusing individual cognitive load while dramatically amplifying adaptive responses to environmental challenges.

This socialized alertness forms a shared cognitive landscape where stories, myths, and ritual enactments embed essential survival knowledge while simultaneously ritualizing and reinforcing communal engagement with both physical environment and kinship networks. The integration of practical knowledge with symbolic narrative creates what anthropologists term "thick" cultural systems—dense webs of meaning that orient individual behavior while maintaining group coherence across generations.

Spatial cognition provides perhaps the most vivid example of this cognitive-cultural integration. Among the San peoples of the Kalahari, landforms, seasonal water sources, and sacred ceremonial places are encoded not through abstract cartographic representations but as living loci intimately intertwined with ancestral presence, multigenerational social memory, and sophisticated ecological knowledge spanning centuries of accumulated observation. This distributed spatial mind painting seamlessly integrates physical geography, temporal awareness of seasonal and cyclical changes, and complex social dimensions involving territorial rights, resource sharing agreements, and ceremonial obligations. The result serves simultaneously as a cornerstone for practical environmental orientation and as the foundation for cultural identity construction and transmission.

Archaeological evidence from Aboriginal Australian sites demonstrates that such sophisticated spatial-cognitive systems can remain stable for tens of thousands of years while continuously adapting to environmental changes. The songline traditions of Aboriginal peoples, documented across the Australian continent, represent perhaps the most complex spatial memory systems ever recorded, encoding navigational information, seasonal resource availability, social obligations, and cosmological understanding within integrated oral traditions that span thousands of miles and multiple language groups.

Alongside sentinel awareness runs the foundational cognitive faculty of pattern recognition—the brain's evolved capacity to transform complex, noisy sensory inputs into meaningful, stable representations that enable prediction and behavioral adaptation. Early humans depended critically on recognizing cyclical and recurring phenomena across multiple temporal scales: animal migration patterns spanning seasons and years, plant fruiting and flowering cycles tied to climate variations, weather pattern changes signaling environmental transitions, and complex social behavioral patterns involving alliance formation, conflict resolution, and resource sharing protocols.

This pattern recognition ability extended far beyond immediate survival applications, enabling the construction of abstract symbolic frameworks that transcended immediate sensory experience. Cognitive linguists George Lakoff and Mark Johnson, drawing on decades of research in cognitive science and neurolinguistics, have demonstrated convincingly that metaphor represents not mere rhetorical ornamentation but a foundational structure of human cognition and language processing. The recognition of underlying environmental and social patterns, combined with humanity's unique capacity for metaphorical projection and analogy construction, allowed early humans to create novel conceptual associations and drive continuous innovation.

Consider, for instance, how the recognition of rotational patterns—observed in celestial movements, seasonal cycles, and mechanical operations—became extended through metaphorical thinking into abstract domains encompassing social organization (cycles of leadership), spiritual understanding (wheel of life concepts), temporal conception (cyclical versus linear time), and technological innovation (from potter's wheels to complex mechanical systems). This demonstrates the human mind's remarkable capacity to extract abstract principles from concrete experiences and apply them creatively across diverse cognitive domains.

Neuroscientific studies conducted using functional magnetic resonance imaging and related techniques highlight the central role of the prefrontal cortex, particularly areas associated with working memory and cognitive control, in enabling what researchers' term "conceptual blending"—the sophisticated capacity to integrate disparate inputs from different cognitive domains into emergent ideas and symbolic representations. This neurological substrate, significantly expanded in humans compared to our closest primate relatives, laid the biological foundation for the construction of dynamic mind paintings: fluid, continuously evolving symbolic systems that orient individuals and groups within increasingly complex landscapes of meaning, social obligation, and environmental management.

The transformative Agricultural Revolution occurring approximately 12,000 years ago marks a profound inflection point in the elaboration and institutionalization of human mind paintings. As human societies transitioned from nomadic foraging strategies to sedentary agricultural production, populations grew exponentially, social hierarchies became increasingly differentiated and formalized, and entirely new categories of ecological and social pressures emerged that demanded novel cognitive and cultural responses.

These new challenges included intensive competition for prime arable land among expanding populations, the rapid spread of infectious diseases facilitated by higher population densities and closer contact with domesticated animals, complex logistical challenges in resource management and food storage across seasonal cycles, and the unprecedented social coordination demands of managing large settled communities with specialized labor divisions and emerging class structures.

Such pressures introduced fundamentally novel socio-cognitive demands that stretched beyond the capacities of traditional hunter-gatherer social organization: articulating and enforcing multiscale governance systems capable of managing thousands rather than dozens of individuals, developing elaborate rituals and ideological frameworks to legitimize emerging social hierarchies and political authority, and constructing comprehensive codified belief systems capable of managing both mundane practical concerns and sacred ceremonial obligations within increasingly complex social environments.

Foremost among the revolutionary developments of this period was the independent invention of writing systems across multiple world regions—Mesopotamian cuneiform, Egyptian hieroglyphics, Indus Valley script, Chinese characters, and Mesoamerican glyphs—each representing a fundamental breakthrough in human cognitive technology. Writing systems accomplished something unprecedented in natural history: the complete externalization of human memory and abstract thought processes, creating durable material repositories that could preserve, systematically refine, and transmit complex ideas across generations without reliance on the biological limitations of human memory or the spatial and temporal constraints of oral tradition.

These writing technologies enabled the creation of permanent records spanning legal codes, commercial transactions, religious knowledge, historical chronicles, and ancestral genealogies, fundamentally transforming the scale and complexity of possible social organization. As media theorist Walter Ong demonstrated in his seminal analysis, the transition from orality to literacy introduced profound changes not merely in information storage capacity but in the fundamental structure of human cognition, social coordination mechanisms, and individual self-understanding processes.

Despite these revolutionary technological and social changes, human sociality retained its fundamentally tribal and hierarchical character, rooted in evolutionary adaptations shaped across hundreds of thousands of years of small-group living. Alpha figures, elder councils, and emergent political authorities continued to regulate group behavior through various mechanisms designed to maintain what might be termed cognitive harmony—a dynamic alignment of beliefs, values, normative expectations, and behavioral patterns that mitigated destructive interpersonal conflicts while solidifying communal bonds necessary for collective survival and prosperity.

However, this cognitive harmony never achieved static perfection or permanent stability. Instead, it existed in constant dialectical tension with cultural drift: the slow, often imperceptible generational modifications in belief systems, ritual practices, linguistic expressions, and customary behaviors that continuously injected adaptive dynamism into social continuity. This process represents far more than random variation or cultural "noise"—it constitutes a fundamental mechanism of cultural evolution enabling human societies to innovate and respond flexibly to changing environmental conditions, social challenges, and technological opportunities.

Cultural drift operates through multiple interrelated mechanisms documented by anthropologists and evolutionary biologists. Individual creativity and innovation introduce novel variants into cultural systems. Generational transmission inevitably involves subtle modifications as knowledge passes from experienced practitioners to novice learners. Geographic isolation led to independent cultural development as communities adapted to different local conditions. Social and environmental pressures select for cultural variants that enhance survival and reproduction while eliminating less adaptive practices.

The archaeological record provides abundant evidence for these cultural evolutionary processes. Variations in ceramic styles, lithic tool traditions, architectural forms, and burial practices among Indigenous Australian communities illustrate the creative potentials of cultural drift operating across thousands of years. Similarly, the documented divergences in dialect, ritual practice, and social organization among historically related hunter-gatherer bands demonstrate how cultural drift enables continuous cultural innovation while maintaining underlying structural continuities.

Contemporary ethnographic and archaeological evidence richly documents mind paintings as fundamentally embodied and material phenomena rather than purely abstract mental constructs. The sophisticated rock art traditions of the San peoples of southern Africa and Australian Aboriginal communities across the continent embody extraordinarily complex symbolic geographies, multigenerational mythic histories, and intricate social organizational systems encoded in durable visual media.

These artistic traditions function simultaneously as practical resource management tools, ceremonial religious artifacts, educational systems for transmitting cultural knowledge, and mnemonic devices supporting oral tradition. They represent what anthropologist Tim Ingold terms "skilled visions"—ways of seeing and knowing that integrate perceptual, cognitive, and practical dimensions of human environmental engagement.

The famous cave paintings at sites like Lascaux in France and Altamira in Spain, created by Paleolithic hunter-gatherers between 15,000 and 30,000 years ago, demonstrate the remarkable sophistication of early human symbolic systems. These artistic achievements required advanced planning, sophisticated material technology, complex social coordination, and profound aesthetic sensibility—capabilities that challenge any simple evolutionary narrative of gradual cognitive development.

Multidisciplinary scientific consensus increasingly situates these hunter-gatherer mind paintings within universal neurocognitive frameworks emergent from neo-cortical constraints and ecological adaptation pressures shared across human populations. This growing understanding challenges both cultural particularism—which would treat cultural diversity as essentially arbitrary—and crude cultural evolutionism—which would rank societies hierarchically according to supposed developmental stages.

Instead, emerging research frameworks emphasize shared cognitive architectures that enable symbolic thinking while preserving full recognition of local cultural diversity and specific historical contingency. This approach successfully bridges biological and cultural levels of analysis, rejecting both reductionist approaches that would eliminate human agency and idealist approaches that would ignore material and evolutionary constraints on cultural development.

Potential philosophical critiques of this framework require careful consideration and robust response. Critics might argue that the metaphorical framing of "mind painting" risks either complete cultural relativism—where all interpretations become equally valid—or oversimplified reductionism that reduces rich cultural phenomena to mere biological mechanisms.

However, this framework consciously embraces complexity and ambiguity while maintaining empirical grounding and analytical precision. Cultural drift is conceptualized as an adaptive evolutionary process that generates genuine innovation rather than mere random variation. Mind painting is understood as active, socially negotiated cognition involving human creativity and agency rather than passive response to environmental stimuli. Human agency is recognized as robust and consequential while acknowledging that it operates within material, social, and cognitive constraints that shape but do not determine cultural outcomes.

The approach defended here avoids both crude materialism—which would reduce cultural phenomena to simple reflections of economic or environmental conditions—and naive idealism—which would treat cultural systems as purely autonomous symbolic constructs unrelated to material conditions. Instead, it articulates a sophisticated dialectical relationship where material conditions provide necessary but not sufficient conditions for cultural development, while cultural innovations can fundamentally transform material conditions and social organization.

In sum, sentinel awareness and pattern recognition constitute the primal cognitive tools from which humanity's earliest and most foundational mind paintings arose during the hunter-gatherer epoch. These formative cognitive landscapes, shaped and refined across hundreds of millennia through intense selective pressures and creative cultural innovation, encode the enduring foundations of human symbolic life: a vivid cognitive canvas continuously enlivened by the creative and cooperative capacities that fundamentally define our species.

This chapter's synthesis of evolutionary biology, cognitive neuroscience, anthropological ethnography, and archaeological evidence establishes the essential foundation for understanding the vast array of human cultural expression—from ancient philosophical systems to contemporary scientific theories—as elaborate historical developments built upon these foundational cognitive structures. The patterns of thought established during humanity's formative hunter-gatherer period continue to influence contemporary human consciousness while enabling the cultural creativity that distinguishes human civilization from all other known phenomena in natural history.

Chapter Two
The Sedentary Brush: Codification and the Birth of Philosophy

The moment humanity chose to settle, to build rather than roam, marked not just a change in lifestyle but a profound transformation in cognition and social organization. This transition—known broadly as the neolithic revolution and anchored by agriculture, permanent dwellings, and food surplus—did more than feed bodies; it fundamentally restructured the architecture of human thought and enabled the flourishing of the human mind in ways previously unimaginable. The stability and surplus time that emerged from this new way of life, previously inconceivable in the constant mobility and immediate survival pressures of nomadic existence, afforded humanity the unprecedented luxury of sustained contemplation that extended far beyond the imperatives of daily survival. This cognitive surplus catalyzed intellectual specialization and gave birth to philosophy as a distinct pursuit of wisdom, marking one of the most significant transformations in human intellectual history.

Archaeological evidence from sites across the Fertile Crescent reveals that the Neolithic Revolution, beginning around 10,000 BCE, introduced not merely new subsistence strategies but entirely new cognitive demands and possibilities. Sedentary life required different mental faculties than nomadic existence—the ability to plan across seasons, to manage complex social hierarchies, and to coordinate labor among specialists who no longer needed to master all survival skills. This cognitive specialization created what we might term "intellectual niches," allowing certain individuals to dedicate their mental resources entirely to abstract thought, pattern analysis, and the systematic organization of knowledge.

Nomadic life had demanded intensely reactive cognition, a mental state of sentinel awareness characterized by constant environmental scanning and immediate response to shifting conditions. This may well explain why we have a lack of focus as focus could have meant death. Early humans devoted the vast majority of their cognitive resources to navigating perilous and unpredictable environments—tracking prey, avoiding predators, locating water sources, reading weather patterns, and finding temporary shelter. Every mental faculty was pressed into service for immediate survival, leaving little bandwidth for extended reflection or systematic inquiry into abstract questions. The cognitive load was distributed but constant, requiring all members of small bands to maintain broad competencies across hunting, gathering, tool-making, navigation, and social coordination.

Settled societies, however, fundamentally altered this cognitive landscape by softening the urgency of immediate survival concerns. Where dense forests once demanded constant vigilance, cultivated fields provided predictable resources; where daily scavenging had consumed mental energy, granaries offered food security; where nomadic groups had required every member to master survival skills, agricultural communities could support specialists. In these new periods of cognitive respite, a revolutionary class of thinkers emerged—not as mystics somehow detached from practical reality, but as specialists who cultivated wisdom and systematic knowledge alongside their neighbors who cultivated crops. Just as some community members developed expertise in metallurgy, pottery, or animal husbandry, others began cultivating the previously unexplored landscape of abstract ideas, ethical questions, and metaphysical inquiries.

The invention and spread of writing systems represented the first great cognitive leap in this intellectual evolution. Writing was far more than a simple recording technology; it fundamentally externalized human memory and thought processes, creating durable repositories that could preserve, refine, and transmit complex ideas across generations without reliance on fragile human memory or the spatial and temporal limitations of oral tradition. Cuneiform tablets from ancient Mesopotamia, Egyptian hieroglyphics carved in stone, and early Chinese characters inscribed on oracle bones all testify to humanity's urgent need to encode increasingly sophisticated concepts in permanent form.

The development of writing followed remarkably similar patterns across independent civilizations. Initially emerging from practical accounting systems—tracking grain stores, livestock inventories, and trade transactions—writing gradually expanded to encode laws, religious beliefs, historical records, and eventually abstract philosophical concepts. In Mesopotamia, the progression from simple token-counting systems to complex cuneiform script capable of expressing any idea demonstrates how cognitive demands drove technological innovation. The earliest writing systems evolved directly from the need to manage the complex resource flows of settled agricultural communities.

Institutions—temples, royal courts, scribal schools, and eventually specialized academies—provided the organizational structure, social legitimacy, and economic resources necessary to transform individual intellectual insights into systematic, enduring frameworks of knowledge. These institutions served as more than mere repositories of information; they created the social architecture within which sustained philosophical inquiry could flourish. The famous Library of Alexandria, the Academy of Plato, and the Lyceum of Aristotle were not simply buildings but cognitive ecosystems that fostered collaborative intellectual labor across generations of scholars.

This institutionalization and codification of thought constituted nothing less than a cultural revolution in human consciousness. It enabled the emergence of what might be termed complex "mind paintings"—intricate, multi-layered symbolic systems that could be systematically revisited, rigorously debated, logically expanded, and creatively reinterpreted across centuries. Unlike the fluid, collectively negotiated oral traditions that had characterized hunter-gatherer societies, these new philosophical frameworks were the products of sustained communal intellectual labor involving scribes who preserved texts, scholars who analyzed and commented on them, priests who interpreted their implications, and rulers who applied their insights. Each contributor added distinctive brushstrokes to an ever-evolving artwork of human understanding.

As sedentary societies grew in size and complexity, the range of goals they pursued expanded dramatically beyond basic survival needs. Where nomadic existence had focused narrowly on securing food, shelter, and physical safety, newly settled communities began pursuing increasingly abstract objectives—social cohesion across large populations, political legitimacy for complex hierarchies, and answers to existential questions about human purpose and cosmic order. These new aspirations required entirely new intellectual tools and cultural technologies.

Elaborate rituals and mythological narratives emerged to bind diverse populations into coherent communities, creating shared identities that transcended kinship ties. Legal codes like Hammurabi's famous law collection established frameworks for managing conflict and coordinating behavior among thousands of individuals who could not rely on personal relationships for social order. Cosmological and theological systems attempted to provide satisfying answers to questions that had little relevance to immediate survival but were increasingly central to the psychological and social fabric of complex civilizations: Why do we exist? What obligations do we have to others? How should society be organized? What happens after death?

The flowering of philosophy in ancient Greece provides perhaps the most vivid example of this cognitive transformation. Greek thinkers like Thales, Heraclitus, Socrates, Plato, and Aristotle created dazzling intellectual tapestries that wove together ethical reflection, metaphysical speculation, logical analysis, and empirical observation into comprehensive systems of thought that continue to influence human thinking millennia later. Plato's Republic explored the relationship between justice in the individual soul and justice in the political community. Aristotle's Metaphysics attempted to understand the fundamental nature of reality itself. These philosophical "mind paintings" were remarkable both for their systematic complexity and their ambition to address the deepest questions of human existence.

Yet these magnificent intellectual achievements were ultimately fragile, intimately bound to the specific societal canvas that sustained them—the institutions, cultural values, economic systems, and shared assumptions of their particular historical moment. Greek philosophy flourished within the unique context of the polis system, where citizen-philosophers could engage in sustained public debate, where economic arrangements provided the foundation for intellectual leisure, and where cultural values prized rational inquiry and rhetorical excellence. When this supporting social fabric was torn by military conquest, imperial transformation, and cultural upheaval, much Greek philosophical knowledge was lost or forgotten, buried beneath centuries of political instability and changing intellectual priorities.

The phenomenon of disappearance, however, is never final in the realm of ideas. Centuries after the decline of classical Greek civilization, these philosophical traditions were gradually rediscovered and reanimated through a complex process of cultural transmission that spanned continents and religious traditions. Islamic scholars in Baghdad, Cordoba, and other intellectual centers preserved, translated, and creatively interpreted Greek philosophical texts during Europe's early medieval period. Figures like Al-Kindi, Al-Farabi, Averroes, and Avicenna did not simply preserve ancient wisdom but actively developed and transformed it, creating synthesis between Greek rationalism and Islamic theology that enriched both traditions.

Later, Renaissance humanists in Italy and Northern Europe encountered these philosophical works through Latin translations of Arabic versions, creating yet another layer of interpretation and cultural translation. Enlightenment thinkers subsequently appropriated Greek philosophical concepts for their own intellectual battles. Each historical moment of "rediscovery" was simultaneously an act of creative reinterpretation, as new generations of thinkers applied ancient insights to contemporary challenges and questions.

This process of transmission and transformation exemplifies what we can identify as Cultural Drift—the inevitable tendency of ideas to evolve, mutate, and adapt as they move across time, cultures, and contexts. Far from representing a failure of accurate preservation or understanding, cultural drift reveals the fundamentally dynamic nature of human thought and the creative vitality of intellectual traditions. The "original" concepts embedded within now-extinct cognitive and cultural frameworks become essentially inaccessible in their full historical specificity and contextual nuance. Every act of interpretation and reappropriation necessarily involves a creative dialogue between past and present, ancient wisdom and contemporary concerns.

Archaeological evidence reinforces this understanding of philosophical development as a fundamentally social and material process. The emergence of specialized scribal schools, the construction of temples, the development of libraries and archives, and the creation of philosophical academies all reflect the material infrastructure necessary for sustained intellectual work. Symbols, metaphors, and conceptual frameworks shift meaning as they move between cultures, as documented in the archaeological record of artistic and textual transmission.

To understand these dynamics properly, we must defend against several potential philosophical objections. Critics might argue that reducing philosophical development to material conditions commits the fallacy of crude economic determinism. This critique misunderstands the framework presented here. The relationship between material conditions and intellectual development is not mechanistically deterministic but dialectical—material conditions provide necessary but not sufficient conditions for philosophical emergence. The neolithic revolution created the possibility space for systematic philosophy, but the specific content and direction of philosophical inquiry remained open to human creativity, cultural values, and intellectual dialogue.

The concept of Cultural Drift might be attacked as leading to complete relativism, where all interpretations become equally valid and objective truth becomes impossible. This criticism fundamentally misunderstands the argument. Cultural Drift does not eliminate the possibility of better or worse interpretations, nor does it deny that some philosophical insights might have enduring validity. Rather, it acknowledges that the meaning and application of ideas necessarily change as they encounter new contexts, problems, and cultural frameworks. This is not relativism but recognition of the historical and contextual nature of all human understanding.

Philosophical idealists might object that this framework reduces ideas to mere epiphenomena of material conditions, denying their autonomous power and intrinsic value. This misrepresents the position argued here. The framework does not claim that ideas are mere reflections of material conditions but rather that ideas and material conditions exist in dynamic, reciprocal relationship. Philosophical "mind paintings" have genuine causal power—they shape social institutions, guide individual behavior, and influence material practices. The emergence of writing systems, for instance, was both enabled by material conditions and itself became a material force that transformed human cognition and social organization.

Critics committed to universal rational truth might argue that acknowledging Cultural Drift undermines the possibility of philosophical progress or objective knowledge. This objection assumes that objectivity requires timeless, context-free truth—an assumption that can be challenged. The framework presented here suggests that philosophical progress occurs precisely through the creative dialogue between inherited wisdom and contemporary challenges. Each generation's reinterpretation of ancient philosophy can potentially reveal new insights, uncover hidden assumptions, or develop implications that were not apparent to earlier thinkers.

The neolithic revolution thus initiated not merely a change in human lifestyle but a fundamental transformation in consciousness itself—the birth of philosophy as systematic inquiry into questions that transcend immediate survival needs. This cognitive revolution established the foundational patterns for how human societies would subsequently organize, preserve, and transmit complex knowledge systems. The "mind paintings" that emerged from this period—systematic philosophies, legal codes, religious frameworks, and scientific methods—continue to shape human civilization as each generation inherits, transforms, and transmits the accumulated wisdom of our sedentary ancestors while creating new frameworks for understanding our place in an ever-changing world.

The patterns established during this pivotal period—the specialization of intellectual labor, the codification of abstract knowledge, the institutionalization of learning, and the creative reinterpretation of inherited wisdom—remain fundamental to human intellectual life. Understanding these origins illuminates not only the historical development of philosophy but also the ongoing processes by which human societies continue to construct, maintain, and transform their collective understanding of reality, meaning, and value.

Chapter Three
The Imperfect Transmission: Cultural Drift and the Fragmentation of Truth

No phenomenon in human history illustrates the inevitability and mechanics of cultural drift more vividly than the historical evolution of Christianity. From its origins in first-century Palestine to its contemporary global manifestations across thousands of denominations, Christianity provides an unparalleled case study in how even the most carefully preserved and institutionally protected "mind paintings" undergo continuous transformation, fragmentation, and creative reinterpretation. This transformation occurs not despite institutional efforts to maintain doctrinal purity, but precisely because cultural drift represents an inherent feature of human cognitive and social processes that no amount of institutional control can completely eliminate.

The very attempt to define orthodoxy—to establish canonical boundaries and condemn heretical deviations—paradoxically demonstrates the pre-existing diversity that such efforts seek to contain. The historical record reveals that Christianity never existed as a single, unified "mind painting" transmitted unchanged from its founder, but rather as a constantly evolving constellation of interpretations, practices, and institutional forms shaped by the cognitive limitations, cultural contexts, and social pressures encountered by successive generations of believers across diverse geographic and cultural contexts.

Cultural drift operates through several interconnected mechanisms that become clearly visible in Christian historical development. Generational transmission necessarily involves interpretation and selective emphasis as older believers communicate their understanding to younger converts who bring their own cultural backgrounds, intellectual frameworks, and experiential contexts to the interpretive process. Geographic dispersion exposes religious ideas to new cultural environments that inevitably influence how those ideas are understood, expressed, and practiced. Linguistic translation requires conceptual adaptation as religious concepts developed in one language and cultural context are rendered comprehensible in fundamentally different linguistic and cultural systems. Political and social pressures create selective advantages for certain interpretations while marginalizing others, leading to evolutionary changes in religious emphasis and practice.

The earliest Christian communities, emerging within decades of Jesus's death, already exhibited remarkable diversity in their understanding of his significance, teachings, and continuing presence. Archaeological evidence from sites across the Mediterranean reveals multiple competing interpretations of Christian identity, practice, and theology that would later be classified as orthodox, heterodox, or heretical by institutional authorities who gained political power in the fourth century.

The Gnostic traditions, now understood through discoveries like the Nag Hammadi library, represented sophisticated theological systems that emphasized direct spiritual knowledge, complex cosmologies involving multiple divine emanations, and radically different interpretations of Jesus's identity and significance. Rather than representing late corruptions of an originally pure Christian message, these traditions appear to have developed simultaneously with what later became orthodox Christianity, drawing on shared scriptural sources and apostolic claims while reaching fundamentally different conclusions about the nature of divine reality, human salvation, and cosmic purpose.

Gnostic texts like the Gospel of Thomas, the Gospel of Philip, and the Gospel of Truth reveal complex theological reflection that addressed philosophical questions about the relationship between matter and spirit, the nature of divine knowledge, and the path to salvation through mystical insight rather than institutional mediation. These texts demonstrate that alternative Christian mind paintings were not crude misunderstandings but sophisticated theological systems that attracted educated converts across the Roman Empire and provided compelling answers to existential questions about human suffering, cosmic purpose, and divine accessibility.

Arianism, the theological position developed by the fourth-century priest Arius, illustrates how cultural drift operates even within institutionally controlled religious environments. Arius argued that Jesus Christ, while divine and sent for human salvation, remained subordinate to God the Father and was not co-eternal with the Father. This position, which attracted widespread support among both clergy and laity across the Eastern Roman Empire, emerged from careful scriptural analysis combined with Greek philosophical frameworks that emphasized strict monotheism and clear hierarchical relationships within divine reality.

The Arian controversy reveals cultural drift operating at multiple levels simultaneously. Linguistically, the transition from Aramaic and Hebrew scriptural concepts into Greek philosophical terminology created opportunities for multiple interpretations of crucial terms describing Jesus's relationship to divine reality. Culturally, the encounter between Jewish monotheistic traditions and Greek philosophical systems generated creative tensions that different Christian communities resolved in divergent directions. Politically, the emergence of Christian imperial patronage under Constantine created new pressures for doctrinal uniformity that had not existed during the previous three centuries of Christian development.

The Council of Nicaea in 325 CE represents a pivotal moment in the institutionalization of cultural drift management rather than its elimination. The council's condemnation of Arianism and affirmation of Christ's co-eternal divinity with the Father did not emerge from pure theological analysis but reflected complex political, cultural, and social factors including imperial preferences, regional power struggles between ecclesiastical centers, and philosophical fashions that influenced how biblical texts were interpreted.

Significantly, the Council of Nicaea succeeded in establishing institutional orthodoxy only through the exercise of imperial power and the threat of exile for dissenting bishops. The fact that only two bishops out of approximately three hundred refused to sign the Nicene Creed reflects political pressure rather than theological consensus, as subsequent decades of continued Arian influence demonstrate. The need for repeated councils—Constantinople in 381, Ephesus in 431, Chalcedon in 451—to clarify and defend Nicene positions reveals the ongoing operation of cultural drift even within officially orthodox communities.

The concept of heresy itself illustrates how religious institutions attempt to manage cultural drift by establishing authoritative boundaries around acceptable interpretation while condemning alternative developments as illegitimate deviations. However, the very proliferation of heresies—Docetism, Adoptionism, Modalism, Pelagianism, Nestorianism, Monophysitism, and hundreds of others—demonstrates the creative vitality of human meaning-making processes that continuously generate new interpretations despite institutional opposition.

Medieval Christianity provides abundant evidence of cultural drift operating within officially orthodox frameworks. The development of scholastic theology, mystical traditions, mendicant orders, cathedral schools, and university systems represented significant innovations in Christian thought and practice that would have been unrecognizable to early Christian communities. The incorporation of Aristotelian philosophy into Christian theology through figures like Thomas Aquinas created synthetic mind paintings that fundamentally transformed Christian intellectual culture while claiming continuity with apostolic tradition.

The Great Western Schism of 1378-1417, during which multiple claimants to papal authority simultaneously exercised ecclesiastical power, reveals how institutional mechanisms for managing cultural drift can themselves become sources of fragmentation and creative innovation. The conciliar movement that emerged to resolve this crisis introduced new theological concepts about ecclesiastical authority and democratic governance that influenced both religious and secular political development.

ALLEN SCHERY

    The Protestant Reformation represents perhaps the most dramatic example of cultural drift accelerating beyond institutional containment. Martin Luther's initial concerns about indulgences and clerical abuse rapidly expanded into fundamental challenges to papal authority, sacramental theology, scriptural interpretation, and ecclesiastical structure. The proliferation of Protestant denominations—Lutheran, Reformed, Anglican, Anabaptist, Presbyterian, Baptist, Methodist, Pentecostal, and thousands of others—demonstrates cultural drift operating with unprecedented speed and creativity once institutional constraints were weakened.

    Each Protestant tradition developed distinctive mind paintings that emphasized different aspects of Christian identity while claiming scriptural authority for their particular interpretations. The doctrine of sola scriptura, intended to provide objective criteria for Christian truth, actually accelerated cultural drift by removing institutional mediations between individual interpreters and sacred texts, leading to exponential multiplication of competing interpretations.

    The missionary expansion of Christianity across Africa, Asia, and the Americas during the colonial period created new opportunities for cultural drift as Christian concepts encountered indigenous cosmologies, social systems, and linguistic frameworks. African Christianity developed distinctive theological emphases on community, ancestral spirituality, and liberation that differ significantly from European traditions. Asian Christianity created synthetic mind paintings that incorporated Buddhist, Confucian, and Hindu philosophical elements while maintaining Christian identity. Latin American Christianity emphasized social justice, popular devotion, and liberation theology in ways that challenged European ecclesiastical authorities.

Contemporary Christianity exhibits cultural drift operating at unprecedented speed and scale due to global communication, democratic governance, theological education, and multicultural encounter. The emergence of prosperity theology, creation spirituality, emerging church movements, liberation theology, feminist theology, and ecological theology represents ongoing creative reinterpretation of Christian tradition in response to contemporary social, intellectual, and environmental challenges.

The proliferation of Christian denominations—currently estimated at over 45,000 distinct groups worldwide—provides quantitative evidence of cultural drift's operation within a single religious tradition. Each denomination represents a distinctive mind painting that emerged from specific historical circumstances, cultural contexts, and interpretive innovations while claiming legitimacy through appeals to scriptural authority, apostolic succession, or spiritual authenticity.

Statistical analysis of denominational development reveals cultural drift operating through predictable patterns. Theological disagreements lead to institutional separation. Geographic expansion creates regional variations. Generational change introduces new priorities and concerns. Educational developments influence interpretive sophistication. Political circumstances affect institutional relationships with state power. Economic factors influence religious practice and social engagement.

The phenomenon of denominational convergence and divergence illustrates cultural drift's dialectical character. Ecumenical movements seek to overcome historical divisions through emphasis on shared beliefs and practices, creating new synthetic mind paintings that transcend traditional boundaries. Simultaneously, ongoing theological development continues generating new sources of disagreement and institutional separation, ensuring that cultural drift remains active even within ecumenical frameworks.

This analysis of Christian historical development requires careful philosophical defense against several potential objections. Religious believers might argue that this framework reduces sacred truth to mere cultural construction, undermining faith claims and spiritual authenticity. However, recognizing cultural drift as an inherent feature of human meaning-making processes need not invalidate religious experience or spiritual insight. Rather, it illuminates how divine truth—if such exists—necessarily encounters human cognitive and cultural limitations that shape its historical expression without necessarily compromising its ultimate validity.

Secular critics might argue that demonstrating cultural drift in religious traditions supports materialist or atheistic interpretations that reduce all religious claims to social construction. However, the framework developed here remains agnostic about ultimate metaphysical questions while focusing on empirically observable processes of cultural transmission and transformation. The operation of cultural drift within religious traditions tells us something important about human cognitive processes without necessarily undermining transcendent truth claims.

Historical scholars might object that this analysis oversimplifies complex theological developments by reducing them to mechanical processes of cultural drift. This objection requires acknowledgment that cultural drift operates alongside other historical factors including individual creativity, institutional power, economic circumstances, and political pressures. The framework presented here illuminates one crucial dimension of historical change without claiming to provide complete causal explanation for all developments.

The contemporary implications of this analysis extend far beyond academic historical study. Understanding cultural drift as an inherent feature of human meaning-making processes can foster intellectual humility about claims to possess unchanging truth while encouraging creative engagement with inherited traditions. Rather than viewing doctrinal diversity as evidence of failure or corruption, this perspective reveals it as testimony to the remarkable human capacity for creative meaning-making within evolving cultural contexts.

For religious communities, recognizing cultural drift can support more honest acknowledgment of historical development while maintaining commitment to core spiritual insights and practices. For secular observers, understanding these processes can foster appreciation for the creative vitality of religious traditions while avoiding simplistic reductionism that ignores their genuine contributions to human flourishing.

The historical record of Christianity provides overwhelming evidence that complex cultural systems inevitably undergo continuous transformation through processes of cultural drift that no amount of institutional control can completely contain. The very existence of orthodoxy and heresy as contested categories demonstrates the pre-existing diversity that such concepts attempt to manage rather than eliminate. The proliferation of thousands of Christian denominations provides quantitative confirmation of ongoing cultural drift operating within a tradition that has invested enormous institutional resources in maintaining doctrinal uniformity.

This phenomenon reflects not the failure of religious institutions but the inherent creativity of human consciousness encountering transcendent questions within finite cultural and cognitive constraints. The fragmentation of religious truth claims demonstrates not the absence of truth but the inevitable limitations of human access to truth and the creative vitality of communities attempting to live authentically within such limitations.

Understanding cultural drift as illustrated through Christian historical development provides essential insight into the broader human project of meaning-making, truth-seeking, and community formation that extends far beyond religious contexts into scientific, political, artistic, and philosophical domains where similar processes of creative interpretation and institutional management operate with comparable complexity and consequence.

The Tower of Babel as a Mind Painting of Cultural Drift

The ancient Tower of Babel narrative emerges from Mesopotamian sources as humanity's earliest systematic attempt to explain cultural and linguistic diversity through symbolic reasoning. Framed as a monumental human endeavor to reach the heavens, the story simultaneously captures an implicit insight into cultural drift—the natural process by which human groups diverge into distinct languages, customs, and social structures as they spread geographically and adapt to varied environments. In crafting this tale, early humans invented a sophisticated "mind painting": a cognitive framework generated by the expanding neocortex to impose narrative coherence on observable social fragmentation despite insufficient empirical data. The builders' hunch—encoded in mythological form—demonstrates the neocortex's evolved capacity for pattern recognition and hypothesis formation, creating rich symbolic meaning from incomplete information.

Modern neuroscience confirms that the human neocortex, particularly its prefrontal regions, evolved to support abstract reasoning, symbolic thought, and complex social cognition. This expanded cortical capacity enabled humans to create elaborate explanatory narratives that served both cognitive and social functions. The Babel story exemplifies how symbolic representation can organize collective understanding even when direct evidence is lacking. Cultural evolution operates through mechanisms analogous to biological evolution—variation, selection, and transmission of cultural traits—yet unlike genetic inheritance, cultural transmission involves active cognitive processing, modification, and creative reinterpretation by individual minds. Mechanisms such as argumentation, selective trust, and ostensive communication illustrate the neocortex's dual role in both generating and transforming cultural content.

From a philosophical anthropological perspective, the Babel metaphor illuminates the fundamental human condition: our drive to create meaning amid uncertainty and our propensity to generate explanatory frameworks that transcend immediate experience. This "anthropological constant" reveals itself whenever humans construct symbolic worlds—mind paintings—that furnish coherence and social cohesion regardless of empirical verification. The story's persistence across millennia demonstrates how generations inherit cultural narratives, modify them through lived experience, and transmit transformed versions onward, reflecting the dynamic interplay between individual cognition and collective meaning-making.

Despite the explanatory power of this evolutionary-cognitive framework, several philosophical objections will arise

First, postmodern critiques warn against ethnocentric universalism, arguing that applying Western scientific paradigms to ancient myths imposes external values and obscures cultural specificity. However, this critique overlooks how the analysis explicitly acknowledges that symbolic expressions vary across cultures. The identified cognitive capacities—pattern recognition, symbolic reasoning—are genuine biological universals embedded in the neocortex's architecture. Recognizing these universals does not negate cultural diversity; rather, it explains the shared human tendency to craft narratives, while leaving open the countless ways such stories are manifested globally.

Second, cultural relativists may charge biological reductionism, asserting that evolutionary neuroscience cannot account for the autonomous realm of cultural meaning. Yet this framework employs methodological naturalism without succumbing to reductive biologism: it recognizes that while the neocortex provides the capacity for symbolic thought, specific cultural contents are historically contingent and socially constructed. Culture and cognition thus engage in a dialectical relationship, with neither fully determining the other.

Third, scientific positivists critique the "mind painting" as unfalsifiable speculation about ancient cognition. In response, we note that the framework is grounded in empirically documented mechanisms—neocortical function, symbolic reasoning, cultural transmission. Although we cannot directly test ancient mental states, the theory generates testable predictions about cognitive biases and cultural universals that ethnographic and experimental research can evaluate.

Fourth, advocates of evolutionary psychology criticism caution against the adaptationist fallacy. This chapter avoids strict adaptationist by acknowledging that symbolic reasoning may have evolved for multiple functions or even arisen as a byproduct of other cognitive developments. The creative application of this capacity in myth-making represents an extension of, rather than a narrow adaptation for, narrative construction.

Fifth, feminist and critical theorists might object that legitimizing patriarchal religious narratives perpetuates oppressive ideologies. However, treating the Babel story as a cultural artifact subject to critical interpretation demystifies its authority. By revealing its cognitive origins, we equip readers to critique the story's social functions and to recognize how dominant narratives emerge, persist, and can be challenged.

Finally, critics concerned with essentialism argue that positing "culture" and "cognition" as distinct categories reifies fluid phenomena. This analysis counters that both culture and cognition are processual—ongoing patterns of activity. Cultural boundaries are porous and contested, and cognitive processes continually reshape cultural meanings in response to new contexts.

Understanding the Tower of Babel as a mind painting born of our neocortex's symbolic capacities offers profound insights into contemporary cultural dynamics. Cultural drift is not a problem to be cured but the natural outcome of human cognition engaging with environmental and social complexity. Recognizing the cognitive roots of cultural diversity fosters appreciation for varied perspectives while highlighting shared human capacities that enable cross-cultural understanding.

Rather than lamenting cultural fragmentation as divine punishment, we can celebrate it as evidence of human cognitive creativity and adaptive flexibility. The ancient storytellers who inscribed the Babel narrative intuited that meaning-making is an intrinsic human endeavor: our capacity to transform fragmentary observations into coherent narratives unites us across time and space. In embracing this legacy, we honor the mind paintings that shape our collective consciousness and the neocortical processes that continue to drive cultural evolution today.

Chapter Four
The Situated and Distributed Canvas – Expanding the Boundaries of Mind Painting

The traditional view of human cognition as a process confined within individual skulls—a series of mental operations occurring in the isolated privacy of brain tissue—has proven increasingly inadequate for understanding how humans actually think, learn, and create meaning in the complex, interconnected world they inhabit. Contemporary advances in cognitive science, anthropology, and philosophy of mind converge on a revolutionary insight: human sense-making, including the construction of "mind paintings," extends far beyond internal neural processes to encompass dynamic interactions with physical environments, social networks, material artifacts, and technological systems.

This chapter explores two interconnected theoretical frameworks that fundamentally expand our understanding of human cognition and cultural meaning-making: situated cognition and distributed cognition. These frameworks reveal mind painting not as an exclusively individual mental product but as an emergent property of complex systems involving brain, body, environment, and social interaction. This expansion of cognitive boundaries has profound implications for understanding how humans have created, maintained, and transformed cultural systems throughout history while operating within the constraints and possibilities articulated by the Primate Principle.

Moving beyond the brain and expanding the canvas of cognitive understanding, situated cognition represents a fundamental challenge to traditional cognitive science models that treat thinking as abstract symbol manipulation occurring independently of bodily experience and environmental context. Developed through the work of scholars like Lucy Suchman, Jean Lave, Etienne Wenger, and Andy Clark, situated cognition demonstrates that knowing is inseparable from doing within specific physical, cultural, and social contexts. Rather than retrieving abstract representations stored in memory, human cognition emerges through dynamic interaction between neural activity, bodily movement, environmental structures, and ongoing activity.

The implications of this perspective are profound. If cognition is fundamentally situated, then the mind paintings that humans create cannot be understood as purely internal mental constructs but must be recognized as products of embodied engagement with specific environments and cultural practices. The stories, beliefs, and conceptual frameworks that organize human experience emerge not from isolated brains but from minds embedded in material and social worlds that both constrain and enable particular forms of thought and meaning-making.

Archaeological evidence from Paleolithic sites across Europe, Africa, and Asia demonstrates the embodied and situated character of early human cognition. The placement of cave paintings at Lascaux, Altamira, and Chauvet reveals sophisticated understanding of how environmental features—cave acoustics, natural rock formations, and lighting conditions—could enhance the psychological and social impact of symbolic representation. These early humans did not simply project internal mental images onto cave walls but crafted their symbolic expressions through careful attention to the affordances provided by specific physical environments.

Ethnographic studies of contemporary hunter-gatherer societies provide detailed insight into how environmental engagement shapes cognitive processes and cultural transmission. Among the Inuit of Arctic Canada, navigation across seemingly featureless ice depends on reading subtle environmental cues—wind patterns, snow formations, sky coloration—that require years of embodied practice to perceive and interpret accurately. This navigational knowledge cannot be reduced to abstract maps stored in memory but exists as embodied skill developed through sustained interaction with challenging Arctic environments.

The Australian Aboriginal concept of "country" illustrates the situated nature of cultural knowledge systems. Aboriginal peoples' understanding of landscape integrates practical ecological knowledge—the location of water sources, seasonal availability of food resources, safe travel routes—with spiritual and social meanings encoded in songline traditions that can span thousands of kilometers across the continent. This knowledge exists not as abstract information but as embodied practice requiring movement through actual landscapes, participation in ceremonial activities, and ongoing relationships with both human and non-human agencies.

Understanding cognition as a collective enterprise reveals how cognitive processes extend across multiple individuals, material artifacts, and technological systems through what researchers term distributed cognition. Rather than viewing thinking as something that happens inside individual brains, distributed cognition demonstrates how complex problem-solving emerges from coordinated interaction among people and tools working together as integrated cognitive systems. This framework, developed primarily through Edwin Hutchins's groundbreaking ethnographic work on naval navigation teams, fundamentally challenges individualistic assumptions about mental processes.

Hutchins's detailed analysis of navigation aboard U.S. Navy ships illustrates how cognitive processes are distributed across multiple participants and artifacts. Determining a ship's position requires coordination among lookouts who take visual bearings, quartermasters who plot these bearings on charts, and officers who integrate multiple sources of information to make navigational decisions. No single individual possesses complete knowledge of the ship's position; instead, this knowledge emerges from the coordinated activity of the entire navigation team working with specialized instruments, charts, and communication protocols.

This distributed cognitive system possesses properties that exceed the capabilities of any individual participant. The system can maintain accurate positional knowledge even when individual team members are replaced, can correct individual errors through redundant information processing, and can adapt to changing conditions through flexible reorganization of roles and responsibilities. The ship's navigation knowledge exists not in any individual mind but in the coordinated patterns of interaction among people and artifacts.

Writing systems represent perhaps the most historically significant example of distributed cognition in human cultural development. The invention of cuneiform, hieroglyphics, and alphabetic scripts created external memory systems that dramatically expanded human cognitive capabilities by enabling the storage, manipulation, and transmission of complex information across space and time. These technologies did not simply record thoughts that occurred in individual minds but fundamentally transformed the kinds of thinking that became possible.

The development of legal codes like Hammurabi's laws or the Roman Twelve Tables created distributed cognitive systems for managing social behavior across large populations. These systems distributed decision-making authority across multiple institutional roles—scribes, judges, administrators—while using written texts as stable reference points that could ensure consistency in legal interpretation and application across different cases and contexts.

Medieval European monasteries exemplify sophisticated distributed cognitive systems for preserving and transmitting knowledge. The monastic scriptoriums that produced illuminated manuscripts distributed intellectual labor across multiple specialists: scribes who copied texts, illuminators who created visual representations, librarians who organized collections, and scholars who provided commentary and interpretation. This system enabled the preservation of classical Greek and Roman knowledge through the medieval period while facilitating its creative reinterpretation within Christian theological frameworks.

Examining situated and distributed mind painting in action through specific case studies reveals the practical operation of these theoretical frameworks across diverse cultural contexts. Indigenous navigation systems provide compelling evidence of how situated and distributed cognition operate together to create sophisticated cultural knowledge systems. Micronesian navigators in the Caroline Islands use a technique called etak that combines embodied spatial awareness with culturally transmitted conceptual frameworks to navigate across hundreds of miles of open ocean without instruments.

The etak system treats navigation not as abstract map-reading but as dynamic awareness of relationships among islands, currents, wave patterns, bird behavior, and celestial movements. Navigators develop this awareness through years of embodied practice involving actual ocean voyages, observation of environmental patterns, and participation in cultural practices that encode navigational knowledge in chants, stories, and ritual activities.

This knowledge is distributed across the navigating community through apprenticeship relationships, specialized roles (master navigators, weather readers, star compass keepers), and material culture (canoe design, sail configurations, provisioning systems) that embody accumulated wisdom about ocean travel. The complete navigational system emerges from interaction among all these components rather than existing as abstract knowledge in any individual mind.

Contemporary digital technologies create unprecedented forms of distributed cognition that are rapidly transforming human cultural systems. Social media platforms like Facebook, Twitter, and TikTok create distributed cognitive systems where individual posts, comments, shares, and algorithmic filtering combine to produce emergent patterns of information flow, opinion formation, and cultural transmission.

These digital systems exhibit classic features of distributed cognition: individual contributions are coordinated through technological infrastructures to produce collective intelligence that exceeds individual capabilities, knowledge is stored and retrieved through external memory systems (databases, search algorithms, recommendation engines), and cognitive processes are distributed across human users and artificial intelligence systems working in coordination.

However, these systems also demonstrate how distributed cognition can produce pathological outcomes. The same mechanisms that enable rapid information sharing and collaborative problem-solving can also facilitate the spread of misinformation, the formation of echo chambers that reinforce existing beliefs, and the manipulation of public opinion through targeted advertising and algorithmic bias.

Revisiting the Primate Principle through the lens of collective and environmental constraints reveals how understanding cognition as situated and distributed fundamentally transforms our comprehension of the cognitive constraints and possibilities imposed by human evolutionary history and neo-cortical architecture. Rather than viewing these constraints as limitations affecting only individual minds, situated and distributed cognition reveal how neo-cortical limitations drive the creation of extended cognitive systems that transcend individual biological boundaries.

The human brain's limited working memory capacity, estimated at approximately seven discrete items, creates powerful incentives for developing external memory systems like writing, notation systems, and digital storage that can maintain and manipulate far larger information sets. The brain's difficulty with abstract reasoning drives the creation of material representations—mathematical notation, scientific instruments, architectural models—that make abstract relationships perceptually accessible through embodied interaction.

Human social psychology, shaped by evolutionary pressures favoring cooperation within small groups, drives the creation of institutional systems that can coordinate behavior across much larger populations. The cognitive mechanisms that promote in-group loyalty and out-group suspicion are managed through legal systems, economic institutions, and political structures that channel these tendencies toward constructive collective action while minimizing destructive conflict.

The Primate Principle thus operates not simply as individual constraint but as generative force driving the creation of increasingly sophisticated distributed cognitive systems. Human cultural evolution can be understood as the ongoing development of extended mind systems that leverage biological cognitive capabilities while transcending their limitations through creative integration of environmental resources, social coordination, and technological mediation.

Defending this theoretical framework and exploring its implications requires addressing several potential philosophical objections. Traditional cognitive scientists might argue that recognizing external factors in cognition violates the explanatory integrity of psychological theory by expanding the boundaries of mental phenomena beyond principled limits. This objection reflects an unjustified commitment to individualistic assumptions about mental processes that ignore how cognition actually operates in natural contexts.

The situated and distributed perspective does not eliminate individual psychological processes but rather situates them within the broader systems that give them meaning and effectiveness. Understanding how individual neural mechanisms contribute to distributed cognitive systems provides more rather than less insight into the organization and function of human psychology.

Philosophers committed to internalist approaches to mind might argue that treating external objects as genuine components of cognitive processes commits a category error by conflating different kinds of phenomena. This objection can be addressed by recognizing that the mind-world boundary is not fixed by biological skin but is dynamically negotiated through ongoing patterns of interaction and functional integration.

The extended mind thesis, developed by Andy Clark and David Chalmers, provides compelling arguments for treating certain external objects as genuine components of cognitive systems when they fulfill functional roles analogous to those played by internal neural processes. A notebook that reliably stores and retrieves information for its user can function as external memory in ways that are cognitively equivalent to internal memory processes.

Cultural critics might argue that emphasizing technological mediation of cognition promotes instrumental rationality while neglecting the humanistic dimensions of cultural life. However, situated and distributed cognition reveal how supposedly "technical" processes are always embedded within cultural meanings, social relationships, and ethical commitments that give them human significance.

The anthropological perspective that informs distributed cognition research reveals how technological systems embody cultural values, social hierarchies, and political arrangements that shape their development and application. Understanding these dimensions requires ethnographic analysis of how people actually use technologies within specific cultural contexts rather than abstract speculation about technological effects.

Recognizing the ever-expanding canvas of human cognition, the frameworks of situated and distributed cognition fundamentally expand the mind painting metaphor to encompass the full range of resources that humans use to create, maintain, and transform cultural meaning systems. Mind paintings emerge not from isolated brains but from dynamic interaction among minds, bodies, environments, social networks, and technological systems that together constitute extended cognitive systems.

This expanded understanding has profound practical implications for educational practice, organizational design, therapeutic intervention, and social policy. If learning is fundamentally situated and distributed, then educational environments must be designed to support embodied engagement with authentic problems rather than abstract transmission of decontextualized information. If organizational intelligence is distributed across people and technologies, then management practices must focus on facilitating coordination and communication rather than controlling individual behavior.

The recognition that human cultural systems are extended cognitive systems also illuminates the challenges facing contemporary global civilization. Climate change, technological disruption, social inequality, and political polarization represent failures of existing distributed cognitive systems to process information accurately, coordinate collective action effectively, and adapt to rapidly changing conditions.

Addressing these challenges requires not just individual behavior change but redesign of the institutional, technological, and cultural systems that constitute our collective intelligence. The mind painting metaphor, expanded to encompass situated and distributed dimensions, provides conceptual tools for understanding how such redesign might proceed through creative integration of human cognitive capabilities with environmental resources and technological affordances.

This chapter establishes the foundation for understanding human cognition and culture as fundamentally extended phenomena that resist reduction to either purely individual psychology or purely social construction. The mind paintings that organize human experience emerge from the dynamic interaction of biological, environmental, social, and technological factors that together constitute the extended cognitive systems within which human life unfolds.

Future chapters will explore how these extended cognitive systems operate across different domains of human experience—scientific research, artistic creation, political organization, economic production—while maintaining focus on the fundamental insight that human sense-making is always already situated within and distributed across the material and social worlds that humans continuously create and inhabit.

Chapter Five
The Divine Canvas: Medieval Philosophy and the Grand Design

The collapse of classical civilization in Western Europe during the fifth and sixth centuries created an unprecedented crisis of meaning that demanded new forms of cognitive organization capable of ordering chaos on a scale previously unimaginable. The fragmentation of political authority, the breakdown of urban culture, the loss of classical learning, and the constant threat of violence from external invasions and internal conflicts combined to create what contemporary sources described as the "ruin of the world." Into this cognitive and cultural vacuum stepped medieval Christianity, offering what would become one of history's most comprehensive and enduring "mind paintings"—a totalizing vision of reality that integrated divine revelation, classical philosophy, and practical governance into a unified framework for understanding existence, society, and human purpose.

Medieval scholasticism, emerging in the eleventh and twelfth centuries and reaching its pinnacle in the thirteenth century through figures like Thomas Aquinas, represents far more than theological speculation divorced from practical concerns. Rather, it constituted a sophisticated cognitive technology designed to manage the fundamental human need for meaning, order, and social coordination within the constraints and possibilities imposed by the Primate Principle. The concept of divine revelation provided the ultimate source of cognitive order and harmony, establishing an authoritative foundation that could subsume earlier philosophical inquiries while preventing the cognitive dissonance that inevitably arises when multiple incompatible worldviews compete for allegiance within the same cultural space.

Understanding medieval philosophy as an elaborate mind painting requires careful analysis that avoids both dismissive secular reductionism and uncritical religious apologetics. This analysis examines not the truth or falsity of medieval religious claims but rather the human cognitive and social processes that drove the construction, maintenance, and transformation of these remarkably sophisticated meaning systems. The framework reveals how adherence to orthodox Christian mind painting secured crucial "bananas"—salvation, social status, political authority, and existential meaning—while heretical deviations from tribal norms led to excommunication, marginalization, and sometimes violent suppression.

The formation of powerful intellectual and social tribes around religious institutions—monasteries, cathedral schools, and eventually universities—created new forms of collective cognition that wielded unprecedented influence over European intellectual and political life. These institutions functioned as "unseen brushes of power and ideology," shaping the mind paintings available to medieval Europeans while channeling enormous resources toward the preservation, transmission, and creative development of Christian philosophical systems. The scholastic method that emerged from these institutions demonstrates how even within totalizing theological frameworks, rational argumentation could be employed to refine and defend the overarching mind painting, seeking logical consistency within its own foundational assumptions while maintaining ultimate commitment to revealed truth.

Moving beyond the monastic preservation of classical learning, the emergence of medieval scholasticism as a comprehensive mind painting system began with the educational revolution of the twelfth century. The translation movement that brought Aristotelian texts from Arabic into Latin created both opportunity and crisis for Christian intellectual culture. These newly available works presented sophisticated philosophical frameworks that addressed fundamental questions about reality, knowledge, and human purpose through rational inquiry rather than divine revelation. The challenge facing medieval intellectuals was how to integrate this powerful pagan philosophy with Christian doctrine without compromising either rational coherence or religious orthodoxy.

The early scholastic response to this challenge reveals the creative flexibility of human mind painting processes operating under external constraints. Rather than rejecting Aristotelian philosophy as incompatible with Christian faith, leading thinkers like Peter Abelard, Anselm of Canterbury, and the masters of the School of Chartres developed increasingly sophisticated methods for reconciling apparent contradictions between reason and revelation. Abelard's "Sic et Non" exemplified this approach by collecting patristic authorities who appeared to contradict each other on important theological questions, then developing dialectical methods for resolving these contradictions through careful attention to context, definition, and logical analysis.

This methodological innovation transformed medieval intellectual culture by establishing formal procedures for managing cognitive dissonance within theological frameworks. Rather than suppressing rational inquiry that might challenge established doctrine, the scholastic method channeled such inquiry toward strengthening and refining orthodox positions through systematic argumentation. The resulting intellectual culture was neither rigidly dogmatic nor freely speculative but occupied a creative middle ground where rational analysis operated within clearly defined boundaries established by religious authority.

The institutional context within which medieval scholasticism developed reveals the distributed and situated character of medieval mind painting. The great monasteries of the early Middle Ages—Monte Cassino, Cluny, St. Denis, Canterbury—functioned as distributed cognitive systems that preserved classical learning while adapting it to Christian purposes. These institutions created specialized roles for scribes, illuminators, librarians, and teachers that distributed intellectual labor across communities of scholars working within shared frameworks of meaning and purpose.

The emergence of cathedral schools in the eleventh century and universities in the twelfth century expanded this distributed cognitive system while introducing new competitive pressures that accelerated intellectual development. Universities like Paris, Oxford, Bologna, and Salamanca attracted scholars from across Europe, creating cosmopolitan intellectual communities that facilitated rapid circulation of ideas while maintaining institutional loyalty to Christian orthodoxy. These institutions developed increasingly sophisticated methods for credentialing intellectual authority through formal degrees, public disputations, and peer review processes that established collective standards for scholarly excellence.

Examining the central figures of medieval scholasticism reveals how individual creativity operated within collective cognitive frameworks to produce innovations that strengthened rather than challenged the overarching Christian mind painting. Augustine of Hippo, writing in the immediate aftermath of Rome's collapse, established foundational principles for integrating classical philosophy with Christian theology. His "De Civitate Dei" constructed a comprehensive historical theology that interpreted all human history as the unfolding conflict between the City of God and the City of Man, providing medieval Christians with a framework for understanding political upheaval, social change, and personal suffering within an ultimately meaningful cosmic narrative.

Augustine's synthesis of Platonic philosophy with Christian doctrine created intellectual tools that would influence European thought for over a thousand years. His analysis of time, memory, and consciousness in the "Confessions" pioneered introspective methods that anticipated modern psychology while remaining grounded in theological assumptions about divine illumination and human sinfulness. His political theory justified both ecclesiastical authority and secular government as necessary responses to human fallenness while maintaining the ultimate superiority of spiritual over temporal power.

Thomas Aquinas represents the pinnacle of medieval scholastic achievement in constructing comprehensive mind paintings that addressed every aspect of human existence within a unified theoretical framework. His "Summa Theologiae," begun while he was regent master at the Dominican studium in Rome, attempted nothing less than a complete synthesis of Aristotelian philosophy with Christian theology that would provide definitive answers to all significant questions about God, creation, human nature, morality, and salvation.

Aquinas's methodological innovations demonstrate the sophistication possible within medieval mind painting systems. His principle that "grace does not destroy nature but perfects it" provided a theoretical foundation for integrating natural reason with supernatural revelation while maintaining the distinct integrity of each. This allowed him to employ Aristotelian logic, metaphysics, and ethics as genuine sources of knowledge about reality while insisting that ultimate truth required divine revelation accessible only through faith and ecclesiastical teaching.

The structure of the Summa illustrates the systematic character of mature scholastic mind painting. Each article begins with objections that present the strongest arguments against the position Aquinas will defend, followed by a brief statement of contrary authority (usually from Scripture or the Church Fathers), then a detailed rational argument establishing the correct position, and finally responses that address each initial objection by showing how apparent contradictions can be resolved through proper understanding. This method enabled scholastic thinkers to engage seriously with intellectual challenges while ultimately strengthening orthodox positions through more sophisticated theological argumentation.

Analyzing "banana acquisition" through adherence to medieval Christian mind painting reveals the complex motivations that sustained scholastic intellectual culture across several centuries. At the most fundamental level, orthodox Christian belief promised eternal salvation—the ultimate "banana" that could justify any temporal sacrifice and rendered all earthly concerns relatively insignificant. This eschatological framework provided powerful psychological resources for coping with the uncertainties, sufferings, and injustices that characterized medieval life while motivating extraordinary investments of time and energy in theological scholarship and spiritual practice.

Beyond individual salvation, adherence to Christian orthodoxy secured numerous temporal benefits that made scholarly careers attractive to ambitious intellectuals. The Church offered one of the few paths to social mobility available to men of humble origins, with ecclesiastical careers providing access to wealth, political influence, and cultural prestige unavailable through secular channels. Universities created new forms of intellectual authority that commanded respect from both secular and religious elites, with master's degrees serving as credentials for appointment to high ecclesiastical offices, royal administrative positions, and lucrative benefices.

The social psychology of medieval intellectual communities reveals how group dynamics reinforced commitment to orthodox Christian mind painting while marginalizing potential dissent. Membership in scholarly communities required public assent to fundamental theological principles, with formal disputations serving as rituals that demonstrated intellectual competence while reinforcing collective identity. The elaborate ceremonies surrounding degree conferrals, inaugural lectures, and academic promotions created powerful psychological incentives for conformity to institutional norms while providing satisfying recognition for scholarly achievement.

Conversely, intellectual deviance from orthodox mind painting carried severe penalties that extended far beyond academic marginalization. Heretical teaching could result in loss of ecclesiastical benefices, excommunication from Christian community, exile from university towns, and in extreme cases prosecution by secular authorities acting at ecclesiastical behest. The cases of Peter Abelard, condemned for theological errors at the Council of Soissons in 1121, and later Meister Eckhart, whose teachings were posthumously condemned by Pope John XXII in 1329, demonstrate how even distinguished scholars could face institutional retaliation for pushing orthodox boundaries too far.

The concept of heresy itself reveals the mechanisms through which medieval institutions policed the boundaries of acceptable mind painting. Unlike modern academic disagreements, medieval theological controversies carried existential stakes that extended beyond professional reputation to encompass salvation, social belonging, and political loyalty. The development of formal inquisitorial procedures in the thirteenth century created institutional machinery for identifying and suppressing theological deviance while providing procedures for reintegrating repentant heretics into orthodox community.

Despite these institutional constraints, or perhaps because of them, medieval scholasticism produced intellectual achievements of remarkable sophistication and enduring influence. The apparent contradiction between institutional orthodoxy and intellectual creativity dissolves when we recognize that creative thinking thrives within well-defined constraints that channel mental energy toward productive problems while providing stable frameworks for evaluating solutions. Medieval scholars working within Christian assumptions produced advances in logic, metaphysics, natural philosophy, political theory, and moral theology that continued to influence European thought long after the medieval synthesis had fragmented.

The scholastic method itself represents a significant innovation in human reasoning that anticipates modern scientific methodology in important respects. The systematic collection of authorities, careful analysis of definitional issues, logical argumentation from clearly stated premises, and honest engagement with objections created intellectual habits that proved transferable to non-theological domains. Many historians of science have noted that the experimental method emerged from medieval universities where scholastic training had established expectations for rigorous argumentation and empirical verification that could be applied to natural philosophical questions.

Defending this analysis against potential objections requires careful articulation of what is and is not being claimed about medieval Christian culture. This framework does not argue that medieval religious beliefs were merely social constructions lacking transcendent referents, nor does it suggest that medieval scholars were cynically manipulating theological doctrine for personal advantage. Rather, it illuminates how genuine religious conviction operates within human cognitive and social systems that shape the expression and development of faith through processes that remain largely unconscious to participants.

Religious believers might object that treating theological systems as "mind paintings" reduces sacred truth to human construction, undermining the possibility of divine revelation and authentic spiritual experience. This objection misunderstands the analytical framework being employed here. Recognizing that human beings inevitably encounter divine truth (if such exists) through culturally mediated cognitive processes does not eliminate the possibility of genuine transcendence but rather illuminates how such encounters necessarily operate within human limitations and possibilities.

The framework developed here remains agnostic about ultimate metaphysical questions while focusing on empirically observable processes of cultural construction, transmission, and transformation. Medieval Christians may have encountered genuine divine revelation that guided their theological development, but this encounter necessarily occurred through human cognitive processes operating within social and institutional contexts that shaped how revelation was understood, articulated, and applied to concrete problems.

Secular critics might argue that the analysis presented here remains too sympathetic to medieval religious culture by failing to emphasize the oppressive and obscurantist dimensions of ecclesiastical authority. This objection reflects contemporary biases that may obscure the genuine achievements of medieval intellectual culture while ignoring the ways in which modern secular institutions employ similar mechanisms for managing intellectual diversity and maintaining ideological orthodoxy.

Contemporary academic institutions, for example, enforce disciplinary boundaries, credentialing requirements, and publication standards that effectively marginalize intellectual approaches deemed methodologically unsound or politically inappropriate. The mechanisms may be less dramatic than medieval excommunication, but the social psychology remains remarkably similar: institutional belonging requires adherence to collective norms that are maintained through peer pressure, professional rewards, and social sanctions applied to deviant behavior.

Historical scholars might object that this analysis oversimplifies the diversity of medieval intellectual culture by focusing primarily on high scholastic achievements while ignoring alternative traditions, mystical movements, and opular religious culture that developed along different trajectories. This criticism has merit and could be addressed through more comprehensive analysis that examines how different medieval mind paintings competed and interacted within the broader cultural landscape.

However, the focus on scholastic philosophy reflects its disproportionate historical influence on subsequent European intellectual development rather than any claim about its exclusivity during the medieval period. The scholastic synthesis established patterns of thinking about the relationship between reason and revelation that continued to influence European culture long after the specific theological conclusions had been challenged or abandoned.

Understanding the complexity and sophistication of medieval mind painting illuminates both the achievements and limitations of human meaning-making systems operating within institutional frameworks designed to provide comprehensive interpretations of reality. Medieval scholasticism succeeded in creating remarkably coherent and psychologically satisfying worldviews that sustained European civilization through several centuries of political instability and cultural transformation. The intellectual tools developed by medieval scholars—logical analysis, systematic theology, political theory, moral philosophy—provided resources that continue to enrich contemporary thinking about fundamental human questions.

At the same time, the medieval example illustrates how even the most sophisticated mind paintings remain vulnerable to historical pressures that can undermine their credibility and effectiveness. The gradual collapse of medieval scholastic authority during the late fourteenth and fifteenth centuries reflected not primarily intellectual inadequacy but rather changing social conditions that made alternative approaches to knowledge more attractive and practically effective. The rise of empirical science, political nationalism, and individual spirituality created new "banana acquisition" opportunities that required different cognitive tools than those provided by traditional scholastic methods.

The enduring significance of medieval philosophy lies not in its specific theological conclusions but in its demonstration of human cognitive creativity operating within institutional constraints to produce comprehensive worldviews capable of organizing complex societies around shared values and purposes. The techniques pioneered by medieval scholars—systematic analysis, logical argumentation, careful attention to textual authority, and creative synthesis of diverse intellectual traditions—remain essential tools for any culture seeking to develop coherent responses to fundamental questions about human existence and purpose.

This understanding of medieval scholasticism as sophisticated mind painting provides essential background for comprehending subsequent developments in European intellectual history that can be interpreted as responses to the perceived limitations or failures of the medieval synthesis. The Renaissance recovery of classical humanism, the Protestant emphasis on individual scriptural interpretation, the Enlightenment celebration of autonomous reason, and the modern development of empirical science all represent attempts to develop alternative mind paintings that might overcome perceived deficiencies in medieval approaches while preserving their genuine insights and achievements.

The lesson for contemporary culture is neither uncritical celebration nor dismissive rejection of medieval intellectual achievements but rather appreciation for the ongoing human challenge of constructing meaning systems that can provide both individual psychological satisfaction and collective social coordination while remaining flexible enough to adapt to changing circumstances and new knowledge. Medieval scholasticism succeeded remarkably well at this task for its historical context while eventually giving way to alternative approaches better suited to different social and intellectual circumstances.

Chapter Six
The Humanist Bridge and Rationalist Foundations

The transition from medieval scholastic mind painting to Enlightenment rationalism did not occur through sudden revolutionary rupture but rather through a gradual transformation that began with the Renaissance recovery of classical learning and the development of humanistic approaches to knowledge, rhetoric, and social criticism. Understanding this crucial bridge period reveals how human meaning-making systems evolve through creative synthesis of inherited traditions with emerging possibilities rather than through simple replacement of old frameworks with entirely new ones.

Renaissance humanism, flourishing from the fourteenth through sixteenth centuries, created the intellectual and institutional foundations that would make Enlightenment rationalism possible while maintaining sufficient continuity with medieval traditions to avoid complete cultural fragmentation. The humanistic mind painting represented neither mere nostalgia for classical antiquity nor simple rejection of Christian culture but rather a sophisticated attempt to integrate the best insights of both traditions within new frameworks adapted to changing social and intellectual circumstances.

The figure of Erasmus of Rotterdam (1466-1536) exemplifies the innovative potential of humanistic mind painting while illustrating the creative tensions that would eventually generate Enlightenment approaches to knowledge and social criticism. Erasmus's intellectual program combined rigorous philological scholarship, satirical social criticism, and irenic theological reflection in ways that prefigured many distinctive features of later Enlightenment thought while remaining grounded in Christian humanistic commitments that distinguished his approach from more radical secular developments.

Erasmus's critical edition of the Greek New Testament, published in 1516, demonstrated how humanistic scholarship could challenge traditional authorities through careful textual analysis and historical investigation without necessarily undermining fundamental religious commitments. His philological methods revealed numerous errors in the Latin Vulgate that had served as the authoritative biblical text for over a thousand years, showing how scholarly inquiry could improve understanding of divine revelation rather than threatening its authority. This approach established precedents for the kind of critical reasoning that would become central to Enlightenment methodology while maintaining integration with religious faith that later secular thinkers would abandon.

"The Praise of Folly," Erasmus's satirical masterpiece, employed classical rhetorical techniques to critique contemporary social and ecclesiastical corruption while avoiding direct theological controversy that might provoke institutional retaliation. The work's ironic persona of Folly herself delivering encomiums to various forms of human stupidity enabled Erasmus to expose the gap between Christian ideals and institutional practices without explicitly challenging religious authority. This literary strategy demonstrated how indirect critique could be more effective than direct confrontation in promoting social reform, establishing patterns of intellectual engagement that would influence Enlightenment writers like Voltaire and Swift.

Erasmus's educational philosophy, articulated in works like "The Education of a Christian Prince" and his numerous pedagogical treatises, advocated for approaches to learning that emphasized critical thinking, historical understanding, and practical wisdom rather than merely technical expertise in scholastic disputation. His curriculum reform proposals stressed the importance of studying classical literature, rhetoric, and history as means of developing judgment and eloquence necessary for effective citizenship and moral leadership. These educational ideals would profoundly influence the development of humanistic education throughout Europe while providing institutional frameworks that could later accommodate Enlightenment emphases on rational inquiry and empirical investigation.

The humanistic movement that Erasmus helped to lead created new forms of intellectual community that transcended traditional institutional boundaries while maintaining connections to established centers of learning. The correspondence networks among humanist scholars, the development of printing technology that facilitated rapid circulation of texts, and the emergence of patronage relationships with secular rulers created alternative structures for intellectual authority that competed with but did not entirely replace ecclesiastical and university institutions.

These developments established precedents for the kind of "public sphere" that would become crucial to Enlightenment intellectual culture while demonstrating how new forms of collective cognition could emerge through technological innovation and social reorganization. The humanistic emphasis on eloquence, civic engagement, and practical wisdom provided models for intellectual activity that extended beyond purely academic concerns to encompass political and social reform, establishing expectations that knowledge should contribute to human flourishing rather than serving merely contemplative or devotional purposes.

The religious reforms initiated by figures like Luther, Calvin, and other Protestant leaders built upon humanistic textual criticism and institutional critique while radicalizing implications that more moderate humanists like Erasmus had sought to contain within traditional frameworks. The Protestant emphasis on individual scriptural interpretation, the critique of ecclesiastical mediation, and the development of vernacular theology all reflected humanistic influences while pushing toward conclusions that would fundamentally transform European religious and political culture.

These developments created both opportunities and challenges that would shape the subsequent emergence of Enlightenment rationalism. The fragmentation of religious authority opened intellectual space for alternative approaches to fundamental questions about reality, knowledge, and human purpose while simultaneously creating urgent needs for new forms of social coordination that could maintain civilization without depending on universal religious consensus.

The humanistic legacy thus provided both positive resources and negative pressures that would influence Enlightenment intellectual development. The scholarly methods pioneered by humanist philologists and historians established standards for critical reasoning and empirical investigation that could be applied to natural philosophical questions. The literary techniques developed by humanist writers created models for social criticism that could challenge traditional authorities while appealing to educated public opinion. The educational reforms promoted by humanist pedagogues created institutional structures that could support new forms of intellectual inquiry while maintaining connections to classical wisdom traditions.

Simultaneously, the religious and political conflicts generated by humanistic critique created pressures for developing more systematic approaches to fundamental questions that could provide stable foundations for knowledge and social order without depending on religious authorities whose credibility had been compromised by sectarian controversy. The need to address skeptical challenges raised by religious disagreement would drive much of the philosophical innovation that characterized seventeenth and eighteenth-century thought.

Understanding Renaissance humanism as the crucial bridge between medieval and Enlightenment mind painting illuminates the evolutionary rather than revolutionary character of major intellectual transformations. Human meaning-making systems change through creative adaptation of inherited resources to new circumstances rather than through complete rupture with previous traditions. The Enlightenment achievement of developing systematic approaches to natural and social questions built upon methodological innovations and institutional developments pioneered by Renaissance humanists while extending their implications in directions that the earlier generation could not have anticipated.

This recognition of historical continuity does not diminish the significance of Enlightenment innovations but rather helps explain both their remarkable achievements and their persistent limitations. By understanding how Enlightenment thinkers inherited and transformed humanistic legacies, we can better appreciate both the creative potential and the cultural constraints that shaped their contributions to human knowledge and social organization.

The seventeenth and eighteenth centuries witnessed an unprecedented transformation in European intellectual culture that fundamentally altered humanity's understanding of knowledge, reality, and social organization. This period, retrospectively termed the Enlightenment, emerged from the cognitive chaos created by multiple converging forces: the Scientific Revolution's challenge to traditional cosmology, global exploration's encounter with diverse cultures and knowledge systems, religious warfare's devastation of social stability, and the gradual collapse of medieval scholastic authority. These disruptions created urgent demands for new "mind paintings" capable of ordering intellectual and social chaos while providing frameworks for understanding the rapidly expanding horizons of human knowledge and possibility.

Recognizing the Scientific Revolution as the catalyst for new cognitive frameworks requires understanding how developments in astronomy, physics, and mathematics created both opportunities and challenges for traditional ways of organizing knowledge and meaning. The Copernican displacement of Earth from the center of the cosmic order, Galileo's telescopic observations of planetary surfaces and stellar multiplicities, Newton's mathematical unification of terrestrial and celestial mechanics, and the discovery of new continents populated by previously unknown peoples all contributed to what historians call the "crisis of European consciousness" that demanded new approaches to fundamental questions about reality, knowledge, and human purpose.

These developments created cognitive dissonance not merely for religious authorities defending traditional cosmologies but for anyone seeking to maintain coherent worldviews capable of integrating expanding empirical knowledge with inherited cultural values and social institutions. The medieval synthesis that had successfully integrated Aristotelian philosophy with Christian theology proved inadequate for accommodating the mathematical precision of Newtonian mechanics, the vastness of astronomical space revealed by improved telescopes, or the cultural diversity encountered through global exploration and colonization.

The response to this crisis involved creating new institutional structures for producing, evaluating, and disseminating knowledge. The emergence of scientific academies like the Royal Society of London (1660) and the French Academy of Sciences (1666) created new forms of collective cognition that distributed research activities across networks of investigators while establishing peer review procedures for evaluating empirical claims and theoretical innovations. These institutions developed protocols for conducting experiments, recording observations, and communicating results that enabled collaborative knowledge production on a scale previously impossible within university or monastic frameworks.

Simultaneously, the expansion of print culture and the development of periodical publications created new venues for intellectual exchange that transcended traditional institutional boundaries. The rise of coffeehouses, salons, and reading societies provided social spaces where educated individuals could encounter diverse perspectives while participating in collective deliberation about scientific, philosophical, and political questions. These developments created what Jürgen Habermas termed the "public sphere"—a realm of social life where private individuals could come together as a public to debate matters of common concern through reasoned argument rather than traditional authority.

The Enlightenment represents far more than a simple rejection of medieval religious authority or an uncritical celebration of human reason. Rather, it constituted a sophisticated attempt to construct comprehensive cognitive frameworks that could integrate empirical observation, rational analysis, and practical application into coherent systems for understanding natural phenomena, human society, and individual consciousness. These new mind paintings operated within the constraints and possibilities imposed by the Primate Principle while seeking to transcend traditional limitations through methodological innovation and institutional reform.

Understanding the Enlightenment as an exercise in collective mind painting illuminates both its remarkable achievements and its inevitable limitations. The period's intellectual giants functioned not as isolated individual geniuses but as members of emerging intellectual communities that created new forms of distributed cognition through scientific societies, philosophical correspondence networks, and publishing enterprises that facilitated unprecedented collaboration across traditional geographic and cultural boundaries.

The tribal conflict that emerged between rationalism and empiricism during this period illustrates how even within broadly shared commitments to reason and empirical investigation, competing methodological approaches generated distinct interpretive communities with their own cognitive practices, institutional allegiances, and claims to intellectual authority. These philosophical tribes competed not merely for abstract theoretical dominance but for practical influence over educational curricula, scientific research programs, and political reform movements that would shape European civilization for centuries to come.

Examining the rationalist tradition through the lens of mind painting reveals how thinkers like René Descartes, Baruch Spinoza, and Gottfried Leibniz attempted to construct comprehensive philosophical systems that could provide certain knowledge about fundamental reality through the exercise of reason alone. Descartes's method of systematic doubt, outlined in his "Discourse on Method" and

"Meditations on First Philosophy," exemplified the rationalist approach to establishing secure foundations for knowledge by subjecting all beliefs to rigorous skeptical examination until discovering truths so clear and distinct that they could not be doubted.

The Cartesian project involved creating a new cognitive architecture that could replace the medieval synthesis while avoiding the perceived unreliability of sensory experience and the confusion created by conflicting authorities. Descartes's dualistic separation of mind and matter, his mechanistic account of physical processes, and his deductive method for deriving complex truths from simple intuitive principles provided a systematic framework for understanding both natural phenomena and human consciousness within a unified theoretical structure.

Descartes's revolutionary impact extended far beyond his foundational epistemological insights to transform the entire framework for scientific investigation and natural philosophy. His rejection of Aristotelian final causes in favor of mechanistic explanation represented a fundamental shift in how Europeans understood the natural world and humanity's place within it. The Cartesian universe operated like a vast machine governed by mathematical laws that could be discovered through rational analysis and empirical investigation, eliminating the need for teleological explanations that had dominated medieval thought.

This mechanistic worldview had profound implications for human self-understanding and social organization. If human bodies functioned according to mechanical principles, then medicine could become a precise science based on anatomical knowledge and physiological experimentation. If the material world operated according to discoverable laws, then technological innovation could provide unprecedented control over natural forces. These insights promised liberation from traditional authorities—whether religious, political, or intellectual—that claimed privileged access to truth through revelation or inherited wisdom.

Descartes's methodological innovations established procedures for systematic doubt and logical reconstruction that would influence scientific methodology for centuries. His requirement that genuine knowledge must achieve mathematical certainty eliminated traditional reliance on probable reasoning and authoritative testimony, establishing new standards for intellectual rigor that privileged demonstrative proof over persuasive argument. This approach created powerful tools for critical evaluation of inherited beliefs while providing frameworks for collaborative knowledge construction across cultural and institutional boundaries.

The political implications of Cartesian philosophy extended well beyond purely intellectual concerns to challenge traditional forms of social authority. If individual reason could discover fundamental truths about reality without dependence on external authorities, then the legitimacy of political and religious institutions required rational justification rather than mere tradition or divine command. This individualistic epistemology provided intellectual foundations for emerging democratic and constitutional movements that would transform European political culture during subsequent centuries.

Spinoza's geometric method, demonstrated in his "Ethics," pushed the rationalist program to its logical extreme by attempting to derive all possible knowledge about God, nature, and human psychology from a small number of basic definitions and axioms through rigorous deductive reasoning. His monistic metaphysics, which identified God with nature itself, eliminated the traditional Christian distinction between creator and creation while providing a deterministic account of all events as necessary consequences of divine nature operating according to mathematical laws.

Leibniz's system of pre-established harmony and his principle of sufficient reason offered alternative approaches to rationalist metaphysics that attempted to preserve both divine providence and human freedom while maintaining the intelligibility of nature through mathematical analysis. His development of calculus, his logical innovations, and his diplomatic efforts to reconcile competing philosophical and religious traditions exemplified the rationalist ambition to achieve comprehensive understanding through systematic theoretical construction.

The empiricist response to these rationalist ambitions reveals alternative strategies for constructing reliable knowledge that emphasized the fundamental role of sensory experience in all genuine learning while maintaining skepticism about claims to achieve certain knowledge through reason alone. John Locke's "Essay Concerning Human Understanding" provided the foundational text for British empiricism by analyzing the origins, nature, and limits of human knowledge through careful examination of how ideas arise in consciousness through sensation and reflection.

Locke's famous characterization of the mind as initially a "tabula rasa" or blank slate directly illustrates the empiricist understanding of how experience literally "paints" our individual and collective mind paintings through the gradual accumulation and association of simple ideas derived from sensory interaction with the external world. This framework provided a naturalistic account of knowledge acquisition that avoided both innate ideas and direct divine illumination while explaining the apparent universality of basic logical and mathematical truths through shared features of human experience and cognitive processing.

Locke's political philosophy, developed in his "Two Treatises of Government," extended his empiricist insights to challenge traditional theories of political authority while providing theoretical foundations for constitutional government and individual rights. His argument that legitimate political power derives from popular consent rather than divine appointment or natural hierarchy directly challenged absolutist political theory while establishing frameworks for limited government that would profoundly influence American and French revolutionary movements.

The concept of natural rights that Locke developed—particularly rights to life, liberty, and property—provided philosophical foundations for challenging arbitrary authority while establishing principled limits on governmental power. His analysis of property rights as originating through individual labor mixing with natural resources offered theoretical justification for commercial society while establishing moral constraints on both individual accumulation and governmental confiscation.

Locke's "Letter Concerning Toleration" addressed one of the most pressing practical problems facing European societies recovering from religious warfare by providing philosophical arguments for religious liberty that could transcend sectarian divisions. His distinction between the civil and religious spheres established theoretical frameworks for managing religious diversity while maintaining social peace and political legitimacy.

This remarkable period established the foundational elements of what would become the broader Enlightenment project: the confidence that human reason and experience could provide reliable guidance for understanding natural phenomena, organizing political life, and promoting individual and collective flourishing. The rationalist emphasis on systematic theoretical construction and the empiricist commitment to experiential grounding would continue to generate creative tensions and synthetic innovations throughout the subsequent century while establishing methodological approaches that continue to influence contemporary intellectual life.

The institutional innovations that emerged during this foundational period—scientific academies, peer review processes, public discourse through print culture, and philosophical correspondence networks—created frameworks for collective knowledge production that would enable the more ambitious social and cultural reforms attempted by later Enlightenment thinkers. Understanding these foundations provides essential context for comprehending both the achievements and limitations of subsequent Enlightenment developments.

Chapter Seven
The Enlightenment Social Revolution

The foundational philosophical achievements of seventeenth-century rationalism and empiricism created intellectual tools and institutional frameworks that would enable eighteenth-century Enlightenment thinkers to address broader questions about social organization, cultural reform, and human progress. This later phase of Enlightenment development moved beyond primarily theoretical concerns about knowledge and reality to engage practical questions about how philosophical insights could be applied to improve human societies, challenge traditional authorities, and expand individual liberty within frameworks of collective welfare.

Among the Enlightenment's most influential public intellectuals, François-Marie Arouet, known as Voltaire (1694-1778), created perhaps the most comprehensive and practically effective "mind painting" for social reform through his masterful integration of philosophical analysis, satirical criticism, and political activism. Voltaire's intellectual program represented a sophisticated synthesis of empirical methodology, religious tolerance, constitutional government, and cultural criticism that provided blueprints for transforming European society along rational and humanitarian lines.

Voltaire's masterpiece "Candide" (1759) illustrates the power of satirical mind painting to challenge entrenched philosophical and religious orthodoxies while offering alternative frameworks for understanding human existence. The novella's systematic demolition of Leibnizian optimism—the philosophical position that "all is for the best in this best of all possible worlds"—demonstrated how literary art could serve as a vehicle for sophisticated philosophical argument while reaching audiences far beyond academic institutions.

The character of Dr. Pangloss, whose absurd rationalizations of obvious evils exemplify the intellectual bankruptcy of systematic optimism, enabled Voltaire to expose the cognitive dissonance between theoretical philosophy and lived experience. Through Candide's journey across a world filled with war, natural disaster, religious persecution, and social injustice, Voltaire revealed the psychological and moral inadequacy of philosophical systems that minimized human suffering in service of abstract metaphysical coherence.

The novella's famous conclusion—"we must cultivate our garden"—offered a practical alternative to both naive optimism and despairing pessimism that emphasized productive work, moderate expectations, and local community as sources of meaning and satisfaction. This philosophy reflected Voltaire's broader commitment to reformist rather than revolutionary approaches to social improvement, emphasizing gradual progress through education, institutional reform, and cultural change rather than dramatic political transformation.

Voltaire's campaign for religious tolerance represents perhaps his most significant contribution to Enlightenment political theory and demonstrates how philosophical principles could be applied to concrete social problems with transformative practical results. His intervention in the Calas affair—defending a Protestant merchant unjustly executed for allegedly murdering his son to prevent his conversion to Catholicism—illustrated how individual cases of injustice could serve as catalysts for broader institutional reform when addressed through sustained public intellectual engagement.

The "Treatise on Tolerance" (1763) that emerged from this campaign provided both theoretical justification for religious liberty and practical arguments for its implementation within existing political structures. Voltaire's analysis revealed how religious persecution violated both natural law and political prudence by creating social instability while contradicting rational principles of justice and utility. His famous declaration that religious intolerance constituted "the right of the tiger" established metaphors that would resonate throughout subsequent human rights discourse.

Voltaire's approach to religious questions exemplified the Enlightenment strategy of managing rather than eliminating religious belief through rational criticism and institutional reform. Rather than attacking religion per se, he distinguished between essential religious truths accessible to natural reason—particularly belief in God and moral responsibility—and sectarian doctrines that generated conflict without corresponding benefits. This position enabled him to maintain broad social support while advocating for specific reforms that would reduce religious violence and expand individual liberty.

His analysis of English society in the "Philosophical Letters" (1734) provided a comprehensive model for how religious diversity could coexist with social stability and economic prosperity when properly managed through appropriate institutional arrangements. Voltaire's famous observation about the London Stock Exchange—where "the Jew, the Mahometan, and the Christian deal with one another as if they were of the same religion, and reserve the name of infidel for those who go bankrupt"—revealed how commercial relationships could transcend religious divisions when structured around mutual benefit rather than ideological agreement.

This economic approach to social harmony reflected Voltaire's broader confidence in human rationality and self-interest as foundations for political order that could supplement or replace traditional religious and cultural bonds. Rather than requiring extensive moral transformation or institutional revolution, Enlightenment reform could proceed through incremental changes that aligned individual incentives with collective benefits while preserving social stability and existing power structures.

The empiricist tradition reached its most sophisticated and challenging expression in the work of David Hume, whose systematic application of empiricist principles led to conclusions that threatened the foundations of both natural science and moral philosophy while revealing fundamental limitations in human cognitive capacity. Hume's analysis of causation, outlined in his "Treatise of Human Nature" and "Enquiry Concerning Human Understanding," demonstrated that our beliefs about causal connections cannot be justified through either rational demonstration or empirical observation but depend on psychological habits formed through repeated experience of regular successions among events.

Hume's "skeptical eraser" functioned as a powerful application of Occam's Razor that systematically eliminated metaphysical commitments that could not be derived from or confirmed by actual experience. His famous problem of induction revealed the logical gap between finite observations of past regularities and infinite claims about future expectations, showing that even our most basic scientific beliefs depend on assumptions that cannot be rationally justified without circular reasoning.

This analysis exposed what Hume recognized as inherent "limits of knowledge" imposed by the neo-cortical constraints that shape human cognitive processing. Our minds are structured to form beliefs about causal connections and to make predictions about future events based on past experience, but these psychological necessities cannot be translated into logical certainties about the actual structure of reality independent of human cognitive processing.

Hume's analysis of moral philosophy extended his skeptical methodology to challenge traditional foundations of ethical reasoning while revealing the psychological and social mechanisms that actually guide human behavior. His famous observation that "reason is and ought to be the slave of the passions" overturned centuries of philosophical tradition by arguing that moral judgments derive from emotional responses rather than rational demonstration, a conclusion that anticipated modern psychological research while raising fundamental questions about the possibility of objective ethical knowledge.

The implications of Humean moral theory for Enlightenment social reform were profound and troubling. If moral beliefs lack rational foundations and depend instead on psychological habits formed through cultural conditioning, then the Enlightenment project of improving society through rational criticism and institutional reform appears to rest on questionable assumptions about human nature and social change. Hume's analysis suggested that moral progress might require transformation of emotional dispositions and social practices rather than merely logical argument and legal reform.

Jean-Jacques Rousseau (1712-1778) represents perhaps the most profound internal critique of Enlightenment assumptions about reason, progress, and human nature while remaining fundamentally committed to the broader project of constructing rational foundations for political legitimacy and social organization. Rousseau's intellectual program reveals the creative tensions within Enlightenment mind painting that would eventually contribute to its transformation and partial replacement by alternative frameworks emphasizing emotion, cultural particularity, and historical development.

Rousseau's famous opening declaration in "The Social Contract" that "man is born free, and he is everywhere in chains" established the fundamental problem that his political philosophy sought to address: how can legitimate political authority exist without destroying the natural freedom that constitutes human dignity? This question challenged core Enlightenment assumptions about the compatibility between rational social organization and individual liberty while demanding more radical solutions than those proposed by moderate reformers like Voltaire.

The concept of the "general will" represents Rousseau's most significant contribution to Enlightenment political theory and illustrates how philosophical mind painting could generate institutional innovations that transcended traditional alternatives between monarchy and anarchy. The general will differs fundamentally from both the aggregate preferences of individual citizens and the imposed will of external authorities by representing the common interest that emerges when citizens deliberate about shared concerns while setting aside their particular interests as private individuals.

However, Rousseau's analysis of existing societies revealed profound obstacles to realizing this democratic ideal. His "Discourse on the Origin of Inequality" demonstrated how the development of private property, social stratification, and cultural sophistication had corrupted natural human goodness while creating artificial needs and competitive relationships that made authentic democratic deliberation increasingly difficult.

This critique challenged fundamental Enlightenment assumptions about the relationship between knowledge, virtue, and happiness. Where thinkers like Voltaire and Diderot assumed that increasing scientific knowledge and cultural refinement would promote human flourishing, Rousseau argued that civilization itself created psychological and social pathologies that required radical institutional transformation to address.

The collaborative encyclopedia project initiated by Denis Diderot (1713-1784) and Jean d'Alembert (1717-1783) represents perhaps the most ambitious attempt in human history to create a comprehensive mind painting that could systematically organize and disseminate all available knowledge for practical application and social improvement. The Encyclopédie, ou dictionnaire raisonné des sciences, des arts et des métiers, published in twenty-eight volumes between 1751 and 1772, demonstrated how Enlightenment ideals could be translated into concrete institutional form through collaborative intellectual labor.

Diderot's vision for the encyclopedia extended far beyond simple compilation of existing information to encompass fundamental transformation of how knowledge was organized, evaluated, and applied to human problems. His manifesto for the project declared that its aim was "to bring together the knowledge scattered over the surface of the earth, to present its overall structure to our contemporaries and to hand it on to those who will come after us, so that our children, by becoming more knowledgeable, will become more virtuous and happier."

The encyclopedia's organizational structure reflected Enlightenment confidence in the unity and systematic character of human knowledge while providing practical tools for cross-referencing and comparative analysis that anticipated modern information management systems. The controversial implications of this approach became evident in articles that challenged religious orthodoxy, political absolutism, and social hierarchy through carefully crafted arguments that appeared to provide neutral scholarly information while advancing radical critiques of existing institutions.

Adam Smith (1723-1790) developed the most sophisticated Enlightenment synthesis of moral philosophy and economic analysis through his systematic investigation of how individual psychological mechanisms could generate beneficial social outcomes without requiring extensive government regulation or moral transformation. His "Theory of Moral Sentiments" (1759) and "The Wealth of Nations" (1776) together constitute a comprehensive mind painting that addresses fundamental questions about human motivation, social coordination, and institutional design.

Smith's analysis of moral sentiments challenged both rational and intuitive approaches to ethics by grounding moral judgment in the human capacity for sympathy—the ability to imagine oneself in another's situation and to experience vicarious emotional responses to their circumstances. The impartial spectator concept provided Smith with a naturalistic foundation for moral judgment that avoided both the dogmatism of revealed religion and the abstraction of purely rational ethics while explaining how moral standards could achieve intersubjective validity across diverse cultural contexts.

Smith's economic analysis extended these insights to explain how market relationships could coordinate the productive activities of countless individuals without requiring comprehensive planning or detailed moral instruction. The famous "invisible hand" mechanism demonstrated how individuals pursuing their own interests within appropriate institutional frameworks would unintentionally promote collective welfare through competitive processes that rewarded efficiency and innovation while punishing waste and incompetence.

The broader Scottish Enlightenment context within which Smith developed his theories reveals the distributed character of Enlightenment intellectual innovation and its connections to specific social and institutional circumstances. Thinkers like Adam Ferguson, Thomas Reid, and Lord Kames contributed to a distinctive approach to social science that emphasized historical development, cultural variation, and the unintended consequences of human action.

The Enlightenment's exclusion of women from formal intellectual institutions and political participation generated internal critiques that challenged core assumptions about rationality, natural rights, and human equality. Mary Wollstonecraft (1759-1797), Olympe de Gouges (1748-1793), and other women intellectuals applied Enlightenment principles to reveal the inconsistency between universal claims about human reason and dignity and practices that systematically denied women educational opportunities and political rights.

Wollstonecraft's "Vindication of the Rights of Woman" (1792) demonstrated how Enlightenment arguments for individual liberty and rational education could be extended to challenge gender hierarchies that subordinated women through artificial restrictions rather than natural differences. De Gouges's "Declaration of the Rights of Woman and the Female Citizen" (1791) directly challenged the exclusions embedded in revolutionary political documents by extending claims about natural rights and political equality to encompass women as well as men.

Understanding the Counter-Enlightenment critiques that emerged even during the eighteenth century reveals the limitations and vulnerabilities of Enlightenment mind painting while anticipating alternative approaches that would gain prominence during the Romantic period and beyond. Edmund Burke's "Reflections on the Revolution in France" (1790) provided the most systematic conservative response to Enlightenment political theory by emphasizing the wisdom embedded in traditional institutions and the dangers of radical rational reconstruction.

Johann Gottfried Herder's cultural philosophy challenged Enlightenment universalism by emphasizing the irreducible diversity of human cultures and the dangers of imposing uniform rational standards across different societies. These critiques would eventually contribute to Romantic and historicist movements that challenged core Enlightenment assumptions about reason, progress, and human nature.

The response to Humean skepticism reveals the creative flexibility of Enlightenment mind painting in developing new approaches that could acknowledge the force of skeptical arguments while maintaining commitment to scientific investigation and social reform. Immanuel Kant's "critical philosophy," developed in his three Critiques, attempted to chart a middle course between rationalist dogmatism and empiricist skepticism by analyzing the necessary conditions that make human experience and knowledge possible.

Kant's "Copernican revolution" in philosophy involved recognizing that objects of experience must conform to the structure of human cognition rather than cognition passively receiving impressions from independently existing objects. The Kantian synthesis preserved the empiricist insight that all knowledge begins with experience while maintaining the rationalist claim that reason contributes essential organizing principles that shape how experience becomes intelligible.

Kant's moral philosophy represents perhaps the most systematic attempt in Enlightenment thought to preserve rational foundations for ethics while acknowledging the force of Humean skeptical arguments about the limits of theoretical knowledge. The categorical imperative provided a formal principle for moral reasoning that claimed universal validity while remaining accessible to ordinary moral agents without specialized philosophical training.

This analysis of Enlightenment social revolution requires explicit defense against several philosophical objections that might question the legitimacy or usefulness of the interpretive framework being employed. However, recognizing the psychological and social processes through which philosophical ideas emerge, develop, and gain acceptance does not invalidate their potential truth value or diminish their intellectual significance.

The framework developed here maintains clear distinctions between causal explanation and normative evaluation while acknowledging the situated character of human knowledge. The mind painting metaphor emphasizes the creative and constructed character of human meaning-making systems without implying that such constructions are arbitrary or purely subjective.

The enduring influence of Enlightenment mind painting on subsequent intellectual development reveals both the creative achievements and persistent limitations of this remarkable cultural transformation. The methodological innovations, institutional structures, and political ideals developed during this period continue to influence contemporary culture while generating new problems that require further creative innovation.

Understanding the Enlightenment not as a final achievement of human rationality but as a particular historical episode in the ongoing human project of creating meaning and order provides essential background for comprehending subsequent developments in human intellectual and social organization while appreciating both the remarkable human capacity for cultural creativity and the inevitable constraints that shape all human meaning-making enterprises.

Chapter Eight

The Logic and Language Canvas – Painting Reality Through Structure and Communication

The human capacity to create systematic frameworks for reasoning and communication represents one of our most sophisticated achievements in constructing "mind paintings" that can order cognitive chaos while enabling complex social coordination across vast temporal and spatial distances. Logic and language function not as direct reflections of reality's inherent structure but as elaborate cognitive technologies designed by and for brains operating within the constraints and possibilities established by the Primate Principle. Understanding these seemingly fundamental aspects of human rationality as culturally constructed systems reveals both their remarkable effectiveness and their inevitable limitations while illuminating the creative processes through which humans continue to develop new tools for thinking and meaning-making.

Before addressing potential objections to this framework, it is essential to acknowledge the apparent self-referential challenge it creates. Critics might argue that using logical reasoning to demonstrate the constructed character of logic commits a performative contradiction—employing the very tools whose objectivity we question to make arguments about their cultural specificity. However, this objection misunderstands the analytical framework being employed here. Recognizing that logical systems emerge from human cognitive processes does not render them invalid or arbitrary, nor does it eliminate their capacity to provide reliable tools for reasoning about their own origins and development.

The framework maintains clear distinctions between describing causal processes and evaluating logical validity. When we analyze how logical systems develop through cultural evolution, we employ logical reasoning not to undermine its effectiveness but to illuminate its remarkable capacity to transcend the biological limitations of individual minds through collective cultural construction. The fact that humans created logical systems demonstrates their creative cognitive achievements rather than revealing fundamental flaws in rational thought. Logic works precisely because it leverages and systematizes cognitive capabilities while creating frameworks that enable collaborative reasoning across diverse cultural contexts.

Logic, traditionally regarded as the bedrock of rational thought and objective reasoning, emerges through this analysis as a highly refined and explicit mind painting that systematizes how humans believe reasoning should work to achieve cognitive harmony while eliminating contradictions within thought processes themselves. The elaborate systems of rules, symbols, and procedures that constitute formal logic represent sophisticated attempts to externalize and standardize the pattern-recognition, abstraction, and sequential-processing capabilities that characterize neo-cortical function.

The historical development of logical systems demonstrates the constructed character of what might appear to be universal rational principles. Aristotelian logic, systematized in the Organon and dominant in European intellectual culture for over two millennia, reflected specific assumptions about reality, language, and thought that seemed natural and necessary to those working within its framework. The Aristotelian emphasis on categorical reasoning, syllogistic argument, and the principle of non-contradiction provided powerful tools for organizing and evaluating arguments while establishing standards for intellectual rigor that shaped European educational and scholarly practice.

However, the emergence of modern mathematical logic during the nineteenth and twentieth centuries revealed the cultural and historical specificity of Aristotelian assumptions while demonstrating that alternative logical systems could be constructed to address different problems and serve different purposes. The work of George Boole, Gottlob Frege, Bertrand Russell, and Alfred North Whitehead created formal systems that treated logic as a calculus whose rules of operation were determined by the structural relationships among symbols rather than their semantic content or correspondence to natural language patterns.

This transformation from Aristotelian to modern formal logic illustrates what can be termed "logical cultural drift"—the process through which communities of thinkers develop new approaches to reasoning that better serve their cognitive and practical needs while building upon but not being determined by previous traditions. The development of propositional logic, predicate logic, modal logic, and non-classical logics like fuzzy logic, paraconsistent logic, and quantum logic demonstrates that there is no single correct way to systematize rational thinking but rather multiple approaches that emphasize different aspects of reasoning while serving different intellectual and practical purposes.

Kurt Gödel's incompleteness theorems provide perhaps the most dramatic demonstration of the inherent limitations within even the most sophisticated logical systems, revealing that any consistent formal system capable of expressing basic arithmetic will contain statements that cannot be proven or disproven within the system itself. The first incompleteness theorem establishes that there will always be true statements that remain unprovable within any such system, while the second theorem demonstrates that the system cannot prove its own consistency without appealing to principles beyond those it contains.

These results initially appeared to threaten the entire foundationalist project in mathematics and logic by showing that no formal system could achieve the complete and self-contained character that David Hilbert and others had sought. However, rather than undermining confidence in logical reasoning, Gödel's theorems actually illuminate the remarkable human capacity for transcending the limitations of any particular formal system through creative theoretical innovation and conceptual expansion.

The incompleteness theorems reveal logic not as a fixed discovery about the nature of reality but as an ongoing cultural project that operates within systematic constraints while remaining open to continued development and refinement. The fact that no single logical system can capture all mathematical truths does not eliminate the possibility of mathematical knowledge but rather demonstrates that such knowledge emerges through the dynamic interaction among multiple formal systems, intuitive insights, and cultural practices that collectively enable mathematical understanding.

Contemporary developments in logic continue to demonstrate its constructed and evolving character. The emergence of computational logic, artificial intelligence applications, machine learning algorithms, and bio-inspired reasoning systems reflects ongoing human creativity in developing reasoning frameworks adapted to new domains and challenges. These innovations reveal logic not as a static reflection of eternal rational principles but as a living cultural tradition that continues to evolve in response to changing intellectual and practical needs.

Ludwig Wittgenstein's later philosophy provides crucial insights into how logical and linguistic systems function as cultural mind paintings embedded within broader forms of social life. Wittgenstein's concept of "language games" reveals how meaning emerges not from fixed correspondences between words and objects but from the rule-governed practices through which linguistic expressions acquire significance within specific contexts of human activity.

The famous example of the builders' language game—in which a builder and assistant coordinate their activities through a minimal vocabulary of "block," "pillar," "slab," and "beam"—illustrates how even the simplest linguistic interactions depend on shared forms of life that provide the cultural context within which words can function meaningfully. The builder's call for a "slab" acquires meaning not through any inherent connection between the sound and the object but through the established practices and expectations that enable the assistant to respond appropriately.

Wittgenstein's broader analysis extends this insight to reveal how our ordinary language consists of countless overlapping language games, each with its own rules and purposes, connected through what he terms "family resemblances" rather than any single essential feature. The word "game" itself illustrates this point—we apply it to board games, card games, ball games, Olympic Games, and war games without being able to identify any single characteristic common to all these activities. Instead, these various activities overlap and crisscross in complex ways that resist systematic definition while maintaining sufficient stability to support reliable communication and social coordination.

The concept of "forms of life" provides the broader cultural context within which language games acquire meaning and significance. Forms of life encompass the shared practices, assumptions, and ways of being in the world that provide the background against which specific linguistic utterances become intelligible. These forms of life are not merely linguistic but involve the entire range of human activities, institutions, and cultural traditions that shape how communities understand themselves and their environments.

This Wittgensteinian analysis reveals how what appears to be purely logical or linguistic activity always operates within specific cultural contexts that provide both the motivation and the criteria for success in reasoning and communication. The meaning of logical connectives like "and," "or," and "if...then" emerges not from abstract definitions but from their role within the language games of reasoning, argumentation, and problem-solving that constitute significant portions of intellectual culture.

The study of language provides even more dramatic evidence for the constructed character of human meaning-making systems while revealing the mechanisms through which different cultural groups develop distinct approaches to conceptualizing and communicating about reality. The Sapir-Whorf hypothesis, also known as the principle of linguistic relativity, suggests that the specific structure of a language influences how its speakers perceive, categorize, and reason about their experiences.

Edward Sapir's foundational insight that "human beings do not live in the objective world alone, nor alone in the world of social activity as ordinarily understood, but are very much at the mercy of the particular language which has become the medium of expression for their society" captures the fundamental recognition that languages function as cultural technologies for organizing experience rather than neutral tools for describing pre-existing reality.

Benjamin Lee Whorf's more specific studies of Hopi temporal concepts, while methodologically limited in some respects, illustrate the kind of systematic differences in conceptual organization that can emerge through linguistic cultural drift. Contemporary research has identified numerous examples of how linguistic differences correlate with cognitive and behavioral variations across cultures, from spatial reasoning and color perception to mathematical thinking and social categorization.

However, the linguistic relativity hypothesis faces significant challenges from Noam Chomsky's theory of Universal Grammar, which argues that all human languages share fundamental structural principles that reflect innate cognitive capacities rather than purely cultural constructions. Chomsky's research program has identified numerous linguistic universals—patterns that appear across unrelated language families and suggest underlying biological constraints on the forms that human languages can take.

The theory of Universal Grammar proposes that children acquire language so rapidly and with such uniformity across diverse cultural contexts because they possess innate knowledge of the basic principles that organize all human languages. The poverty of the stimulus argument suggests that the linguistic input available to children is too limited and variable to account for their consistent success in acquiring complex grammatical systems without extensive explicit instruction.

Recent research has identified specific parameters that distinguish different languages while operating within universal constraints established by the human language faculty. The pro-drop parameter, for example, determines whether languages require explicit subjects in all sentences (like English) or allow them to be omitted when contextually recoverable (like Spanish and Italian). Children must set this and other parameters based on the linguistic input they receive, but the range of possible parameter settings appears to be severely constrained by Universal Grammar.

This tension between linguistic relativity and Universal Grammar reflects a deeper question about the relationship between biological and cultural factors in human cognitive development. However, rather than viewing these approaches as mutually exclusive, we can understand them as addressing different aspects of human linguistic capacity while both remaining compatible with the mind painting framework.

Universal Grammar may establish the basic cognitive architecture that makes cultural linguistic constructions possible without determining their specific content or development. The fact that all human languages employ certain universal principles—such as hierarchical phrase structure, long-distance dependencies, and systematic sound-meaning correspondences—demonstrates the remarkable biological foundations that enable cultural meaning-making rather than eliminating its constructed character.

Within the constraints established by Universal Grammar, different linguistic communities have developed remarkably diverse approaches to organizing and expressing human experience. These differences operate at multiple levels—lexical, grammatical, and pragmatic—that collectively create distinct linguistic mind paintings while remaining comprehensible across cultural boundaries through the shared biological foundations of human language capacity.

Contemporary research in color perception provides instructive examples of how biological and cultural factors interact in linguistic development. Brent Berlin and Paul Kay's influential study of color terms across languages revealed systematic patterns in how different cultures organize the color spectrum through their vocabulary. While all humans share the same basic color vision system, languages differ dramatically in how many color terms they possess and how those terms divide the visible spectrum.

Some languages have only two basic color terms (roughly corresponding to light and dark), while others have eleven or more. However, the emergence of new color terms follows predictable patterns across cultures, suggesting underlying biological constraints on how color categories can be organized while allowing for significant cultural variation in their specific implementation.

These findings support a nuanced view of linguistic relativity that acknowledges both universal constraints and cultural variations in how humans organize their conceptual systems. Languages provide different cognitive palettes for attending to and remembering color distinctions, with speakers of languages that have more refined color vocabularies showing enhanced discrimination abilities in those specific regions of the color spectrum.

Semiotics, the systematic study of signs and symbols, provides additional insight into how human meaning-making operates through constructed rather than natural relationships between signifiers and their referents. Charles Sanders Peirce's triadic model of the sign—consisting of the sign vehicle (the physical form), the object (what is signified), and the interpretant (the meaning created in someone's mind)—reveals the complex cultural processes through which arbitrary relationships between symbols and meanings become sufficiently stable to support reliable communication while remaining flexible enough to adapt to changing circumstances and needs.

Ferdinand de Saussure's dyadic model, emphasizing the arbitrary relationship between signifier and signified, demonstrates how linguistic and other symbolic systems depend on networks of differences rather than positive connections to reality. The meaning of any particular sign emerges from its systematic relationships to other signs within the same cultural system rather than from any direct correspondence between the sign and external objects or experiences.

This semiotic understanding illuminates how different cultural groups can develop systematically different approaches to interpreting and responding to their experiences while maintaining internal consistency and practical effectiveness. Iconic relationships (where signs resemble their referents), indexical relationships (where signs are causally connected to their referents), and symbolic relationships (where signs are arbitrarily associated with their referents) create different types of meaning that serve different communicative and cognitive functions while being susceptible to different types of cultural evolution and historical change.

Contemporary developments in cognitive linguistics, particularly the work of George Lakoff and Mark Johnson on conceptual metaphor, reveal how abstract reasoning depends on systematic mappings from concrete bodily and cultural experience. Their analysis demonstrates that seemingly objective logical and mathematical concepts—such as categories, causation, and numerical relationships—emerge from embodied metaphorical projections rather than direct apprehension of abstract logical structures.

The conceptual metaphor "argument is war," for example, systematically structures how English speakers understand and engage in intellectual debate through military terminology—we attack positions, defend claims, shoot down arguments, and defeat opponents. This metaphorical structure influences not only how we talk about reasoning but how we actually conduct intellectual activity, creating cultural patterns of competitive argumentation that might seem natural to English speakers but reflect specific cultural constructions of intellectual engagement.

Cross-cultural studies reveal that different linguistic communities employ different metaphorical systems for organizing the same abstract domains, creating systematic differences in reasoning patterns and problem-solving approaches. These differences suggest that even the most abstract logical and mathematical thinking remains grounded in culturally specific ways of understanding bodily experience and social interaction.

Developments in artificial intelligence and computational linguistics provide additional evidence for the constructed character of logical and linguistic systems while revealing their functional effectiveness across different material substrates. Machine learning systems can acquire sophisticated language processing capabilities and logical reasoning abilities without possessing human biological architecture, demonstrating that these capacities emerge from complex system-level interactions rather than from any essential connection to human neural organization.

Neural network approaches to language processing reveal how systematic grammatical and semantic patterns can emerge from statistical regularities in large datasets without requiring explicit representation of grammatical rules or logical principles. These systems develop internal representations that capture important linguistic generalizations while remaining quite different from traditional formal approaches to grammar and logic.

However, the success of artificial systems does not eliminate the significance of cultural construction in human meaning-making but rather demonstrates the remarkable human achievement in creating tools and techniques that can be implemented across diverse material contexts. The fact that computers can perform logical operations and process human languages reflects the effectiveness of human-created systems rather than revealing their independence from cultural development.

Contemporary neurolinguistic research provides additional insight into how cultural linguistic experience literally reshapes brain structure and function during development and throughout life. Studies using neuroimaging techniques reveal systematic differences in brain organization between speakers of different languages, particularly in areas responsible for processing grammatical structures, phonological patterns, and semantic relationships.

Speakers of tonal languages like Mandarin Chinese show enhanced neural responses to pitch variations compared to speakers of non-tonal languages like English, while speakers of languages with complex case systems show different patterns of activation in areas responsible for processing grammatical relationships. These findings demonstrate that cultural linguistic experience shapes neural development in ways that can influence cognitive processing beyond purely linguistic tasks.

However, these neuroplasticity effects operate within constraints established by the basic architecture of human brain organization. All human brains possess specialized areas for language processing that develop according to similar principles regardless of which specific language is acquired, while cultural variation in linguistic experience influences the detailed organization and connectivity patterns within these universal systems.

This analysis of logic and language as sophisticated mind painting systems requires explicit defense against several additional philosophical objections beyond the performative contradiction charge already addressed. Critics might argue that the apparent universality of mathematical truths—such as the fact that 2+2=4 in all cultures—demonstrates that at least some logical principles transcend cultural construction and reflect objective features of reality.

This objection raises important questions about the relationship between cultural construction and cross-cultural validity. However, the universality of certain mathematical relationships can be understood as reflecting the shared constraints imposed by human cognitive architecture rather than direct access to mind-independent mathematical objects. The fact that all human cultures that develop numerical systems discover the same basic arithmetical relationships demonstrates the consistency of human pattern-recognition capabilities rather than the mind-independence of mathematical truth.

Moreover, even apparently universal mathematical concepts show significant cultural variation in their development, representation, and application. Different cultures have developed different numeral systems, geometric concepts, and approaches to mathematical reasoning that reflect specific cultural needs and aesthetic preferences while remaining capable of translation and comparison through shared human cognitive capacities.

The translation challenge poses another potential objection to the cultural construction framework. Critics might argue that if meanings were genuinely culture-specific, successful translation between languages would be impossible, yet we regularly achieve effective cross-cultural communication through translation and interpretation practices.

However, the possibility of translation does not require that different languages carve up experience in identical ways but only that they remain sufficiently related through shared human experience and cognitive architecture to enable mutual understanding through creative interpretive work. Translation is indeed a creative cultural practice that involves constructing bridges between different meaning systems rather than simply transferring identical contents from one neutral container to another.

The most successful translations often require extensive cultural explanation and creative adaptation rather than word-for-word correspondence, demonstrating both the genuine differences between linguistic meaning systems and the human capacity for transcending these differences through interpretive creativity and cultural exchange.

Evolutionary objections might argue that human logical and linguistic capacities evolved through natural selection for their adaptive effectiveness in tracking environmental regularities and enabling social coordination, suggesting that these systems succeed because they correspond to objective features of reality rather than merely expressing cultural constructions.

This objection correctly identifies the evolutionary origins of human cognitive capacities while misunderstanding their implications for cultural construction. The fact that human brains evolved cognitive mechanisms capable of pattern recognition, social communication, and abstract reasoning provides the biological foundation that makes cultural meaning-making possible without determining its specific content or development.

Evolution equipped humans with cognitive tools that are sufficiently flexible and powerful to support diverse cultural constructions rather than hard-wired representations of environmental features. The remarkable diversity of human cultures and the continuing development of new logical and linguistic systems demonstrate the creative potential inherent in human cognitive architecture rather than its limitation to specific environmental correspondences.

Understanding logical and linguistic systems as cultural mind paintings reveals both the remarkable human capacity for developing sophisticated tools for organizing thought and communication and the inevitable constraints that shape all human meaning-making enterprises. These systems provide powerful resources for managing complexity, enabling cooperation, and extending individual cognitive capabilities through collective cultural processes while remaining open to continued development and refinement through ongoing human creativity.

The analysis presented here aims to contribute to more sophisticated and effective approaches to logical reasoning and linguistic communication by providing theoretical frameworks that can illuminate both their strengths and their limitations while supporting continued innovation and development. Recognizing that logical and linguistic systems are human constructions rather than discoveries of eternal truths encourages both intellectual humility about current achievements and confidence in human capacity for continued cultural innovation.

This recognition provides essential background for understanding how human cultures continue to develop new approaches to reasoning and communication that can address emerging challenges while building upon the achievements of previous generations. The mind painting framework illuminates both the creative processes through which such innovations emerge and the constraints and possibilities that shape their development and application across different cultural contexts.

The study of logic and language as cultural mind paintings demonstrates the broader applicability of this theoretical framework for understanding human cultural achievement while revealing the ongoing human project of creating meaning and order within the constraints and possibilities established by our evolutionary inheritance. These insights provide resources for continuing intellectual and cultural development while maintaining appreciation for both human creativity and the systematic character of the challenges we face in organizing complex societies and managing increasingly sophisticated technological systems.

Understanding the constructed character of logical and linguistic systems does not diminish their remarkable effectiveness but rather enhances our appreciation for the creative processes through which humans continue to develop tools that transcend biological limitations while serving essential functions in organizing thought, enabling communication, and coordinating complex social activities across diverse cultural contexts and historical circumstances.

Chapter Nine
The American Palette – Pragmatism and the Utility of Thought

The emergence of American pragmatism in the late nineteenth century represents a revolutionary transformation in philosophical thinking that explicitly recognizes the functional character of human mind paintings while providing systematic frameworks for evaluating their effectiveness in achieving practical goals. This distinctively American contribution to philosophy—developed through the pioneering work of Charles Sanders Peirce, William James, John Dewey, George Herbert Mead, Oliver Wendell Holmes Jr., and Jane Addams—offers profound insights into the nature of truth, knowledge, and inquiry that directly support the theoretical framework advanced throughout this analysis while challenging traditional approaches that claim validity through abstract coherence or external authority rather than demonstrated utility in ordering chaos and acquiring essential "bananas."

Pragmatism emerged from specific cultural circumstances that enabled its founders to develop new approaches to fundamental philosophical questions without the constraints imposed by European academic traditions. The aftermath of the Civil War, the rapid industrialization and urbanization of American society, the influence of evolutionary theory, and the practical demands of building democratic institutions within a diverse and changing society all contributed to creating intellectual conditions where pragmatic approaches to knowledge and truth could develop and flourish.

The movement's origins can be traced to discussions at the so-called "Metaphysical Club" that met in Cambridge, Massachusetts around 1870-1874, where young intellectuals including Peirce, James, Oliver Wendell Holmes Jr., Chauncey Wright, and Nicholas St. John Green engaged in vigorous debates about the nature of knowledge, meaning, and truth. These discussions occurred within a broader cultural context that emphasized practical problem-solving, democratic participation, and scientific investigation over abstract theoretical speculation, creating favorable conditions for developing philosophical approaches that emphasized the functional consequences of ideas rather than their correspondence to eternal principles or their internal logical consistency.

Charles Sanders Peirce (1839-1914) established the foundational principles of pragmatic thinking through his development of what he termed the "pragmatic maxim," first articulated in his 1878 essay "How to Make Our Ideas Clear." This maxim proposed that the meaning of any concept could be clarified by examining its practical consequences: "Consider what effects, which might conceivably have practical bearings, we conceive the object of our conception to have. Then, our conception of these effects is the whole of our conception of the object."

This apparently simple formulation contains profound implications that directly illuminate the constructed character of human mind paintings while providing criteria for evaluating their effectiveness. Peirce's insight recognizes that human concepts function not as passive reflections of external reality but as active tools for organizing experience and guiding behavior within the constraints and possibilities established by our cognitive architecture and social circumstances.

Peirce's categories of Firstness, Secondness, and Thirdness provide a systematic framework for understanding how human experience organizes itself through increasingly sophisticated levels of relationship and meaning. Firstness encompasses immediate qualitative experience—pure possibility and feeling without reference to anything else. Secondness involves dyadic relationships of action and reaction, resistance and effort, existence and struggle. Thirdness represents the realm of signs, laws, habits, and general relationships that enable prediction and understanding across different situations and contexts.

This categorical analysis reveals how human mind paintings operate through the progressive integration of immediate experience (Firstness), practical interaction with resistant reality (Secondness), and systematic symbolic organization that enables general understanding and effective prediction (Thirdness). The categories demonstrate how even our most abstract conceptual constructions remain grounded in embodied experience while achieving sufficient generality to function across diverse circumstances.

Peirce's semiotics—his systematic study of signs and meaning-making processes—reveals how human understanding operates through complex networks of interpretive relationships rather than direct correspondences between mental representations and external objects. His triadic model of the sign (consisting of the representamen, object, and interpretant) demonstrates how meaning emerges through dynamic processes that involve both individual cognitive activity and collective cultural development.

The concept of the "community of inquirers" represents Peirce's most significant contribution to understanding how reliable knowledge can emerge through collective cultural processes operating within the constraints of human cognitive limitations. Peirce argued that truth should be understood not as correspondence to mind-independent reality but as the opinion that would be reached by competent investigators if they pursued inquiry far enough using appropriate methods.

This approach recognizes that individual human minds operate within severe cognitive constraints while demonstrating how collaborative inquiry can transcend these limitations through the development of shared methods, institutional frameworks, and cumulative traditions of investigation. The community of inquirers functions as a distributed cognitive system that can achieve levels of reliability and sophistication impossible for isolated individual minds while remaining grounded in the practical consequences that determine the effectiveness of different approaches to organizing experience.

Peirce's fallibilism—the recognition that any particular belief or theory might prove inadequate and require revision in light of future experience—acknowledges the inherent limitations of human knowledge while maintaining confidence in the long-term effectiveness of properly conducted inquiry. This position avoids both the dogmatism that claims certainty for particular beliefs and the skepticism that denies the possibility of reliable knowledge, instead emphasizing the ongoing, self-correcting character of inquiry as a cultural process.

William James (1842-1910) developed pragmatic insights in directions that more explicitly emphasized their implications for individual psychology and religious experience while maintaining focus on the practical consequences that determine the value of different beliefs and theories. James's famous declaration that "the ultimate test for us of what a truth means is the conduct it dictates or inspires" captures the pragmatic emphasis on functional effectiveness rather than abstract correspondence as the criterion for evaluating ideas.

James's revolutionary concept of the "stream of consciousness," developed in his "Principles of Psychology" (1890), provides crucial support for understanding mind paintings as dynamic, flowing constructions rather than static representations. Consciousness does not consist of discrete ideas or sensations but rather flows as a continuous stream of experience that is selective, personal, constantly changing, and always focused on objects beyond itself. This analysis reveals how human mind paintings emerge through the ongoing activity of attention and selection rather than through passive reception of external impressions.

The stream of consciousness demonstrates how human experience actively constructs rather than merely discovers the objects of its attention. What we experience as objective reality emerges through the selective activity of consciousness organizing its stream of experience according to interests, purposes, and habitual patterns that reflect both individual psychology and cultural conditioning. This insight directly supports the mind painting framework by revealing the active, constructive character of all human experience.

James's "will to believe" doctrine addresses fundamental questions about how individuals should respond to situations where evidence remains inconclusive while decisions cannot be postponed. In cases involving what James termed "live, forced, and momentous" options—situations where individuals must choose between alternatives that both remain psychologically compelling while having significant consequences for their lives—James argued that practical considerations legitimately influence belief formation even in the absence of conclusive theoretical evidence.

This analysis directly illuminates the role of "banana acquisition" motivations in human belief formation while providing criteria for distinguishing legitimate from illegitimate influences of practical considerations on cognitive processes. James recognized that human beings inevitably operate within situations that require action despite incomplete information, making it necessary to develop approaches to belief formation that can acknowledge practical constraints while maintaining commitment to evidential standards where they remain applicable.

James's investigations of religious experience, documented in his masterwork "The Varieties of Religious Experience," demonstrate how pragmatic criteria can be applied to evaluate claims that traditional epistemological approaches struggle to address effectively. Rather than attempting to determine the metaphysical truth of religious beliefs through abstract theoretical analysis, James examined their practical consequences for individual psychological well-being and social functioning.

Oliver Wendell Holmes Jr. (1841-1935) extended pragmatic principles into legal theory and practice through his revolutionary analysis of how law functions as a social institution that must adapt to changing circumstances while maintaining sufficient stability to coordinate collective behavior. Holmes's famous opening declaration in "The Common Law" (1881) that "the life of the law has not been logic; it has been experience" captures the pragmatic understanding that legal systems achieve their effectiveness through ongoing experimental adaptation rather than through deductive application of abstract principles.

Holmes's legal pragmatism recognizes that law functions as a sophisticated form of social mind painting that must balance competing demands for predictability and adaptability while serving the practical needs of complex societies. Legal rules and standards emerge through collective processes that integrate past experience, current circumstances, and anticipated consequences rather than through purely logical deduction from fundamental principles.

The concept of external standards represents Holmes's most significant contribution to legal theory and demonstrates how pragmatic approaches can address problems that remain intractable within traditional jurisprudential frameworks. Holmes argued that legal liability should be determined by objective, community-based standards of conduct rather than by the subjective moral culpability of particular individuals. This approach enables legal systems to coordinate social behavior through publicly accessible criteria while avoiding the impossible task of determining individual psychological states.

Holmes's analysis of negligence illustrates how legal pragmatism operates through institutional mechanisms that enable collective learning and adaptation. The division of responsibility between judge and jury reflects the need to integrate expert knowledge of legal principles with practical understanding of community standards and particular circumstances. This institutional structure enables legal systems to develop increasingly sophisticated approaches to complex problems while remaining responsive to changing social conditions.

The common law system that Holmes analyzed exemplifies pragmatic inquiry operating at the institutional level. Legal precedents function as hypotheses about effective approaches to recurring social problems, subject to testing and revision through subsequent application and analysis. Successful precedents become established elements of legal doctrine, while unsuccessful approaches are abandoned or modified based on demonstrated inadequacy for achieving intended purposes.

George Herbert Mead (1863-1931) made perhaps the most fundamental contribution to understanding how individual mind paintings emerge through social interaction and communication. Mead's analysis of the social construction of the self reveals how human consciousness and identity develop through the capacity to take the role of others and to view oneself from external perspectives.

Mead's distinction between the "I" and the "Me" illuminates the dynamic process through which individual identity emerges from social interaction while maintaining creative spontaneity. The "Me" represents the organized set of attitudes and expectations that individuals internalize through their participation in social groups and institutions. This internalized social perspective enables individuals to anticipate how others will respond to their actions while coordinating their behavior with collective activities and shared purposes.

The "I" represents the creative, spontaneous response that individuals make to social situations based on their unique perspective and emerging circumstances. The "I" prevents the "Me" from resulting in rigid conformity by introducing elements of novelty and innovation that can lead to social change and individual growth. The dynamic interaction between "I" and "Me" generates the ongoing process of self-development that continues throughout human life.

Mead's analysis of role-taking reveals how children develop the capacity for self-consciousness through progressive stages that mirror their expanding social participation. In the play stage, children learn to adopt the perspectives of specific significant others, developing empathy and understanding through imaginative identification with parents, teachers, and peers. This process enables children to begin seeing themselves as others see them while learning the basic social skills necessary for effective interaction.

The game stage represents a more sophisticated level of role-taking that requires children to understand and coordinate multiple perspectives simultaneously. Playing organized games requires understanding not only one's own role but also the roles of all other participants and the general rules that organize the entire activity. This capacity for taking the role of the "generalized other" enables individuals to participate effectively in complex social institutions while internalizing shared cultural values and expectations.

Mead's concept of symbolic interaction demonstrates how human communication transcends the simple stimulus-response patterns that characterize animal behavior through the development of significant symbols that have shared meanings across different participants in social interaction. Language enables humans to communicate not only about immediate circumstances but also about absent objects, future possibilities, and abstract relationships that exist only through cultural construction.

The capacity for symbolic interaction enables humans to engage in what Mead termed "minded behavior"—the ability to delay immediate responses while considering alternative possibilities and their likely consequences. This capacity for reflection and deliberation transforms human action from mere reaction to environmental stimuli into creative problem-solving that can address novel situations through innovative combinations of established patterns and emerging possibilities.

Mead's social psychology reveals how individual mind paintings emerge through the internalization of social perspectives and cultural meanings while remaining open to creative reconstruction through ongoing interaction and communication. This analysis demonstrates that even our most personal and individual mental processes remain fundamentally social in their origins and structure while providing foundations for continued innovation and cultural development.

Jane Addams (1860-1935) developed pragmatic principles in directions that explicitly addressed issues of social justice, gender equality, and democratic participation through her work as the founder and leader of Hull House, one of America's most influential social settlements. Addams's "applied philosophy" demonstrates how pragmatic insights can be translated into effective institutional innovations that address concrete social problems while contributing to broader cultural transformation.

Addams's concept of "lateral progress" challenges traditional approaches to social reform that focus on individual moral improvement or abstract policy recommendations without addressing the structural conditions that create and perpetuate social problems. Lateral progress requires inclusive advancement that benefits all community members rather than merely elite groups, emphasizing collective problem-solving and democratic participation rather than charitable intervention by privileged classes.

The Hull House experiment provided Addams with extensive practical experience in applying pragmatic principles to address complex urban problems created by rapid industrialization and massive immigration. Rather than imposing predetermined solutions based on abstract theoretical principles, Hull House developed programs and services through ongoing dialogue with neighborhood residents and careful attention to the actual consequences of different approaches.

Addams's educational philosophy exemplifies pragmatic approaches to learning and development through its emphasis on experiential education, cultural appreciation, and democratic participation. Hull House programs integrated practical skill development with intellectual stimulation and cultural enrichment while maintaining respect for the diverse backgrounds and perspectives that immigrants brought to American society.

The settlement's educational offerings included not only English language instruction and citizenship preparation but also art classes, dramatic productions, musical performances, and cultural celebrations that honored the traditions of different immigrant communities. This approach recognized that effective education must build upon learners' existing knowledge and experience rather than attempting to replace their cultural backgrounds with standardized curricula.

Addams's feminist pragmatism addressed the exclusion of women from traditional political and intellectual institutions through practical innovations that demonstrated women's capacity for effective public leadership while expanding opportunities for meaningful participation in social reform. Her concept of "municipal housekeeping" extended traditional domestic responsibilities into the public sphere by arguing that effective urban governance required the same attention to cleanliness, health, safety, and moral development that women brought to family life.

This rhetorical strategy enabled Addams to advocate for women's suffrage and expanded political participation without directly challenging traditional gender roles, demonstrating the pragmatic effectiveness of working within existing cultural frameworks while gradually transforming them through practical demonstration of their limitations and possibilities for extension.

Addams's peace advocacy, which earned her the Nobel Peace Prize in 1931, exemplified pragmatic approaches to international relations through its emphasis on practical cooperation, mutual understanding, and institutional innovation rather than abstract moral appeals or idealistic visions of world government. Her work with the Women's International League for Peace and Freedom demonstrated how grassroots organizing and cross-cultural dialogue could contribute to reducing international tensions and building foundations for lasting peace.

Contemporary neo-pragmatism, developed through the work of philosophers like Richard Rorty, Hilary Putnam, and Cornel West, extends classical pragmatic insights to address current intellectual and cultural challenges while maintaining focus on the practical consequences of different approaches to knowledge and social organization. These thinkers demonstrate the continued relevance of pragmatic thinking for addressing contemporary philosophical problems while contributing to ongoing cultural conversations about science, democracy, and human flourishing.

Richard Rorty's anti-foundationalism challenges the traditional philosophical project of discovering secure foundations for knowledge and morality, arguing instead that human intellectual activities achieve their purposes more effectively when they focus on practical problem-solving rather than theoretical justification. Rorty's "philosophy without mirrors" abandons the correspondence theory of truth in favor of approaches that emphasize the usefulness of different vocabularies and theoretical frameworks for addressing particular purposes and audiences.

Hilary Putnam's internal realism provides sophisticated accounts of how truth and objectivity can be preserved within pragmatic frameworks without requiring correspondence to mind-independent reality. Putnam's analysis demonstrates that our most successful scientific and mathematical concepts gain their objectivity through their functional effectiveness within human practices of inquiry and reasoning rather than through their reflection of abstract metaphysical structures.

Cornel West's prophetic pragmatism extends pragmatic insights to address issues of racial justice and cultural diversity through approaches that integrate intellectual rigor with moral commitment and political engagement. West's work demonstrates how pragmatic principles can support rather than undermine struggles for social justice while providing theoretical frameworks for understanding the relationship between cultural identity and universal human values.

The pragmatic emphasis on practical consequences and functional utility requires explicit defense against several philosophical objections that critics have raised since the movement's inception. The most fundamental challenge involves the apparent circularity of pragmatic arguments about truth and knowledge. Critics argue that if pragmatists define truth in terms of utility or practical effectiveness, they cannot then argue for pragmatism on the grounds that it is more useful or effective than alternative approaches without committing circular reasoning.

However, this objection misunderstands the pragmatic position and reflects assumptions about philosophical argument that pragmatists explicitly reject. Pragmatists do not claim that their approach is true in some mind-independent metaphysical sense that exists apart from human practices and purposes. Rather, they argue that pragmatic approaches prove more effective for addressing the kinds of problems that motivate philosophical inquiry in the first place.

The apparent circularity dissolves when we recognize that all philosophical positions must ultimately appeal to criteria that they themselves help to establish and defend. Traditional correspondence theories of truth face analogous challenges in providing non-circular justifications for their own criteria of truth and knowledge. The question is not whether philosophical positions can avoid all circularity but whether they provide frameworks that enable productive inquiry and effective action.

Pragmatic approaches demonstrate their value through their capacity to illuminate problems that remain intractable within traditional philosophical frameworks while generating insights and methods that prove useful for addressing practical challenges. The test of pragmatism lies not in its conformity to predetermined philosophical criteria but in its demonstrated effectiveness for the purposes that philosophical thinking is supposed to serve.

The "success objection" represents a more sophisticated challenge to pragmatic approaches. Critics argue that many false beliefs prove practically successful—flat earth theories worked adequately for local navigation, religious beliefs provide psychological comfort regardless of their metaphysical truth, and even harmful ideologies like Nazism achieved short-term effectiveness for their adherents. If utility is the test of truth, critics contend, then pragmatism cannot distinguish between beneficial and harmful practical success or between local effectiveness and genuine knowledge.

This objection requires careful analysis of what pragmatists mean by "practical consequences" and "long-term inquiry processes." Pragmatic evaluation demands attention to the full range of consequences that flow from adopting different beliefs and practices, including their effects on human flourishing, social cooperation, environmental sustainability, and the continued possibility of inquiry and learning. These criteria are both demanding and objective even though they remain grounded in human purposes and values rather than correspondence to mind-independent metaphysical principles.

The pragmatic framework provides robust tools for criticizing harmful but locally effective beliefs by examining their broader consequences for human flourishing and social cooperation. Nazi ideology, for example, can be criticized not only on moral grounds but also on pragmatic grounds because it systematically undermined the conditions necessary for sustained human development, international cooperation, and continued learning about effective approaches to social organization.

Religious beliefs present more complex challenges because they often serve essential human functions—providing meaning, motivation, social cohesion, and resources for coping with suffering and uncertainty—while making claims about ultimate reality that transcend empirical investigation. Pragmatic approaches to religion evaluate these beliefs according to their demonstrated capacity to enable individuals and communities to live meaningful and constructive lives while remaining open to revision based on changing circumstances and improved understanding.

The criterion of "long-term effectiveness within a community of inquirers" distinguishes pragmatic truth from mere local utility by emphasizing the self-correcting character of genuine inquiry. Beliefs and practices that prove effective only within limited contexts or time periods will eventually encounter circumstances that reveal their limitations and require modification or replacement. Genuine knowledge emerges through processes of inquiry that remain open to correction and improvement based on expanding experience and more sophisticated understanding.

The theoretical science objection challenges pragmatic approaches by pointing to pure mathematics and theoretical physics as domains where immediate practical consequences seem irrelevant to evaluating truth claims. Critics argue that mathematical theorems and theoretical scientific hypotheses often lack immediate practical applications while nevertheless representing genuine knowledge that pragmatic criteria cannot adequately address.

However, this objection misunderstands both the nature of theoretical inquiry and the scope of pragmatic evaluation.

Theoretical mathematics and physics achieve their effectiveness precisely through their capacity to provide powerful tools for understanding and manipulating natural phenomena, even when specific applications may not be immediately apparent. The pragmatic test focuses on the long-term consequences of adopting different theoretical frameworks rather than requiring immediate practical application of every hypothesis or theorem.

Mathematical and theoretical scientific knowledge demonstrates its utility through its essential role in ongoing processes of inquiry and technological development rather than through direct application to immediate practical problems. The remarkable effectiveness of mathematics and theoretical physics in enabling prediction and control of natural phenomena provides strong evidence for their pragmatic value while demonstrating the sophisticated character of genuine inquiry processes.

Moreover, theoretical inquiry serves essential functions within communities of inquirers by developing conceptual tools and methodological approaches that enable more effective investigation of practical problems. The apparent lack of immediate practical consequences reflects the complex, cumulative character of human knowledge rather than any fundamental limitation of pragmatic approaches to evaluation and justification.

The infinite regress objection argues that if beliefs are evaluated according to their practical consequences, we must also evaluate the consequences by some standard, which requires further evaluation, leading to an infinite regress that makes pragmatic evaluation impossible. Critics contend that pragmatism cannot provide ultimate foundations for evaluation because every standard of evaluation must itself be evaluated according to some further standard.

However, this objection reflects the foundationalist assumptions that pragmatism explicitly rejects. Pragmatic approaches operate through what philosophers call "reflective equilibrium"—the ongoing process of adjusting beliefs, values, and methods in response to their demonstrated consequences while maintaining overall coherence and effectiveness. This process does not require ultimate foundations but rather depends on the self-correcting character of inquiry within communities committed to ongoing learning and improvement.

The apparent threat of infinite regress dissolves when we recognize that pragmatic evaluation operates within established practices of inquiry that provide provisional starting points for evaluation while remaining open to revision based on their demonstrated consequences. These practices have been developed through centuries of collective experience and continue to evolve in response to new challenges and improved understanding.

The democratic assumption critique argues that Dewey and other pragmatists simply assume that democratic institutions and values are good without providing adequate justification for this assumption. Critics contend that if pragmatism judges institutions according to their practical effectiveness, it must remain open to the possibility that authoritarian systems might prove more effective for achieving various social goals.

This objection requires careful analysis of what Dewey and other pragmatists mean by "effectiveness" and how democratic values relate to the broader framework of pragmatic evaluation. Democratic institutions and practices are justified pragmatically not because they conform to abstract moral principles but because they provide more reliable and sustainable approaches to addressing complex social problems while maintaining conditions necessary for continued inquiry and adaptation.

Authoritarian systems may achieve short-term effectiveness in addressing specific challenges, but they systematically undermine the conditions necessary for ongoing learning and adaptation by restricting the flow of information, suppressing criticism and dissent, and concentrating decision-making power in ways that prevent effective responses to changing circumstances. Democratic institutions, despite their evident limitations, provide better frameworks for collective learning and self-correction over the long term.

The pragmatic defense of democracy emphasizes its instrumental value for enabling effective collective inquiry and problem-solving rather than its intrinsic moral worth. This approach provides more robust foundations for democratic institutions because it focuses on demonstrated effectiveness rather than abstract ideological commitments while remaining open to institutional reforms that better serve democratic purposes.

Educational applications of pragmatism have generated substantial empirical research demonstrating the effectiveness of experiential learning, collaborative inquiry, and student-centered approaches to education. Contemporary research in cognitive science and educational psychology provides strong support for Dewey's insights about the importance of active engagement, meaningful contexts, and social interaction for effective learning and development.

Dewey's Laboratory School at the University of Chicago provided concrete demonstrations of how pragmatic educational principles could be successfully implemented while achieving superior results compared to traditional approaches. Students who participated in the Laboratory School's experimental programs showed enhanced creativity, critical thinking abilities, and social cooperation while achieving strong academic performance across traditional subject areas.

The school's integrated curriculum, which organized learning around practical projects and real-world problems rather than abstract subject divisions, enabled students to develop sophisticated understanding of complex topics while maintaining motivation and engagement throughout their educational experience. These approaches continue to influence contemporary educational reform efforts that emphasize project-based learning, interdisciplinary studies, and authentic assessment.

Sociological and psychological research on belief formation and attitude change provides additional empirical support for pragmatic approaches by demonstrating the central role of practical consequences in shaping human cognition and behavior. Studies of cognitive dissonance, social influence, and cultural learning reveal how beliefs and practices that serve adaptive functions tend to persist and spread while those that generate harmful consequences are gradually modified or abandoned.

Cross-cultural research demonstrates that different societies develop remarkably diverse approaches to fundamental questions about reality, value, and social organization while facing similar underlying challenges posed by human nature and environmental constraints. This diversity supports pragmatic recognition of the constructed character of cultural meaning systems while revealing the universal human capacity for developing effective responses to shared problems.

Understanding American pragmatism as an explicit recognition of the functional character of human mind paintings illuminates both its distinctive contributions to philosophical thinking and its continued relevance for addressing contemporary intellectual and practical challenges. Pragmatic approaches demonstrate that ideas, theories, and beliefs gain their significance through their capacity to serve essential human functions rather than through their correspondence to mind-independent metaphysical principles or their internal logical consistency.

This insight provides powerful tools for evaluating competing approaches to knowledge, morality, politics, and education while maintaining appreciation for the remarkable human capacity to develop increasingly sophisticated and effective cultural technologies for organizing experience and coordinating social activity. The pragmatic framework supports rather than undermines human intellectual and moral achievements by revealing the creative processes through which they emerge and the practical purposes they serve.

The continued development and application of pragmatic insights offers resources for addressing contemporary challenges while building upon the substantial achievements of previous generations. Understanding human culture as an ongoing experimental process of developing and testing different approaches to fundamental problems enables both intellectual humility about current achievements and confidence in human capacity for continued innovation and improvement.

The pragmatic recognition that truth emerges through collective inquiry processes operating within cultural and institutional contexts provides foundations for maintaining both scientific rigor and democratic openness while addressing the complex challenges that contemporary societies face.

This approach enables productive engagement with diversity and disagreement while maintaining commitment to evidence-based reasoning and constructive problem-solving.

American pragmatism thus represents not merely a philosophical school but a sophisticated understanding of human cultural activity that illuminates the processes through which individuals and communities continue to develop new approaches to fundamental challenges while building upon the substantial achievements that previous generations have created through their own experimental efforts at ordering chaos and acquiring the essential bananas that enable human flourishing.

The pragmatic tradition demonstrates how philosophical thinking can remain intellectually rigorous while engaging constructively with practical problems and contributing to ongoing cultural development. This integration of theoretical sophistication with practical engagement provides models for contemporary intellectual work that seeks to address complex social challenges while maintaining high standards for evidence and argumentation.

The recognition that human mind paintings achieve their effectiveness through their functional utility rather than their correspondence to external reality provides both realistic understanding of human cognitive limitations and confident appreciation for human creative capacities. This balanced perspective enables continued philosophical and cultural development while avoiding both the arrogance that claims certainty about ultimate questions and the skepticism that denies the possibility of reliable knowledge and effective action.

Chapter Ten
Beyond Homo Sapiens – Non-Human and Artificial Mind Paintings

The emergence of sophisticated pattern recognition, problem-solving capabilities, and communicative systems across diverse biological species and artificial intelligence systems reveals that mind painting—the active construction of meaningful frameworks for organizing experience and guiding behavior—extends far beyond human cognition into realms that challenge traditional boundaries between intelligent and non-intelligent entities. This expansion of our theoretical framework illuminates both the evolutionary continuity that links human cognition to broader biological processes and the emerging possibilities for non-biological intelligence that may transcend traditional limitations of organic cognitive architectures.

Understanding mind painting as a phenomenon that operates across multiple types of cognitive systems—biological, technological, and hybrid—requires careful analysis of how different species and artificial agents construct meaningful relationships between sensory input, internal representations, and behavioral outputs while working within distinct constraints and possibilities imposed by their specific architectures and environments. This comparative approach reveals both universal features of effective information processing and the remarkable diversity of solutions that different systems have developed for addressing fundamental challenges of survival, reproduction, and goal achievement.

The theoretical framework developed throughout this analysis gains substantial support from examining how non-human animals and artificial intelligence systems demonstrate sophisticated forms of pattern recognition, symbolic communication, social coordination, and adaptive learning that parallel human cognitive achievements while revealing alternative approaches to organizing experience and constructing meaning within different material and cultural constraints.

Animal Cognition and Evolutionary Mind Paintings

The systematic study of animal cognition reveals remarkable continuities between human and non-human approaches to information processing, problem-solving, and social coordination while illuminating the distinctive features that characterize different cognitive architectures. Contemporary research across multiple species—including primates, cetaceans, corvids, parrots, and elephants—demonstrates that sophisticated pattern recognition, tool use, symbolic communication, and cultural transmission occur throughout the biological world, suggesting that mind painting represents a fundamental strategy for managing complexity and uncertainty that emerges naturally from the constraints and possibilities inherent in evolved nervous systems.

Primates, as humanity's closest evolutionary relatives, provide particularly compelling evidence for the continuity between human and non-human mind painting while revealing both shared cognitive foundations and species-specific elaborations that reflect different ecological niches and social structures. The tool-use behaviors observed across multiple primate species—from chimpanzee termite fishing and nut cracking to capuchin monkey stone tool use and orangutan leaf manipulation—demonstrate sophisticated understanding of causal relationships, planning capabilities, and cultural transmission mechanisms that parallel human technological development while operating within different constraints and serving different adaptive functions.

Jane Goodall's pioneering observations of chimpanzee tool use at Gombe revealed not only the sophisticated motor skills and planning abilities required for successful termite fishing but also the cultural transmission mechanisms through which young chimpanzees acquire these techniques through extended observation and practice with experienced adults. The regional variations in tool-use patterns across different chimpanzee populations—including differences in ant-dipping techniques, honey gathering methods, and nut-cracking procedures—demonstrate that primate cultures develop distinctive approaches to common problems while maintaining sufficient flexibility to adapt to local environmental conditions.

The discovery of "proto-symbolic" communication systems among great apes provides additional evidence for the evolutionary foundations of human language and meaning-making systems. The gestural communication observed in wild chimpanzees, bonobos, and gorillas involves intentional signaling between individuals using hand movements, body postures, and facial expressions that convey specific meanings within social contexts. These gestural systems demonstrate several key features that characterize human language: intentionality (gestures are directed toward specific audiences), reference (gestures refer to objects or events beyond immediate sensory experience), and cultural transmission (gesture meanings are learned through social interaction rather than being innately determined).

Research by Michael Tomasello and his colleagues has revealed that great ape gestural communication involves sophisticated understanding of others' mental states, including their attention, intentions, and knowledge. Apes modify their gestural communication based on whether recipients are paying attention, repeat or modify gestures when initial attempts fail to achieve intended effects, and use different gestural strategies depending on their relationship with recipients and the social context of interaction.

Cetaceans represent perhaps the most remarkable example of non-human cultural mind painting, with evidence suggesting that whale and dolphin populations develop complex cultural traditions that are transmitted across generations through social learning rather than genetic inheritance. The discovery of distinct "dialects" in the vocalizations of different killer whale pods reveals sophisticated acoustic communication systems that serve both social coordination and cultural identification functions.

The remarkable complexity of sperm whale communication, documented through advances in underwater recording technology, suggests that these marine mammals may possess communication systems that rival human language in their structural sophistication. Sperm whales produce complex sequences of clicks (called "codas") that vary systematically across different social groups and geographic regions, with evidence suggesting that these acoustic patterns serve functions analogous to human names, social identifiers, and cultural markers.

Cetacean intelligence extends beyond communication to encompass sophisticated problem-solving abilities, self-recognition, and empathetic responses to other individuals' distress. Bottlenose dolphins demonstrate mirror self-recognition—a cognitive capacity previously thought to be limited to humans, great apes, and elephants—while also showing evidence of complex social cooperation, teaching behaviors, and innovative problem-solving approaches that spread through populations via cultural transmission.

The tool-use behaviors observed in several dolphin populations provide particularly compelling evidence for cetacean cultural innovation and transmission. Dolphins in Shark Bay, Australia, have developed techniques for using marine sponges as protective tools while foraging on the seafloor, with this behavior being transmitted from mothers to offspring through extended social learning rather than genetic inheritance. The regional specificity of this behavior and its transmission patterns demonstrate that cetacean cultures can develop and maintain sophisticated technological traditions that enhance foraging effectiveness while reflecting local ecological conditions.

Corvids and parrots represent remarkable examples of convergent evolution in cognitive capabilities, demonstrating that sophisticated intelligence can emerge from neural architectures that differ dramatically from mammalian brain organization. Despite lacking the neocortical structures that characterize mammalian cognition, these avian species demonstrate tool use, planning abilities, episodic memory, and social reasoning that rival those observed in great apes while revealing alternative neurological pathways for achieving complex cognitive functions.

New Caledonian crows provide perhaps the most striking example of non-human technological sophistication, manufacturing and using tools with a precision and complexity that surpasses many human societies' technological achievements. These remarkable birds not only use naturally occurring materials as tools but also modify twigs, leaves, and other objects to create specialized implements for extracting insects from crevices and obtaining food from otherwise inaccessible locations.

The tool-making behaviors of New Caledonian crows demonstrate several features that characterize human technology: sequential modification of materials to achieve desired functional properties, standardized manufacturing procedures that produce tools with consistent characteristics, and cultural transmission of technological knowledge across generations. Different crow populations have developed distinct tool-making traditions that reflect local environmental conditions while maintaining sophisticated understanding of the physical principles that determine tool effectiveness.

Corvid cognitive abilities extend beyond tool use to encompass sophisticated social reasoning, planning capabilities, and episodic memory that demonstrate remarkable parallels to human cognitive achievements. Scrub jays demonstrate "mental time travel" by planning for future needs and remembering specific past events, while also showing evidence of understanding others' mental states and adjusting their behavior accordingly to achieve social and foraging goals.

The "Machiavellian intelligence" observed in corvid social interactions reveals sophisticated understanding of deception, cooperation, and competition that enables these birds to navigate complex social relationships while pursuing individual and group objectives. Ravens demonstrate alliance formation, tactical deception, and reconciliation behaviors that parallel those observed in primate societies while reflecting the specific ecological and social constraints that characterize corvid environments.

Parrots, particularly African grey parrots, demonstrate remarkable symbolic communication abilities that approach human language use in their sophistication and flexibility. The famous research with Alex the African grey parrot conducted by Irene Pepperberg revealed that these birds can learn and use symbolic labels not merely through associative conditioning but through genuine understanding of categorical relationships, numerical concepts, and abstract properties like color, shape, and material.

Alex demonstrated the ability to combine learned symbols in novel ways to describe new objects and situations, showing evidence of compositional understanding that enables creative expression rather than mere repetition of trained responses. His ability to answer questions about absent objects, demonstrate numerical competence with quantities up to six, and express preferences and emotions through learned symbols suggests that parrot cognition involves sophisticated representational abilities that parallel key features of human language and thought.

The cultural transmission mechanisms observed across these diverse species reveal that non-human mind paintings emerge through social learning processes that enable populations to develop, maintain, and modify sophisticated behavioral traditions across generations. These cultural systems demonstrate both stability and flexibility, maintaining core features that serve essential adaptive functions while allowing for innovation and adaptation to changing environmental conditions.

However, critical analysis reveals important limitations in non-human mind painting that distinguish animal cognition from human cultural systems. While animals demonstrate sophisticated pattern recognition, tool use, and social coordination, their cognitive systems appear to operate within more restricted domains of abstraction and generalization than human thinking typically achieves. Animal communication systems, despite their impressive complexity, lack the recursive, compositional properties that enable human language to generate unlimited novel expressions from finite symbolic resources.

The absence of cumulative cultural evolution in non-human species represents perhaps the most significant limitation of animal mind painting relative to human cultural systems. While animals can learn from others and maintain behavioral traditions across generations, they do not appear to engage in the kind of progressive elaboration and improvement of cultural knowledge that characterizes human technological and intellectual development.

These limitations reflect the specific cognitive constraints that operate within different neural architectures while revealing the distinctive features that enable human mind painting to achieve unprecedented levels of abstraction, creativity, and cumulative cultural development. Understanding these constraints illuminates both the evolutionary foundations of human cognition and the remarkable innovations that enable human cultures to transcend biological limitations through collaborative knowledge construction and technological enhancement.

Artificial Intelligence as Synthetic Mind Painting

The development of artificial intelligence systems represents humanity's most ambitious attempt to create non-biological mind painting through technological means, generating new forms of pattern recognition, problem-solving, and information processing that operate according to principles that both parallel and diverge from biological cognitive architectures. Contemporary AI systems demonstrate increasingly sophisticated capabilities for processing vast amounts of information, recognizing complex patterns, generating creative outputs, and adapting to novel situations in ways that challenge traditional distinctions between intelligent and non-intelligent systems.

Large language models like GPT-4, Claude, and their successors represent particularly striking examples of artificial mind painting, demonstrating abilities to process and generate human-like text that exhibits apparent understanding, creativity, and reasoning across diverse domains of knowledge and application. These systems achieve their performance through training on massive datasets of human-generated text, developing internal representations that capture statistical patterns in language use while enabling flexible generation of responses that often appear to demonstrate genuine comprehension and insight.

The transformer architecture that underlies most contemporary language models operates through sophisticated attention mechanisms that enable these systems to identify relevant relationships among different parts of input sequences while maintaining contextual awareness across extended conversations and complex reasoning tasks. This architectural innovation enables AI systems to exhibit behavior that appears to involve understanding of meaning, logical reasoning, and creative expression even though their underlying computational processes operate through statistical pattern matching rather than the kind of semantic understanding that characterizes human cognition.

Machine learning systems demonstrate forms of pattern recognition and adaptive learning that parallel key features of biological mind painting while revealing the potential for non-biological intelligence to achieve sophisticated performance through fundamentally different computational approaches. Neural networks trained through supervised, unsupervised, and reinforcement learning can develop internal representations that enable effective performance on tasks ranging from image recognition and natural language processing to strategic game-playing and robotic control.

The remarkable success of deep learning systems in achieving superhuman performance on specific cognitive tasks—including chess, Go, protein folding prediction, and mathematical theorem proving—demonstrates that artificial intelligence can transcend human cognitive limitations in certain domains while revealing the potential for hybrid human-AI systems that combine biological and artificial cognitive capabilities in complementary ways.

Computer vision systems demonstrate sophisticated visual pattern recognition capabilities that enable artificial agents to identify objects, understand spatial relationships, and navigate complex environments with accuracy and efficiency that rivals or exceeds human visual processing. These systems achieve their performance through hierarchical feature detection mechanisms that extract increasingly abstract representations from raw sensory input, enabling recognition of objects and scenes across diverse viewing conditions and contexts.

Robotics applications of artificial intelligence reveal how synthetic mind painting can be embodied in physical systems that interact with complex environments while adapting their behavior based on sensory feedback and learning from experience. Autonomous vehicles, manufacturing robots, and exploration rovers demonstrate sophisticated sensorimotor coordination, spatial reasoning, and adaptive problem-solving that enable effective performance in dynamic, uncertain environments.

The integration of multiple AI systems through distributed computing architectures creates emergent forms of collective intelligence that parallel the distributed cognition observed in biological social systems while achieving scales of coordination and information processing that transcend individual cognitive limitations. These hybrid systems demonstrate how artificial mind painting can operate across networks of interconnected agents while maintaining coherent goal-directed behavior and adaptive learning capabilities.

However, critical analysis reveals fundamental limitations in current artificial intelligence systems that distinguish synthetic mind painting from biological cognition. Most importantly, AI systems appear to lack genuine consciousness, intentionality, and subjective experience, operating through computational processes that simulate intelligent behavior without the phenomenal awareness that characterizes human and other biological minds.

The absence of genuine understanding in AI systems becomes apparent when these systems are tested beyond their training distributions or required to engage in tasks that demand genuine semantic comprehension rather than sophisticated pattern matching. While AI systems can generate human-like responses and achieve impressive performance on many cognitive tasks, they often fail in ways that reveal their fundamental lack of genuine understanding of meaning, causation, and contextual relevance.

The "Chinese Room" argument developed by philosopher John Searle illuminates this limitation by demonstrating that systems can exhibit intelligent behavior through purely syntactic manipulation of symbols without genuine semantic understanding. AI systems process information through computational operations that manipulate symbolic representations according to learned rules and patterns, but these operations do not necessarily involve the kind of semantic understanding that enables genuine comprehension of meaning.

Contemporary AI systems lack the embodied experience that appears to be essential for genuine understanding and consciousness. Biological minds develop through extended interaction with physical and social environments, acquiring understanding through sensorimotor experience, emotional responses, and social relationships that provide the foundation for meaningful cognition. AI systems, despite their impressive performance, operate through disembodied computational processes that lack this experiential foundation.

The absence of genuine creativity and consciousness in AI systems becomes apparent when examining their inability to experience genuine emotions, form genuine social relationships, or engage in the kind of autonomous goal-setting that characterizes conscious agents. While AI systems can simulate these capacities, they do not appear to experience the subjective states and intentional attitudes that provide the foundation for genuine agency and consciousness.

However, emerging developments in AI research suggest possibilities for overcoming some of these limitations through approaches that incorporate embodied experience, emotional modeling, and social interaction into artificial intelligence systems. Neuromorphic computing architectures that more closely model biological neural networks may enable forms of artificial cognition that approach genuine understanding and consciousness rather than merely simulating intelligent behavior.

The development of artificial general intelligence (AGI) represents the ambitious goal of creating AI systems that can match or exceed human cognitive capabilities across diverse domains while potentially achieving forms of genuine understanding and consciousness. While current AI systems excel in specific domains, they lack the general intelligence, adaptability, and consciousness that characterize human cognition.

Comparative Analysis and Theoretical Implications

Systematic comparison of human, animal, and artificial mind painting reveals both universal features of effective information processing and distinctive characteristics that distinguish different types of cognitive systems. All successful mind painting systems demonstrate sophisticated pattern recognition, adaptive learning, goal-directed behavior, and the ability to generate appropriate responses to novel situations within their domains of competence.

The capacity for abstraction represents a key dimension along which different mind painting systems vary significantly. Human cognition demonstrates unprecedented abilities to operate with abstract concepts, logical relationships, and hypothetical scenarios that extend far beyond immediate sensory experience. Animal cognition shows varying degrees of abstraction, with great apes and corvids demonstrating sophisticated abstract reasoning while other species operate within more concrete, stimulus-bound cognitive frameworks.

Artificial intelligence systems demonstrate remarkable capabilities for processing abstract patterns and relationships within their training domains while often failing to achieve the kind of flexible, general-purpose abstraction that characterizes human thinking. AI systems can manipulate abstract symbols and patterns with superhuman precision and speed, but they typically lack the contextual understanding and flexible generalization that enable human cognition to apply abstract knowledge across diverse domains and situations.

Social cognition represents another crucial dimension for comparing different mind painting systems. Human cognition is fundamentally social, developing through extended social interaction and cultural transmission while achieving its highest expressions through collaborative cultural construction. Animal social cognition varies dramatically across species, with highly social species like primates, cetaceans, and corvids demonstrating sophisticated understanding of others' mental states and complex social coordination abilities.

Current AI systems largely lack genuine social cognition, operating through computational processes that can simulate social interaction without genuine understanding of others' mental states or authentic social relationships. However, emerging research on multi-agent AI systems and social robotics suggests possibilities for developing forms of artificial social cognition that may approach genuine social understanding and relationship formation.

Cultural transmission mechanisms distinguish human mind painting from both animal cognition and current AI systems through their capacity for cumulative cultural evolution. Human cultures can progressively elaborate and improve their knowledge, technologies, and institutions across generations, achieving unprecedented levels of sophistication through collaborative cultural construction. Animal cultures demonstrate impressive stability and local adaptation but lack the progressive elaboration that characterizes human cultural evolution.

AI systems currently depend entirely on human-provided training data and objectives, lacking the autonomous cultural development that characterizes biological intelligence. However, emerging approaches to artificial cultural evolution and multi-generational AI training suggest possibilities for developing AI systems that can engage in autonomous cultural development and knowledge creation.

Embodied cognition represents a fundamental distinction between biological and artificial mind painting systems. Biological cognition emerges through extended embodied experience that provides the foundation for understanding spatial relationships, causal connections, and meaningful interactions with the physical and social environment. Current AI systems operate through largely disembodied computational processes that lack this experiential foundation.

However, developments in robotics, sensorimotor AI, and embodied artificial intelligence suggest possibilities for creating AI systems that acquire knowledge through embodied experience rather than purely abstract computational processes. These approaches may enable artificial systems to achieve more genuine understanding and more flexible, adaptive behavior through embodied interaction with complex environments.

Defending Against Philosophical Objections

The extension of mind painting analysis to non-human animals and artificial intelligence systems requires robust defense against several potential philosophical objections. Critics might argue that attributing "mind painting" to non-conscious entities like current AI systems or to animals with limited cognitive capabilities commits the fallacy of anthropomorphism by projecting human characteristics onto fundamentally different types of systems.

However, this objection misunderstands the theoretical framework being employed. The mind painting concept does not require consciousness, subjective experience, or human-like cognition but rather focuses on the functional characteristics of systems that construct meaningful relationships between input patterns and behavioral outputs. The framework explicitly acknowledges different levels and types of cognitive organization while identifying common functional features that enable effective information processing across diverse types of systems.

The comparative approach reveals both universal constraints that operate across all effective information processing systems and distinctive features that characterize different cognitive architectures. Understanding these similarities and differences illuminates both the evolutionary foundations of human cognition and the emerging possibilities for artificial intelligence while avoiding both excessive anthropomorphism and inappropriate reductionism.

Critics might argue that current AI systems lack genuine intelligence and consciousness, making it inappropriate to characterize their computational processes as forms of mind painting. While this criticism correctly identifies important limitations in current AI systems, it misses the theoretical value of analyzing how these systems achieve impressive performance through sophisticated pattern recognition and adaptive learning mechanisms.

The mind painting framework provides analytical tools for understanding how different types of systems—biological and artificial—construct effective responses to complex information processing challenges while remaining explicit about the distinctive features that characterize conscious versus non-conscious processing. This approach enables productive theoretical development while maintaining appropriate distinctions between different types of cognitive systems.

The framework's emphasis on functional effectiveness rather than specific implementation details provides advantages for analyzing diverse types of cognitive systems while avoiding premature commitment to particular theories about consciousness, understanding, or intelligence. This functional approach enables comparison across different types of systems while remaining open to emerging developments in our understanding of consciousness, artificial intelligence, and animal cognition.

Critics concerned about technological determinism might argue that emphasizing artificial intelligence capabilities promotes inappropriate optimism about AI development while minimizing legitimate concerns about AI safety, alignment, and social impact. However, the analysis presented here explicitly acknowledges current limitations in AI systems while providing theoretical frameworks for understanding both their capabilities and their limitations.

The comparative approach reveals that current AI systems achieve impressive performance within specific domains while lacking the general intelligence, consciousness, and genuine understanding that characterize human cognition. This recognition supports appropriate caution about AI development while enabling productive theoretical analysis of how different types of cognitive systems achieve their distinctive capabilities.

Understanding the limitations of current AI systems provides essential background for developing more sophisticated and safer AI technologies that can better serve human needs while avoiding potential risks associated with poorly understood or inadequately controlled artificial intelligence systems. The mind painting framework contributes to these goals by providing analytical tools for understanding both the capabilities and limitations of different types of cognitive systems.

Evolutionary Continuity and Future Possibilities

The comparative analysis of human, animal, and artificial mind painting reveals both the evolutionary continuity that links human cognition to broader biological processes and the emerging possibilities for transcending biological limitations through technological innovation. Human cognitive capabilities emerge from evolutionary processes that built upon foundations established in other primate species while achieving distinctive innovations that enable unprecedented levels of abstraction, cultural transmission, and technological sophistication.

Understanding human cognition within this broader evolutionary context provides essential perspective on both the achievements and limitations of human mind painting while revealing the biological foundations that make cultural innovation possible. Human cognitive architecture reflects millions of years of evolutionary development that shaped neural mechanisms for pattern recognition, social coordination, and adaptive learning while providing the foundation for cultural innovations that transcend biological constraints.

The study of animal cognition continues to reveal impressive cognitive capabilities across diverse species while illuminating alternative approaches to information processing and social organization that may inform the development of more sophisticated and flexible artificial intelligence systems. Biological evolution has produced remarkable diversity in cognitive strategies that reflect different ecological niches and social environments while achieving effective solutions to common information processing challenges.

Contemporary developments in artificial intelligence suggest possibilities for creating synthetic mind painting systems that may eventually match or exceed human cognitive capabilities while potentially achieving forms of consciousness and understanding that rival biological intelligence. However, these possibilities remain speculative and require continued research and development to determine their feasibility and implications.

The potential convergence of biological and artificial intelligence through brain-computer interfaces, neural prosthetics, and other hybrid technologies suggests possibilities for creating new forms of mind painting that combine the distinctive advantages of biological and artificial cognitive systems. These hybrid approaches may enable cognitive capabilities that transcend the limitations of either purely biological or purely artificial systems while creating new challenges for understanding consciousness, identity, and agency.

The ongoing development of artificial intelligence systems raises important questions about the future of human cognition and cultural development. As AI systems become increasingly capable of performing cognitive tasks that were previously the exclusive domain of human intelligence, human societies will need to adapt their educational, economic, and social institutions to maintain meaningful roles for human cognition while leveraging the capabilities of artificial intelligence systems.

The mind painting framework provides theoretical resources for understanding these developments while maintaining appreciation for both human cognitive achievements and the emerging possibilities for artificial intelligence. This approach supports continued innovation while promoting appropriate caution about the implications of advanced AI systems for human society and individual well-being.

Understanding mind painting as a phenomenon that extends beyond human cognition to encompass diverse forms of biological and artificial intelligence provides essential perspective on humanity's place within the broader landscape of intelligent systems while revealing both the distinctive achievements of human culture and the emerging possibilities for transcending traditional cognitive limitations through technological innovation and cultural development.

The comparative analysis demonstrates that while human mind painting achieves unprecedented levels of sophistication through its capacity for abstraction, cultural transmission, and collaborative knowledge construction, it remains grounded in biological processes that link human cognition to the broader evolutionary development of intelligence throughout the natural world. This recognition supports both intellectual humility about human cognitive limitations and appreciation for the remarkable creative potential that emerges through cultural collaboration and technological innovation.

The emerging possibilities for artificial intelligence and hybrid biological-artificial systems suggest that the future of mind painting may involve forms of intelligence that transcend current human capabilities while remaining grounded in the functional principles that enable effective information processing and adaptive behavior. Understanding these principles provides essential resources for navigating the challenges and opportunities that emerge as human society continues to develop increasingly sophisticated cognitive technologies while maintaining commitment to human flourishing and cultural development.

Chapter Eleven
The Mind's Inner Canvas – Psychology, Neuroscience, and the Biased Brush

The systematic investigation of human psychological processes and neurological mechanisms reveals that mind painting operates through sophisticated but inherently constrained cognitive architectures that introduce systematic biases, emotional influences, and unconscious drives into all human meaning-making activities. Understanding these "brushes" and "canvases" that shape our mental constructions illuminates both the remarkable achievements of human cognition and its inevitable limitations while providing essential insights into why certain types of mind paintings prove more compelling than others and how therapeutic interventions can facilitate adaptive reconstruction of maladaptive cognitive frameworks.

The exploration of psychology and neuroscience as they relate to mind painting requires explicit acknowledgment that this investigation itself represents a form of metacognition—the mind studying itself through the very cognitive processes it seeks to understand. This apparent circularity does not undermine the validity of psychological and neuroscientific insights but rather demonstrates the remarkable human capacity for self-reflection and systematic investigation of our own cognitive limitations and possibilities.

However, critics might argue that if human cognition is as biased and limited as psychological research suggests, then psychology itself—as a human enterprise—cannot achieve the objectivity necessary for reliable scientific knowledge. This "bias bias" objection appears to create an infinite regress: if psychologists are subject to the same cognitive biases they study, how can their research be trusted?

This challenge requires careful analysis of how scientific methodology enables collective transcendence of individual cognitive limitations. While individual researchers remain subject to cognitive biases, confirmation bias, and motivated reasoning, the scientific enterprise achieves greater reliability through institutional mechanisms designed specifically to counteract these limitations. Peer review processes expose research to criticism from diverse perspectives, replication requirements test the robustness of findings across different laboratories and populations, and meta-analytic techniques integrate results from multiple studies to identify consistent patterns while reducing the influence of individual researcher biases.

The history of psychological science demonstrates this self-correcting character through numerous examples where initial findings have been revised or overturned based on improved methodology, larger samples, and more sophisticated analyses. The "replication crisis" in psychology, rather than undermining confidence in psychological science, actually demonstrates its capacity for self-correction by identifying problems and implementing reforms to improve research practices.

Moreover, psychological research has achieved remarkable practical success in areas ranging from clinical treatment and educational improvement to organizational effectiveness and public health interventions. These practical achievements provide evidence for the validity of psychological insights that extends beyond purely theoretical considerations while demonstrating the capacity of scientific methodology to generate useful knowledge despite individual cognitive limitations.

Psychology functions as humanity's most sophisticated "banana acquisition" tool for self-understanding, enabling greater awareness of mind painting processes even though these investigative activities necessarily operate through the same constrained cognitive architectures they seek to analyze. This metacognitive capacity represents one of the most distinctive achievements of human intelligence while remaining subject to the same biases and limitations that characterize all human cognitive activity.

Dual-Process Architecture: System 1 and System 2 Thinking

Daniel Kahneman and Amos Tversky's groundbreaking research on human judgment and decision-making revealed fundamental features of cognitive architecture that directly illuminate how mind painting operates through the interaction of two distinct processing systems with different capabilities, limitations, and operating principles. This dual-process framework provides comprehensive understanding of why human reasoning simultaneously demonstrates remarkable sophistication and systematic biases while revealing the underlying mechanisms through which cognitive and motivational factors influence all mental activity.

System 1 thinking operates automatically, quickly, and effortlessly, processing information through associative networks that generate impressions, intuitions, and immediate responses based on learned patterns and emotional associations. This fast, unconscious processing system handles the vast majority of routine cognitive tasks—including object recognition, language comprehension, social interaction, and familiar motor skills—while requiring minimal cognitive resources and operating largely outside conscious awareness.

System 1 capabilities include innate skills shared with other animals—such as perceiving spatial relationships, detecting emotional expressions, and avoiding immediate dangers—as well as sophisticated abilities acquired through extensive practice and cultural learning. Expert chess players can recognize promising moves through System 1 pattern recognition, while native speakers process complex grammatical structures automatically without conscious effort.

However, System 1 processing introduces systematic biases that reflect both its evolutionary origins and its reliance on heuristic shortcuts for efficient information processing. The availability heuristic leads System 1 to judge probability based on how easily relevant examples come to mind rather than actual statistical frequencies. The representativeness heuristic generates judgments based on similarity to mental prototypes rather than base rate information. These and other systematic biases reflect the adaptive functions that System 1 serves while revealing its limitations for tasks requiring statistical reasoning or abstract logical analysis.

System 2 thinking operates slowly, deliberately, and effortfully, allocating conscious attention to mental activities that demand analytical reasoning, complex computations, or novel problem-solving. This controlled processing system enables humans to override automatic System 1 responses when circumstances require careful analysis, systematic planning, or adherence to logical rules that conflict with intuitive impressions.

System 2 activities include tasks such as comparing complex alternatives, performing mathematical calculations, learning new skills, monitoring one's own thinking for errors, and implementing self-control in situations where immediate impulses conflict with longer-term goals. The subjective experience of agency, choice, and concentration primarily reflects System 2 operations, even though this controlled processing depends heavily on information and impressions generated by System 1.

The division of labor between these two systems optimizes cognitive performance by minimizing the mental effort required for routine activities while providing mechanisms for overriding automatic responses when circumstances demand careful analysis. System 1 handles familiar situations efficiently while System 2 intervenes when problems become too difficult for automatic processing or when stakes are sufficiently high to justify the mental effort required for deliberate reasoning.

This dual-process architecture directly supports the mind painting framework by revealing how human cognition actively constructs rather than passively receives the contents of experience. System 1 continuously generates interpretive frameworks that organize sensory input according to learned associations and emotional valences, while System 2 can modify these constructions through deliberate analytical thinking when motivated to do so.

However, System 2 processing remains heavily influenced by System 1 inputs and operates within severe capacity limitations that constrain its effectiveness. Mental effort is a limited resource that becomes depleted through use, leading to "ego depletion" effects where sustained self-control or analytical thinking reduces the capacity for subsequent effortful processing. These limitations ensure that even deliberate reasoning often relies on System 1 processes for generating initial impressions and maintaining ongoing cognitive operations.

Contemporary research on Prospect Theory, developed by Kahneman and Tversky, demonstrates how these dual processing systems interact to generate systematic patterns in human decision-making that deviate predictably from rational choice theory. The theory reveals that people evaluate potential outcomes relative to reference points rather than absolute values, demonstrate loss aversion by weighting losses more heavily than equivalent gains, and show probability weighting that overemphasizes small probabilities while underweighting moderate and high probabilities.

These systematic deviations from normative rationality reflect the operation of cognitive and emotional mechanisms that served adaptive functions in ancestral environments while creating systematic biases in contemporary decision contexts. Understanding these patterns enables both better individual decision-making and more effective design of choice architectures that can help people make decisions more aligned with their own long-term interests.

The Neurological Canvas: Brain Architecture and Cognitive Constraints

Contemporary neuroscience reveals that human mind painting operates within constraints imposed by the specific architecture of mammalian brains that evolved to address challenges related to survival, reproduction, and social coordination rather than objective truth-seeking or abstract theoretical reflection. The neocortex—the evolutionarily recent brain structure that enables sophisticated pattern recognition, abstraction, and symbolic manipulation—provides both remarkable cognitive capabilities and systematic limitations that shape all human thought processes.

The discovery of neuroplasticity—the brain's capacity to reorganize and rewire its neural connections throughout life in response to experience, learning, and environmental changes—provides crucial insights into how mind paintings develop and can be modified through therapeutic intervention, educational programs, and deliberate practice. This plasticity enables the brain to adapt its structure and function to changing circumstances while maintaining sufficient stability to preserve learned skills and knowledge.

Neuroplasticity operates through multiple mechanisms that range from changes in synaptic strength and connectivity to large-scale reorganization of cortical maps and the generation of new neurons in specific brain regions. Learning new skills, recovering from brain injury, and adapting to sensory deficits all involve plastic changes that demonstrate the brain's remarkable capacity for self-modification while revealing the biological foundations that make cultural learning and individual development possible.

The hierarchical organization of cortical processing creates systematic biases toward certain types of pattern recognition while making others more difficult or unlikely. Visual processing systems, for example, demonstrate remarkable capabilities for object recognition and scene understanding while remaining vulnerable to specific types of illusions and misinterpretations that reveal the constructed character of visual experience.

Split-brain research conducted by Roger Sperry, Michael Gazzaniga, and their colleagues reveals how different hemispheres of the brain contribute distinctive capabilities to overall cognitive function while creating potential conflicts between different processing systems. The left hemisphere typically specializes in language, sequential processing, and analytical reasoning, while the right hemisphere contributes spatial processing, holistic pattern recognition, and emotional integration.

These hemispheric specializations create both enhanced capabilities and systematic limitations in human cognition while revealing how unified conscious experience emerges from the integration of diverse neural systems with different processing characteristics. The interpreter function identified in left-hemisphere processing demonstrates how brains continuously construct explanatory narratives that integrate diverse experiences into coherent stories, even when these narratives must incorporate inconsistent or incomplete information.

The discovery of mirror neurons in macaque monkeys and their human analogues illuminates how social cognition operates through embodied simulation mechanisms that enable understanding of others' actions and intentions through internal modeling rather than abstract inference. These findings reveal how empathy, social learning, and cultural transmission operate through neurological mechanisms that blur traditional boundaries between self and other while creating systematic biases toward anthropomorphic interpretation of complex phenomena.

Global Workspace Theory, developed by Bernard Baars and subsequently refined through neuroimaging research, provides comprehensive accounts of how conscious experience emerges from the integration and broadcasting of information across diverse brain networks. According to this framework, consciousness arises when information becomes globally accessible across different brain systems, enabling flexible responses and reportable experience.

Integrated Information Theory, developed by Giulio Tononi, offers mathematical approaches to understanding consciousness that attempt to quantify the amount of integrated information generated by different types of systems. While this theory remains controversial, it provides frameworks for thinking about consciousness that extend beyond purely biological systems while maintaining precision about the computational requirements for conscious experience.

The predictive coding framework, also known as the Bayesian brain hypothesis, provides perhaps the most comprehensive account of how neural systems actively construct experience rather than passively receiving and processing external information. According to this framework, brains function as sophisticated prediction machines that continuously generate hypotheses about incoming sensory data while using prediction errors to update and refine their internal models of reality.

This predictive processing operates through hierarchical mechanisms where higher-level brain areas generate predictions about lower-level sensory input while lower-level areas signal prediction errors back up the hierarchy when actual input differs from predicted input. Successful predictions require minimal neural resources, while significant prediction errors trigger increased neural activity and model updating that can lead to revised understanding and behavioral adaptation.

The predictive coding framework directly supports the mind painting metaphor by revealing how brains actively construct rather than discover the objects of experience. What we experience as objective reality emerges through ongoing predictive processes that integrate prior expectations with current sensory input according to learned statistical regularities rather than through direct perception of mind-independent external objects.

Contemporary research in predictive processing demonstrates how individual differences in prediction mechanisms can create systematic variations in how different people experience and interpret the same physical stimuli. These differences help explain phenomena ranging from individual variations in pain perception to cultural differences in categorical thinking and aesthetic judgment while revealing the constructed character of all human experience.

The default mode network—a set of brain regions that show high activity during rest and introspective thinking—provides additional insight into how minds actively construct meaning even in the absence of external task demands. This network appears to be involved in self-referential thinking, mental time travel, theory of mind, and the integration of diverse cognitive processes into coherent narratives about identity and experience.

Dysfunction in default mode network activity has been associated with various psychological disorders, including depression, anxiety, and schizophrenia, suggesting that the capacity for constructive self-reflection and narrative integration represents both a distinctive achievement of human cognition and a potential source of psychological difficulties when these processes become maladaptive.

Unconscious Drives and the Hidden Palette

The systematic investigation of unconscious psychological processes reveals that mind painting operates through mechanisms that remain largely inaccessible to conscious awareness while exerting profound influences on thought, emotion, and behavior. Understanding these unconscious influences illuminates both the sophisticated character of human psychological organization and the systematic limitations that constrain conscious rational reflection.

Sigmund Freud's pioneering analysis of unconscious mental processes revealed that much human behavior reflects the operation of psychological mechanisms that remain outside conscious awareness while serving essential functions related to motivation, defense, and adaptation. Freud's structural model of the mind—comprising the id, ego, and superego—provides frameworks for understanding how unconscious drives, conscious rational planning, and internalized social standards interact to generate the complex patterns of thought and behavior that characterize human psychology.

The id represents the reservoir of unconscious instinctual drives—particularly those related to sexuality, aggression, and immediate gratification—that provide the motivational energy for all psychological activity while operating according to the "pleasure principle" that seeks immediate satisfaction without regard for reality constraints or social consequences. These primitive drives remain active throughout life while being channeled and transformed through the development of more sophisticated psychological structures.

The ego develops through interaction with environmental constraints and serves to mediate between unconscious drives and external reality according to the "reality principle" that delays immediate gratification in favor of more effective long-term strategies for need satisfaction. The ego employs various defense mechanisms—including repression, projection, sublimation, and rationalization—to manage conflicts between unconscious desires and conscious social expectations.

The superego represents the internalization of social standards, moral principles, and parental expectations that guide behavior according to idealized rather than merely practical considerations. The superego can generate feelings of guilt, shame, and moral obligation that influence behavior even when external authorities are absent, demonstrating how social expectations become integrated into individual psychological organization.

Carl Jung's analytical psychology extended and transformed Freudian insights while developing more sophisticated accounts of how unconscious processes contribute to psychological development and creative expression. Jung's distinction between the personal unconscious and the collective unconscious reveals different levels of unconscious organization that operate according to different principles while both influencing conscious experience.

The personal unconscious contains material that was once conscious but has been forgotten or repressed, along with subliminal perceptions and undeveloped aspects of personality that remain available for potential conscious integration. This level of unconscious organization resembles Freud's conception while placing greater emphasis on its potential for psychological growth and creative expression rather than its primarily defensive and conflictual character.

The collective unconscious represents Jung's most distinctive theoretical contribution and refers to deeper layers of unconscious organization that are shared across all human beings and contain archetypal patterns that influence behavior, emotion, and meaning-making across different cultures and historical periods. These archetypes—including the Shadow, Anima/Animus, and Self—function as organizing principles that shape individual development while connecting personal experience to broader patterns of human meaning-making.

The Shadow archetype represents the rejected, repressed, or undeveloped aspects of personality that individuals typically disown while projecting onto others. Integration of shadow material requires acknowledging and accepting aspects of oneself that contradict idealized self-concepts while developing more complete and authentic self-understanding.

The Anima (in men) and Animus (in women) represent the unconscious feminine and masculine aspects of personality that serve as bridges between conscious ego-consciousness and deeper unconscious contents. These archetypal figures often appear in dreams and fantasies while influencing romantic attraction and creative inspiration in ways that can either promote or hinder psychological development depending on how consciously they are engaged.

The Self archetype represents the potential for psychological wholeness and integration that serves as the organizing principle for individuation—Jung's term for the lifelong process of psychological development that involves the progressive integration of unconscious contents into a more complete and authentic personality structure.

Contemporary research in cognitive and social psychology provides substantial empirical support for unconscious psychological processes while revealing their pervasive influence on perception, judgment, decision-making, and social behavior. Studies of implicit cognition demonstrate that people possess unconscious attitudes and stereotypes that can influence behavior in ways that contradict conscious beliefs and intentions.

Implicit association tests reveal unconscious biases related to race, gender, age, and other social categories that operate automatically and outside conscious awareness while influencing hiring decisions, medical treatment, legal judgments, and interpersonal interactions. These findings demonstrate that unconscious psychological processes continue to shape social behavior even in societies that have consciously rejected explicit prejudice and discrimination.

Priming studies demonstrate that exposure to subtle environmental cues can unconsciously influence subsequent thoughts, emotions, and behaviors in ways that people do not recognize or acknowledge. These effects suggest that much human behavior reflects the operation of automatic psychological processes that respond to contextual influences outside conscious awareness while serving adaptive functions related to social coordination and environmental navigation.

Cognitive Biases: The Systematic Distortions of Mental Brushwork

The systematic study of human judgment and decision-making reveals that mind painting operates through cognitive mechanisms that introduce predictable distortions and limitations into all information processing activities. These cognitive biases represent not random errors or failures of rational thinking but rather systematic features of human psychological architecture that reflect both evolutionary adaptations and the constraints imposed by limited cognitive resources.

Confirmation bias represents perhaps the most pervasive and significant limitation in human information processing, creating systematic tendencies to seek, interpret, and remember information that supports existing beliefs while avoiding or discounting information that challenges established convictions. This bias operates through multiple psychological mechanisms including selective attention, biased interpretation, and selective memory that work together to maintain cognitive consistency while protecting self-esteem and reducing psychological discomfort.

The prevalence of confirmation bias creates substantial challenges for objective inquiry and rational decision-making while serving important psychological functions related to cognitive efficiency and social coordination. Maintaining consistent belief systems reduces the cognitive effort required for information processing while enabling effective coordination with others who share similar beliefs and values.

Contemporary research reveals that confirmation bias operates even among highly trained scientists, professionals, and experts who are explicitly committed to objective analysis and evidence-based reasoning. These findings demonstrate that cognitive biases represent fundamental features of human psychological architecture rather than simply failures of education or training that can be easily eliminated through intellectual development.

However, awareness of confirmation bias can enable individuals and institutions to develop strategies for reducing its harmful effects while maintaining its beneficial functions. Scientific methodology, peer review processes, and diverse research teams represent institutional innovations designed to counteract individual cognitive biases through collaborative knowledge construction and systematic error correction.

The availability heuristic creates systematic biases in probability judgment by leading people to estimate the likelihood of events based on how easily relevant examples come to mind rather than on actual statistical frequencies. This mental shortcut often provides reasonably accurate judgments while requiring minimal cognitive effort, but it can generate significant errors when memorable events are not representative of overall patterns.

Media coverage, personal experience, and cultural narratives can create availability biases that lead to overestimation of dramatic but rare events (like terrorist attacks or airplane crashes) while underestimating common but mundane risks (like heart disease or automobile accidents). These biases influence individual behavior and public policy in ways that can reduce overall welfare while reflecting natural human tendencies to focus attention on vivid and emotionally significant events.

Anchoring bias demonstrates how initial numerical information can inappropriately influence subsequent judgments even when the anchor is obviously irrelevant to the task at hand. Studies reveal that people adjust insufficiently from initial anchors when making numerical estimates, leading to systematic biases that persist even when people are warned about the anchoring effect and offered monetary incentives for accuracy.

The anchoring effect operates through both conscious deliberation and unconscious priming mechanisms, suggesting that it reflects fundamental features of how human minds process numerical information rather than simply errors in conscious reasoning. Understanding anchoring bias can improve negotiation strategies, financial decision-making, and other activities where numerical judgments play important roles.

Framing effects reveal how the presentation of identical information in different ways can systematically influence choices and judgments. The famous Asian disease problem demonstrates that people prefer options framed as gains over those framed as losses even when the outcomes are objectively equivalent, reflecting a fundamental feature of human psychology known as loss aversion.

These framing effects operate across diverse domains including medical decision-making, financial choices, consumer behavior, and political preferences while revealing how the linguistic and contextual presentation of information shapes cognitive processing independent of its logical content. Understanding framing effects enables more effective communication and decision-making while revealing the constructed character of all human preference and judgment.

The representativeness heuristic leads people to make probability judgments based on similarity to mental prototypes rather than on base rate information or statistical reasoning. While this approach often yields reasonable judgments with minimal cognitive effort, it can generate systematic errors including the conjunction fallacy, base rate neglect, and insensitivity to sample size.

These biases reflect the human tendency to think in terms of narrative coherence and causal explanation rather than abstract statistical relationships. Understanding representativeness bias can improve statistical reasoning and decision-making while revealing how human minds naturally organize information according to meaningful patterns rather than mathematical relationships.

The Dunning-Kruger effect demonstrates how people with limited knowledge or competence in specific domains systematically overestimate their abilities while those with greater expertise tend to underestimate their relative competence. This bias reflects the meta-cognitive requirements for accurate self-assessment: people need sufficient knowledge to recognize the limitations of their own understanding.

The fundamental attribution error reveals systematic biases in how people explain others' behavior, with tendencies to attribute actions to personal characteristics rather than situational factors. This bias reflects the accessibility of information about others' behavior compared to information about the situational constraints they face, while also serving social functions related to moral evaluation and social coordination.

Hindsight bias creates systematic distortions in memory and judgment that lead people to overestimate how predictable past events were once their outcomes become known. This "knew it all along" effect impairs learning from experience by reducing recognition of genuine uncertainty and the role of chance in outcomes.

The sunk cost fallacy leads people to continue investing in failing projects or relationships based on past investments rather than future prospects. This bias reflects loss aversion and commitment escalation mechanisms that can prevent adaptive disengagement when circumstances change.

Status quo bias creates resistance to change that can prevent beneficial adaptations while maintaining stability in situations where change might be costly or risky. This bias reflects both cognitive and motivational factors that favor maintaining existing arrangements over exploring alternatives.

Social Psychology and Tribal Mind Paintings

Henri Tajfel's Social Identity Theory provides crucial insights into how individual mind paintings become integrated with group-based identity systems that create systematic biases favoring in-group members while disadvantaging out-group members. Tajfel's research demonstrated that even minimal group membership—based on arbitrary and meaningless criteria—can generate significant in-group favoritism and out-group discrimination.

The minimal group paradigm revealed that people randomly assigned to groups based on preference for abstract art or judgments about the number of dots in displays consistently allocated more rewards to in-group members than out-group members, even when they had no prior interaction with other group members and no prospect of future contact. These findings demonstrate that group categorization alone is sufficient to trigger biased processing that favors in-group interests.

Social Identity Theory proposes that group membership provides individuals with social identity that contributes to self-esteem and meaning through three interrelated processes: social categorization (dividing the world into us and them), social identification (adopting the identity of the group one belongs to), and social comparison (comparing one's group favorably to other groups to maintain positive distinctiveness).

These processes create systematic biases that influence perception, memory, and judgment in ways that support group cohesion while potentially creating conflict with other groups. In-group members are seen as more variable and positively evaluated than out-group members, who are often perceived as homogeneous and negatively stereotyped.

John Turner's Self-Categorization Theory extended Social Identity Theory by analyzing how different levels of identity—personal, interpersonal, and group—become activated in different contexts. When group identity becomes salient, individuals shift toward thinking of themselves in terms of shared group characteristics rather than personal uniqueness, leading to depersonalization that facilitates group coordination while potentially reducing empathy for out-group members.

Leon Festinger's Cognitive Dissonance Theory reveals how psychological discomfort arising from inconsistent beliefs or behaviors motivates cognitive and behavioral changes that restore consistency. This drive for consistency can lead to rationalization of questionable decisions, selective exposure to confirming information, and resistance to evidence that challenges important beliefs.

Cognitive dissonance reduction serves important functions in maintaining psychological coherence and social relationships while potentially impeding learning and adaptation when circumstances change. Understanding dissonance processes can improve decision-making while revealing the motivational factors that influence belief formation and maintenance.

Attribution Theory, developed through the work of Fritz Heider, Harold Kelley, and others, examines how people explain the causes of behavior and events. The fundamental attribution error demonstrates systematic tendencies to attribute others' behavior to personal characteristics while attributing one's own behavior to situational factors.

These attributional biases serve social functions by enabling moral evaluation and social coordination while potentially creating misunderstandings and conflicts when people misinterpret the causes of behavior. Cultural differences in attribution patterns reveal how these biases can be modified through social learning and cultural values.

Stereotype threat, identified by Claude Steele and his colleagues, demonstrates how awareness of negative stereotypes about one's group can impair performance through anxiety and cognitive interference. These effects reveal how social identity processes can create self-fulfilling prophecies that maintain group inequalities while demonstrating the power of situational factors to influence individual performance.

Irving Janis's research on groupthink reveals how group cohesion and conformity pressures can lead to poor decision-making through suppression of dissent, illusions of unanimity, and stereotyping of out-groups. These dynamics can cause groups to make decisions that individual members would recognize as flawed if they were deciding independently.

Developmental Psychology and the Formation of Mind Paintings

Jean Piaget's comprehensive research on cognitive development reveals how mind painting capabilities emerge through systematic stages that reflect both biological maturation and environmental interaction. Piaget's stage theory demonstrates how children's thinking progresses through qualitatively different organizational structures that enable increasingly sophisticated understanding of physical and social reality.

The sensorimotor stage (birth to 2 years) involves learning through direct sensory experience and motor activity, with gradual development of object permanence and basic causal understanding. During this stage, infants construct basic schemas for understanding physical objects and spatial relationships through active exploration and manipulation.

The preoperational stage (2 to 7 years) involves the emergence of symbolic thinking and language while remaining limited by egocentrism, centration, and inability to understand conservation. Children during this stage begin constructing mental representations that can extend beyond immediate sensory experience while remaining constrained by perceptual salience and difficulty coordinating multiple perspectives.

The concrete operational stage (7 to 11 years) enables logical thinking about concrete objects and relationships while remaining limited in ability to reason about abstract hypothetical situations. Children develop understanding of conservation, classification, and seriation while beginning to coordinate multiple perspectives and consider reversible operations.

The formal operational stage (11+ years) enables abstract logical reasoning about hypothetical situations and systematic experimental thinking. This stage represents the culmination of cognitive development while remaining limited by individual differences in education, cultural support, and domain-specific expertise.

Erik Erikson's psychosocial development theory reveals how identity formation occurs through successful resolution of stage-specific crises that integrate individual needs with social expectations. Each stage presents challenges that require developing new capacities while building upon previous achievements to construct coherent identity and effective social functioning.

Erikson's eight stages span the entire lifespan and demonstrate how identity construction continues through adulthood as individuals face new challenges and opportunities for growth. The successful resolution of each crisis contributes to the development of specific virtues or strengths that support continued development while providing resilience for addressing future challenges.

Contemporary research on theory of mind reveals how children develop understanding of others' mental states through systematic stages that enable increasingly sophisticated social cognition. The false belief task demonstrates how children gradually develop understanding that others can hold beliefs that differ from reality and from their own knowledge.

These developments enable increasingly sophisticated forms of social coordination and cultural learning while revealing the cognitive foundations that make complex human societies possible. Understanding theory of mind development illuminates both the remarkable achievements of human social cognition and the systematic limitations that constrain empathy and perspective-taking.

Neurotransmitter Systems and Chemical Influences on Mind Painting

The discovery of how different neurotransmitter systems influence cognition, emotion, and behavior reveals that mind painting operates through complex biochemical processes that can be modified through both endogenous changes and external interventions. Understanding these chemical influences illuminates the biological foundations of psychological experience while providing insights into how therapeutic interventions can facilitate adaptive changes in maladaptive mind paintings.

The dopamine system plays crucial roles in motivation, reward processing, and learning while contributing to attention, motor control, and executive functioning. Dysfunction in dopamine systems has been associated with various psychological disorders including depression, schizophrenia, and attention-deficit/hyperactivity disorder, while therapeutic interventions that modify dopamine function can improve symptoms and functioning.

Dopamine neurons respond to unexpected rewards and reward-predicting stimuli while contributing to reinforcement learning that shapes both adaptive and maladaptive behavior patterns. Understanding dopamine function provides insights into addiction, motivation, and behavioral change while revealing the biological mechanisms that underlie reward-seeking behavior and goal-directed action.

The serotonin system influences mood, anxiety, sleep, and social behavior while contributing to impulse control and cognitive flexibility. Serotonin dysfunction has been implicated in depression, anxiety disorders, and aggression, while therapeutic interventions that increase serotonin availability often improve mood and social functioning.

Serotonin receptors are distributed throughout the brain and body while showing particular concentrations in areas involved in emotional regulation and social cognition. Recent research on psychedelic substances that act on serotonin receptors reveals potential therapeutic applications for treatment-resistant depression, post-traumatic stress disorder, and other conditions while providing insights into the neurochemical foundations of consciousness and meaning-making.

The norepinephrine system contributes to attention, arousal, and stress responses while influencing memory consolidation and emotional processing. Dysfunction in norepinephrine systems has been associated with depression, anxiety, and attention disorders, while therapeutic interventions can improve focus and emotional regulation.

The GABA system provides the primary inhibitory neurotransmission in the brain while contributing to anxiety regulation, sleep, and seizure control. Anxiety disorders often involve dysfunction in GABA systems, while therapeutic interventions that enhance GABA function can reduce anxiety and improve emotional regulation.

Understanding neurotransmitter systems reveals how chemical factors influence all aspects of mind painting while providing opportunities for therapeutic intervention when these systems become dysregulated. However, the complexity of brain chemistry ensures that simple chemical explanations remain insufficient for understanding the full range of human psychological experience.

Emotional Coloring and Motivational Brushstrokes

The integration of emotion and cognition in human psychological functioning reveals that mind painting necessarily involves affective as well as cognitive components that influence attention, memory, judgment, and decision-making in ways that cannot be separated from purely rational information processing. Contemporary neuroscience demonstrates that emotion and cognition operate through interconnected brain networks that influence each other at all levels of psychological organization.

The limbic system—including structures such as the amygdala, hippocampus, and anterior cingulate cortex—plays crucial roles in emotional processing, memory formation, and attention regulation while maintaining extensive connections to prefrontal regions involved in executive control and abstract reasoning. These anatomical connections ensure that emotional processes influence cognitive activities while cognitive processes can modulate emotional responses through top-down regulatory mechanisms.

Antonio Damasio's research on patients with damage to ventromedial prefrontal cortex reveals that impaired emotional processing leads to profound deficits in practical decision-making despite preserved logical reasoning abilities. These findings challenge traditional assumptions about the relationship between emotion and rationality while demonstrating that effective decision-making requires the integration of emotional and cognitive information rather than the elimination of emotional influences.

The somatic marker hypothesis proposes that emotional responses to potential outcomes influence decision-making through bodily signals that guide attention toward advantageous choices while steering behavior away from harmful options. This emotional guidance system operates both consciously and unconsciously while providing essential information for navigating complex social and practical decisions that involve significant uncertainty and multiple competing values.

Mood states systematically influence cognitive processing through multiple mechanisms including attention allocation, memory retrieval, and judgment formation. Positive moods tend to promote creative thinking, risk-taking, and optimistic judgments while negative moods enhance analytical thinking, cautious decision-making, and critical evaluation of information.

These mood-congruent processing effects can create systematic biases in information processing while also serving adaptive functions that adjust cognitive strategies to environmental demands. Understanding mood effects on cognition can improve decision-making while revealing how emotional states influence the construction of mind paintings in ways that extend beyond rational information processing.

Motivated reasoning demonstrates how desires and preferences unconsciously influence information processing in ways that support preferred conclusions while maintaining the subjective experience of objective rational analysis. People engage in more extensive and creative reasoning when defending preferred positions than when evaluating unwelcome conclusions, leading to systematic biases that protect self-esteem and valued beliefs while compromising accuracy and objectivity.

However, motivated reasoning serves important psychological functions including maintaining coherent self-concepts, preserving important social relationships, and reducing cognitive dissonance that can interfere with effective action. Understanding motivated reasoning can improve critical thinking while acknowledging the psychological needs that make completely objective analysis both impossible and potentially counterproductive.

Cultural Psychology and Universal vs. Particular Mind Paintings

Cross-cultural research in psychology reveals both universal features of human cognition and systematic cultural variations that challenge assumptions about the universality of psychological processes identified primarily through research on Western, educated, industrialized, rich, and democratic (WEIRD) populations. Understanding cultural influences on mind painting illuminates the interaction between biological constraints and cultural learning while revealing both the diversity and commonality of human psychological experience.

Richard Nisbett's research on cultural differences in cognition demonstrates systematic variations between East Asian and Western approaches to attention, categorization, and causal reasoning. East Asians show greater attention to contextual relationships and holistic patterns while Westerners focus more on focal objects and categorical relationships. These differences reflect cultural emphases on interdependence versus independence while revealing how cultural values become embedded in basic cognitive processes.

Cross-cultural studies of moral reasoning reveal both universal moral concerns—including care, fairness, loyalty, authority, and sanctity—and systematic cultural variations in their relative importance and application. Jonathan Haidt's moral foundations theory demonstrates how different cultures emphasize different moral considerations while revealing the psychological foundations that make moral reasoning possible across diverse cultural contexts.

Cultural variations in self-concept reveal different approaches to understanding personal identity and its relationship to social groups. Independent self-construals emphasize personal uniqueness and individual achievement, while interdependent self-construals emphasize social relationships and group harmony. These differences influence motivation, emotion, and social behavior while revealing how cultural values become integrated into individual psychology.

However, cross-cultural research also reveals substantial universals in human psychology that reflect shared biological heritage and common challenges faced by all human societies. Universal emotions, basic cognitive processes, and social behaviors demonstrate the species-typical foundations that enable cultural learning while constraining the range of viable cultural variations.

The tension between cultural universalism and cultural relativism in psychology requires careful analysis that acknowledges both the reality of cultural differences and the existence of universal human nature. Understanding this balance provides frameworks for avoiding both cultural imperialism and relativistic approaches that deny the possibility of cross-cultural understanding and communication.

Critics might argue that Western psychology imposes culturally specific concepts—such as individual autonomy, mental illness categories, and therapeutic goals—on other cultures in ways that constitute cultural imperialism disguised as scientific objectivity. This critique requires serious consideration while maintaining confidence in the possibility of cross-cultural psychological science that respects cultural differences while identifying universal principles.

Neurodiversity and Individual Differences in Mind Painting

Contemporary understanding of neurodevelopmental differences reveals that variations in brain structure and function create diverse approaches to information processing and social interaction that challenge traditional assumptions about normal and abnormal psychological functioning. The neurodiversity movement advocates for understanding conditions like autism, ADHD, dyslexia, and other neurological differences as natural variations rather than deficits requiring correction.

Research on autism spectrum disorders reveals distinctive cognitive profiles that include enhanced attention to detail, superior performance on certain visual-spatial tasks, and different approaches to social communication while challenging assumptions about the necessity of typical social interaction patterns for meaningful human relationships and achievement.

Attention-deficit/hyperactivity disorder research demonstrates how differences in attention regulation and impulse control can create both challenges and advantages depending on environmental demands and cultural values. Understanding ADHD as a neurodevelopmental difference rather than simply a disorder provides opportunities for developing educational and workplace accommodations that leverage strengths while addressing difficulties.

Dyslexia research reveals how differences in phonological processing can coexist with superior visual-spatial abilities and creative thinking while requiring alternative approaches to reading and writing instruction. These findings demonstrate how learning differences can reflect alternative cognitive architectures rather than simply deficient processing. Also, dyslexia might be an ancient survival function of pattern recognition. (see my book "The Pattern Seeking Ape")

The neurodiversity perspective challenges traditional medical model approaches that focus on eliminating differences in favor of approaches that accommodate diversity while providing support for areas of genuine difficulty. This shift in perspective requires balancing recognition of real challenges and needs for support with appreciation for the value of cognitive diversity.

Understanding neurodiversity illuminates both the biological foundations that constrain human cognitive variation and the cultural factors that determine which variations are valued or stigmatized. This perspective provides resources for developing more inclusive approaches to education, employment, and social participation while maintaining recognition of genuine needs for support and intervention.

Therapeutic Repainting: Clinical Applications and Psychological Change

The systematic application of psychological insights to address mental health problems reveals how maladaptive mind paintings can be identified and modified through therapeutic interventions that help individuals develop more effective and satisfying approaches to understanding themselves and their environments. Various therapeutic approaches demonstrate different strategies for facilitating psychological change while illuminating common principles that underlie effective mental health treatment.

Cognitive-behavioral therapy (CBT) focuses explicitly on identifying and modifying dysfunctional thought patterns that contribute to emotional distress and behavioral problems. CBT approaches assume that psychological symptoms often result from systematic cognitive distortions that create maladaptive interpretations of experience while maintaining through selective attention and confirmation bias.

Common cognitive distortions include all-or-nothing thinking, overgeneralization, mental filtering, discounting positive experiences, jumping to conclusions, magnification and minimization, emotional reasoning, should statements, labeling, and personalization. These thinking patterns create systematic biases that maintain psychological distress while preventing individuals from developing more balanced and effective approaches to common life challenges.

CBT interventions help clients identify these cognitive distortions while developing more balanced and realistic thinking patterns that reduce emotional distress and improve behavioral effectiveness. Techniques such as thought records, behavioral experiments, and exposure exercises enable clients to test the accuracy of negative thoughts while developing alternative interpretations that support psychological well-being and effective functioning.

Aaron Beck's cognitive theory of depression demonstrates how systematic negative biases in attention, memory, and interpretation create and maintain depressive episodes through the cognitive triad of negative thoughts about self, world, and future. Beck's research reveals how these biases operate automatically while being amenable to modification through systematic therapeutic intervention.

The effectiveness of CBT across diverse psychological disorders demonstrates that therapeutic change can occur through systematic modification of cognitive mind paintings without requiring extensive exploration of unconscious processes or childhood experiences. However, CBT approaches acknowledge that cognitive change often requires behavioral change and emotional processing rather than purely intellectual insight.

Behavioral approaches developed from B.F. Skinner's operant conditioning principles focus on modifying maladaptive behaviors through systematic manipulation of environmental contingencies. These approaches demonstrate how behavior patterns can be changed through careful analysis of antecedents, behaviors, and consequences while providing practical tools for addressing problems ranging from phobias and addictions to parenting and organizational management.

Albert Bandura's social learning theory reveals how much human behavior is acquired through observation and imitation rather than direct conditioning, while his research on self-efficacy demonstrates the importance of confidence in one's ability to perform specific behaviors for motivation and achievement. These insights provide frameworks for therapeutic interventions that enhance personal agency while addressing learned helplessness and low self-esteem.

Psychodynamic approaches to therapy focus on identifying and resolving unconscious conflicts that contribute to psychological symptoms while promoting greater self-awareness and emotional integration. These approaches assume that current difficulties often reflect the operation of unconscious patterns that developed during childhood and continue to influence adult behavior in ways that remain outside conscious awareness.

Transference phenomena—where clients unconsciously experience their therapist in ways that reflect important early relationships—provide opportunities for exploring how past experiences continue to influence current perceptions and relationships. Working through transference enables clients to develop more conscious awareness of unconscious patterns while creating opportunities for developing new and more satisfying relationship patterns.

The therapeutic relationship itself serves as a corrective emotional experience that enables clients to internalize new models of interpersonal interaction while developing greater capacity for emotional regulation and authentic self-expression. The gradual development of trust and intimacy within the therapeutic relationship provides a safe context for exploring difficult emotions and experiences while developing new capacities for psychological integration.

Humanistic and existential approaches to therapy emphasize the importance of authentic self-expression and personal meaning-making while supporting clients' natural tendencies toward psychological growth and self-actualization. These approaches assume that psychological symptoms often reflect disconnection from authentic values and experiences rather than specific cognitive distortions or unconscious conflicts.

Person-centered therapy, developed by Carl Rogers, provides unconditional positive regard, empathy, and genuineness to create therapeutic conditions that support clients' natural capacity for psychological healing and growth. This approach demonstrates that therapeutic change can occur through supportive relational experiences that enable clients to develop greater self-acceptance and authentic self-expression.

Existential approaches address fundamental human concerns about meaning, freedom, responsibility, and mortality while helping clients develop more authentic and satisfying approaches to these universal challenges. These therapies recognize that psychological symptoms often reflect deeper existential struggles that require philosophical as well as psychological exploration.

Contemporary integrative approaches to therapy combine insights and techniques from multiple therapeutic traditions while adapting treatment approaches to individual client needs and preferences. These approaches recognize that different therapeutic methods may be more effective for different types of problems while maintaining focus on common factors that promote psychological change across diverse therapeutic contexts.

The therapeutic alliance—the collaborative relationship between therapist and client—represents perhaps the most important predictor of therapeutic success across different treatment approaches. Effective therapeutic relationships provide safety, support, and challenge that enable clients to explore difficult experiences while developing new capacities for self-understanding and behavioral change.

However, critics raise legitimate concerns about the cultural specificity of many therapeutic approaches and their potential for imposing dominant cultural values disguised as mental health treatment. The concept of mental illness itself reflects cultural assumptions about normal and abnormal behavior that may not apply across different cultural contexts.

These concerns require careful consideration while maintaining confidence in the possibility of developing culturally responsive therapeutic approaches that respect cultural differences while addressing genuine psychological suffering. Understanding cultural influences on psychological experience provides resources for developing more effective and culturally appropriate therapeutic interventions.

Defending Against Philosophical Objections

The analysis of psychological and neurological foundations of mind painting requires robust defense against several potential philosophical objections beyond those already addressed. Critics concerned about free will might argue that emphasizing brain chemistry, unconscious drives, and systematic biases eliminates human agency and moral responsibility by suggesting that behavior is determined by factors outside conscious control.

However, this objection reflects a false dichotomy between complete rational autonomy and mechanistic determinism. Understanding the psychological and neurological mechanisms that influence thought and behavior enhances rather than eliminates human agency by providing knowledge that can be used to make more conscious and effective choices while acknowledging the realistic constraints within which all human decision-making operates.

A compatibilist position maintains that free will and moral responsibility remain meaningful concepts even within a scientific understanding of human psychology and neurology.

What matters for moral responsibility is not the absence of causal influences but the capacity for rational reflection, emotional regulation, and value-guided choice that distinguish mature human agents from children, individuals with severe mental illness, or those acting under extreme duress.

The framework developed here maintains clear distinctions between causal explanation and moral evaluation while recognizing that effective moral responsibility requires realistic understanding of human psychological limitations and possibilities. Awareness of cognitive biases and unconscious influences can enable individuals and institutions to develop strategies for making more rational and ethical decisions while acknowledging that complete objectivity remains impossible.

Critics concerned about the measurement problem might argue that psychology cannot adequately measure what matters most—consciousness, meaning, values, and subjective experience—because these phenomena are inherently subjective and resist quantification. This objection challenges the entire enterprise of scientific psychology while questioning whether rigorous knowledge about human experience is possible.

However, this criticism underestimates the capacity of psychological science to develop reliable methods for investigating subjective phenomena through multiple approaches including behavioral measures, self-report instruments, physiological assessments, and neuroimaging techniques.

While these methods have limitations and cannot capture all aspects of human experience, they can provide useful knowledge that enhances understanding and enables practical applications.

The phenomenological tradition in psychology demonstrates how subjective experience can be systematically investigated while maintaining respect for its distinctive character. The development of validated measures for psychological constructs like personality, intelligence, and psychopathology demonstrates that meaningful quantification of psychological phenomena is possible while acknowledging the limitations of any particular measurement approach.

Contemporary advances in neuroscience provide increasingly sophisticated methods for investigating the neural correlates of consciousness, emotion, and meaning-making while remaining appropriately modest about the explanatory gap between neural activity and subjective experience. Understanding these correlations provides useful knowledge for addressing psychological problems while acknowledging the continued mystery of consciousness.

The hard problem of consciousness—explaining how subjective experience arises from neural activity—remains unsolved and may represent a fundamental limitation of scientific approaches to understanding mind. However, this limitation does not invalidate the substantial practical knowledge that psychology and neuroscience have achieved about the functions and mechanisms of human cognition and behavior.

Critics might argue that therapeutic approaches represent forms of social control that impose dominant cultural values while disguising coercion as healthcare. This critique questions whether therapeutic interventions genuinely serve client interests or primarily function to maintain social conformity and reduce behaviors that challenge existing power structures.

This concern requires serious consideration while maintaining confidence in the genuine benefits that effective therapy can provide for individuals experiencing psychological distress. The key distinction lies between therapeutic approaches that respect client autonomy and cultural values while addressing genuine suffering versus those that impose external standards of normality without regard for client preferences and cultural contexts.

Ethical therapeutic practice requires informed consent, cultural sensitivity, and respect for client values while providing effective interventions for addressing psychological problems that interfere with individual functioning and well-being. The development of culturally adapted therapeutic approaches demonstrates the possibility of providing effective treatment while respecting cultural diversity and individual autonomy.

The growth of client-centered and collaborative therapeutic approaches demonstrates movement away from authoritarian models toward approaches that prioritize client empowerment and self-determination. These developments address legitimate concerns about therapeutic coercion while maintaining commitment to providing effective treatment for genuine psychological difficulties.

Critics concerned about the medicalization of normal human experience argue that expanding definitions of mental illness pathologize natural variations in personality and behavior while creating artificial needs for professional intervention. This critique questions whether many psychological problems represent genuine disorders or simply cultural disapproval of nonconformity.

However, this criticism can be addressed through careful attention to functional impairment and individual distress rather than simple statistical deviance or social disapproval. Genuine psychological disorders typically involve significant impairment in functioning and subjective distress rather than merely unusual behavior or cultural nonconformity.

The distinction between problems in living and mental disorders remains important while acknowledging that the boundary between them can be unclear and culturally influenced. What matters is providing appropriate support for individuals experiencing genuine difficulties while avoiding unnecessary pathologizing of normal human diversity.

Understanding the psychological and neurological mechanisms that influence human mind painting reveals both the constraints and possibilities that shape human meaning-making while providing resources for enhancing individual and collective functioning within realistic appreciation of human limitations and possibilities.

The systematic investigation of psychological and neurological mechanisms reveals that mind painting operates through sophisticated but constrained cognitive architectures that introduce systematic biases and limitations into all human meaning-making activities. Understanding these mechanisms enhances rather than diminishes human agency and achievement while providing essential resources for continued individual and cultural development within realistic appreciation of human psychological possibilities and constraints.

Contemporary neuroscience reveals that human brain architecture evolved to address specific survival and reproductive challenges rather than to achieve abstract truth or objective knowledge. This evolutionary history creates systematic limitations and biases that influence all human cognitive activities while providing the foundation for remarkable achievements in art, science, philosophy, and social cooperation.

Understanding these evolutionary influences illuminates both the constraints and possibilities that shape human mind painting while supporting realistic approaches to cognitive enhancement and cultural development. Rather than eliminating human creativity and achievement, evolutionary psychology provides frameworks for understanding how these distinctive capacities emerge from and build upon biological foundations.

The recognition that psychology functions as humanity's most sophisticated tool for self-understanding demonstrates the remarkable human capacity for transcending biological constraints through cultural innovation and collaborative knowledge construction. This metacognitive achievement enables continued improvement in psychological understanding while acknowledging the inevitable limitations that constrain all human knowledge-seeking activities.

The integration of psychological and neuroscientific insights with the mind painting framework provides comprehensive understanding of how human meaning-making systems emerge from and operate within biological constraints while achieving unprecedented levels of sophistication through cultural development and individual creativity. This understanding supports both intellectual humility about human cognitive limitations and appreciation for the remarkable achievements that emerge through individual and collective human efforts at understanding and improving the conditions of human existence.

Chapter Twelve
Society's Canvas – Politics, Ideology, and the Power of Shared Paintings

Karl Marx and the Material Foundation of Social Mind Paintings

Karl Marx's historical materialism provides the most systematic analysis of how economic structures shape social consciousness and political organization, revealing that what appear to be autonomous cultural and ideological systems actually reflect underlying material conditions and class relationships that operate according to discoverable scientific laws. Marx's revolutionary insight demonstrates that social mind paintings do not emerge from pure intellectual activity but rather from the practical necessities of human survival and production within specific economic arrangements that determine the range of viable cultural possibilities.

The base-superstructure model represents Marx's fundamental contribution to understanding how economic organization shapes all other aspects of social life. The economic base consists of the forces of production (technology, natural resources, human labor power) and the relations of production (the social organization of economic activity, particularly class relationships based on ownership or non-ownership of productive resources). This material foundation generates a superstructure of political institutions, legal systems, cultural practices, and ideological frameworks that serve to legitimize and reproduce the existing economic arrangements.

Marx's famous formulation in the "Preface to A Contribution to the Critique of Political Economy" establishes the causal priority of material conditions: "The mode of production of material life conditions the general process of social, political and intellectual life. It is not the consciousness of men that determines their existence, but their social existence that determines their consciousness."

This materialist approach directly challenges idealist philosophies that treat ideas, values, and beliefs as autonomous forces that shape social reality according to their own internal logic. Marx demonstrates that even the most abstract philosophical and religious systems reflect the practical interests and lived experiences of particular social classes while serving specific functions in maintaining or challenging existing power relationships.

The concept of false consciousness reveals how subordinate classes often accept ideological frameworks that justify their own exploitation by presenting existing social arrangements as natural, inevitable, or divinely ordained rather than historically contingent products of specific economic systems. Workers under capitalism may embrace individualist ideologies that blame personal failings for economic difficulties while obscuring the systematic exploitation inherent in wage labor relationships.

However, Marx's analysis avoids crude economic determinism by recognizing the relative autonomy of superstructural elements and their capacity to influence the economic base through dialectical interaction. Political movements, cultural innovations, and ideological developments can accelerate or retard economic transformation while remaining ultimately constrained by material possibilities and class interests.

The theory of commodity fetishism demonstrates how capitalist economic relationships mystify social relations by making them appear as relationships between things rather than between people. When workers sell their labor power for wages, the social relationship of exploitation becomes obscured by the apparently equal exchange of labor for money, hiding the fundamental asymmetry in power and control over the production process.

Marx's analysis of capitalism reveals systematic contradictions that generate ongoing instability and crisis while creating conditions for revolutionary transformation. The falling rate of profit, overproduction crises, and increasing concentration of capital create objective pressures that no amount of ideological manipulation can permanently resolve, suggesting that capitalist mind paintings ultimately depend on material conditions that they cannot fully control.

The concept of class struggle provides the dynamic mechanism through which historical change occurs as different classes develop competing ideologies that reflect their material interests while struggling for political and economic control. These conflicts cannot be resolved through purely intellectual argument or moral appeal but require practical political action that addresses underlying economic contradictions.

Contemporary developments in global capitalism, technological automation, and environmental crisis demonstrate both the continuing relevance of Marxist analysis and the emergence of new contradictions that require creative theoretical development within historical materialist frameworks. Understanding how digital technologies, financial markets, and ecological constraints shape contemporary class relationships provides resources for developing updated analyses of capitalist mind paintings.

Émile Durkheim and the Sacred Foundations of Social Order

Émile Durkheim's sociological analysis reveals how shared moral beliefs and collective rituals create the social solidarity necessary for large-scale cooperation while demonstrating that even seemingly secular modern societies require quasi-religious foundations that transcend individual rational calculation. Durkheim's investigation of social facts illuminates how collective mind paintings operate as external constraints on individual behavior while serving essential functions in maintaining social integration and psychological well-being.

Social facts exist as external realities that exercise coercive power over individuals independently of their personal beliefs or preferences. These collective phenomena include legal systems, moral codes, religious practices, economic institutions, and cultural traditions that individuals encounter as objective features of their social environment rather than as products of their own creation or choice.

The concept of collective consciousness (conscience collective) captures how shared beliefs, values, and emotional responses create unified social perspectives that enable coordination across diverse individuals while providing meaning and identity that transcends personal experience. This collective consciousness operates through symbols, rituals, and narratives that connect individual lives to broader social purposes while maintaining cultural continuity across generations.

Durkheim's distinction between mechanical and organic solidarity reveals how different types of social organization create different forms of collective consciousness and social integration. Mechanical solidarity characterizes traditional societies where social cohesion emerges from shared beliefs, common experiences, and similar social positions that create strong collective consciousness but limited individual autonomy.

Organic solidarity develops in complex modern societies where social integration depends on functional interdependence created by extensive division of labor rather than cultural similarity. This form of solidarity enables greater individual freedom and social diversity while requiring sophisticated institutional mechanisms to coordinate specialized activities and maintain social cooperation.

The analysis of anomie demonstrates how weakening of collective moral regulation can generate psychological distress and social instability even when material conditions improve. Durkheim's research on suicide rates revealed that social integration and moral regulation provide essential resources for individual psychological health that cannot be replaced by purely economic or technological solutions.

Religious phenomena provide the clearest examples of how collective consciousness creates and maintains social solidarity through shared participation in sacred activities that reinforce group identity while providing transcendent meaning that justifies social cooperation. Even apparently secular rituals and symbols serve similar functions by creating emotional bonds and shared purposes that enable collective action.

The sacred-profane distinction reveals how societies create special categories of experience that are set apart from ordinary practical activity and invested with extraordinary significance that commands respect and reverence. These sacred elements serve as focal points for collective identity while providing standards for evaluating and organizing social relationships.

Durkheim's analysis of modern education demonstrates how secular institutions can serve quasi-religious functions by transmitting shared values, creating national identity, and legitimizing social hierarchies through ritualized activities that generate emotional commitment to collective ideals. Schools function as temples of the modern state religion of individualism and citizenship.

The concept of collective effervescence captures how group gatherings can generate intense emotional experiences that create and reinforce social bonds while providing direct experience of collective power that transcends individual limitations. These experiences provide the emotional foundations for social solidarity while demonstrating the reality of collective consciousness.

Contemporary applications of Durkheimian analysis to political movements, consumer culture, and digital communities reveal how modern societies continue to require shared symbols and collective rituals while adapting traditional mechanisms of social integration to new technological and cultural circumstances.

Michel Foucault and the Micropolitics of Power/Knowledge

Michel Foucault's genealogical analysis revolutionizes understanding of political power by revealing how modern societies operate through subtle disciplinary mechanisms that shape individual consciousness and behavior rather than relying primarily on direct coercion or ideological manipulation. Foucault's power/knowledge framework demonstrates that political control operates through the production of truth and the formation of subjects rather than simply through the repression of pre-existing desires and interests.

The concept of disciplinary power reveals how modern institutions create "docile bodies" through sophisticated techniques of surveillance, examination, and normalization that operate below the threshold of conscious awareness while shaping individual identity and social relationships. Unlike sovereign power that operates through spectacular displays of force, disciplinary power works through continuous observation and gentle correction that makes resistance appear unnecessary or impossible.

The Panopticon serves as Foucault's central metaphor for modern disciplinary society where the possibility of constant surveillance creates self-regulating behavior even when actual observation is intermittent or absent. This architectural model reveals how power becomes most effective when it is invisible and internalized rather than visible and external.

Disciplinary mechanisms operate through three primary techniques: hierarchical observation that makes individuals visible to authority while keeping authority hidden from view; normalizing judgment that evaluates behavior according to standards of normalcy rather than simple legal compliance; and examination that combines observation with judgment to create knowledge about individuals while reinforcing their subjection to institutional authority.

The power/knowledge nexus demonstrates that modern political control operates through the production of scientific and professional knowledge about human behavior rather than through the suppression of truth or the imposition of false beliefs. Psychology, medicine, criminology, and other human sciences serve political functions by creating categories of normal and abnormal behavior while providing techniques for managing and modifying deviant populations.

Biopower extends disciplinary techniques to entire populations through statistical analysis, public health measures, and demographic management that treats collective human life as an object of political intervention and optimization. This form of power operates through the administration of bodies and the management of life itself rather than through the traditional sovereign right to take life or let live.

Governmentality reveals how modern political power operates through the "conduct of conduct" that shapes the conditions within which individuals make choices rather than dictating specific behaviors through direct command. This governmental rationality creates freedom as a necessary condition for effective control while maintaining overall direction of social development.

The concept of subjectification demonstrates how modern power relations create the very subjects who appear to be their targets rather than simply acting upon pre-existing individuals. Disciplinary and governmental techniques produce particular types of persons—criminals, mental patients, citizens, consumers—who embody the categories through which power operates.

Foucault's analysis of sexuality reveals how apparently private and natural aspects of human experience actually reflect complex historical processes of knowledge production and subject formation that serve political functions while creating the illusion of discovering rather than constructing human nature.

The genealogical method exposes how contemporary institutions and practices that appear rational and necessary actually emerged through contingent historical processes that could have developed differently, revealing possibilities for alternative forms of social organization that are obscured by dominant truth regimes.

Resistance operates not through direct opposition to power but through creative practices that exploit the gaps and contradictions within disciplinary systems while developing alternative forms of subjectivity and relationship that escape capture by dominant technologies of control.

Antonio Gramsci and the Cultural Dimension of Political Hegemony

Antonio Gramsci's analysis of cultural hegemony provides crucial insights into how ruling classes maintain political dominance through intellectual and moral leadership rather than relying primarily on economic coercion or state violence. Gramsci's prison writings reveal how political power operates through the construction of common sense that makes existing social arrangements appear natural and beneficial while marginalizing alternative perspectives and possibilities.

Hegemony represents the capacity of dominant groups to universalize their particular interests and values while securing active consent from subordinate groups rather than merely passive compliance with superior force. This cultural dominance operates through educational institutions, mass media, religious organizations, and intellectual activity that shape popular consciousness in ways that support existing power relationships.

The concept of historic bloc reveals how successful hegemonic projects require the integration of economic, political, and cultural elements into coherent arrangements that can address the needs and aspirations of diverse social groups while maintaining overall direction by dominant classes.

These blocs are not simply imposed from above but must be constructed through ongoing cultural and political work that adapts to changing circumstances.

Civil society functions as the primary terrain where hegemonic struggles occur through the competition between different cultural and political projects that seek to win popular support while establishing their vision as the foundation for social organization. This sphere mediates between the economy and the state while serving as the location where consent is organized and alternative perspectives developed.

The role of intellectuals becomes crucial in hegemonic processes as they serve to articulate and disseminate the worldviews that justify existing arrangements while also potentially developing critical perspectives that challenge dominant common sense. Traditional intellectuals associated with established institutions and organic intellectuals emerging from particular social classes play different roles in maintaining or transforming cultural hegemony.

Gramsci's analysis of passive revolution reveals how dominant groups can maintain their position by adapting to popular pressures through limited reforms that preserve essential power relationships while appearing to address subordinate group concerns. This strategy enables ruling classes to neutralize opposition while avoiding fundamental changes in social organization.

The war of position strategy emphasizes the importance of cultural and educational work in preparing for political transformation rather than relying on direct confrontation with state power. This approach recognizes that lasting political change requires the development of alternative hegemonic visions that can win popular support before attempting to seize control of governmental institutions.

Common sense represents the contradictory mixture of inherited beliefs, practical experience, and dominant ideological elements that shapes popular consciousness while containing both conservative and progressive possibilities. Political strategy must engage with existing common sense rather than dismissing it while working to develop its critical and transformative potential.

The analysis of Fordism demonstrates how new forms of economic organization require corresponding cultural changes that reshape work, consumption, and daily life in ways that support increased productivity while managing potential sources of social conflict. This cultural transformation involves both coercion and consent as workers are induced to accept new forms of discipline and regulation.

Contemporary applications of Gramscian analysis to neoliberalism, globalization, and populist movements reveal how cultural hegemony continues to play crucial roles in political dominance while adapting to new technological and economic circumstances that create opportunities for counter-hegemonic projects.

Benedict Anderson and the Construction of Imagined Communities

Benedict Anderson's analysis of nationalism demonstrates how modern political communities depend on shared cultural imagination rather than direct personal relationships or common territorial experience. Anderson's concept of "imagined communities" reveals how print capitalism and mass media create the conditions for large-scale social solidarity while exposing the constructed rather than natural character of national identity and political belonging.

The imagination of national community operates through simultaneous shared experiences created by mass media consumption that enable millions of people to think of themselves as participating in common activities despite never meeting or directly interacting with most other community members. Newspaper reading creates the experience of shared simultaneous activity that provides the foundation for national consciousness.

Print capitalism serves as the technological foundation for national imagination by creating unified fields of exchange and communication that transcend local dialects and regional differences while making possible the development of standardized national languages that can serve as vehicles for cultural and political identification.

The concept of homogeneous empty time reveals how national imagination requires temporal frameworks that enable people to situate their individual lives within broader historical narratives that connect past, present, and future through stories of national development and destiny. This temporal imagination makes possible both historical consciousness and future-oriented political projects.

Anderson's analysis of creole nationalism demonstrates how colonial societies developed new forms of political identity that combined European cultural elements with local territorial attachments while creating precedents for anti-imperial movements that would later spread throughout the colonized world.

The role of intellectuals becomes crucial in creating and disseminating national narratives through literature, journalism, and educational activity that translates abstract political concepts into emotionally compelling stories that can mobilize popular support for political projects while creating shared cultural reference points.

Museums, monuments, and national ceremonies serve to materialize abstract national identities through concrete symbols and rituals that provide focal points for collective identification while creating sacred spaces that reinforce emotional attachment to political communities.

The analysis of official nationalism reveals how established states attempt to mobilize national sentiment to support their legitimacy while competing with popular nationalist movements that may challenge existing political arrangements in the name of authentic national identity and self-determination.

Anderson's framework illuminates both the progressive potential of anti-imperial nationalism and the dangerous possibilities of exclusionary ethnic nationalism that mobilizes popular sentiment against minority populations while serving elite interests in maintaining political and economic dominance.

Contemporary developments in global communications, migration, and transnational organizations create new challenges for national imagination while potentially enabling new forms of political community that transcend traditional territorial boundaries without necessarily eliminating the need for collective identity and shared cultural frameworks.

James C. Scott and the Hidden Transcripts of Resistance

James C. Scott's analysis of everyday resistance reveals how subordinate groups develop hidden forms of opposition to domination that operate below the threshold of open political confrontation while maintaining dignity and agency within oppressive circumstances. Scott's framework demonstrates that political resistance operates through cultural practices and symbolic activities as well as through direct organizational challenges to state power.

The concept of hidden transcripts captures the critique of power that subordinate groups develop and share among themselves while maintaining public performances of deference and compliance when interacting with dominant groups. These hidden transcripts provide psychological resources for resistance while creating cultural foundations for potential collective action.

Public transcripts represent the open interaction between dominant and subordinate groups that typically involve ritualized displays of power and deference designed to maintain existing hierarchies while allowing subordinate groups to survive within oppressive arrangements. These public performances often contain subtle forms of resistance and criticism that remain invisible to dominant groups.

The analysis of foot-dragging, dissimulation, false compliance, and other forms of everyday resistance demonstrates how subordinate groups can limit the effectiveness of domination without engaging in open rebellion that would provoke violent repression. These tactics enable survival and limited agency while preserving possibilities for more direct resistance when circumstances become favorable.

Scott's study of peasant resistance reveals how rural populations develop sophisticated strategies for limiting landlord and state extraction while maintaining community solidarity and traditional cultural practices against modernizing pressures. These resistance strategies often involve appeals to moral economy principles that challenge purely market-based relationships.

The concept of weapons of the weak emphasizes how subordinate groups use available cultural and material resources to resist domination rather than requiring revolutionary organization or ideological transformation. These everyday practices can accumulate into significant constraints on elite power while preparing ground for more organized resistance movements.

The analysis of state legibility demonstrates how modern governments attempt to make their populations and territories more visible and controllable through standardization, mapping, and administrative rationalization that often destroys local knowledge and adaptive practices while creating vulnerabilities to resistance and failure.

High modernist ideology represents the belief that rational scientific planning can improve human welfare through comprehensive social engineering that ignores local knowledge and cultural preferences while imposing universal solutions that often generate unintended consequences and popular resistance.

The concept of metis captures the practical wisdom that emerges from local experience and cultural tradition rather than formal scientific knowledge, demonstrating how this informal knowledge often proves more effective than expert planning while providing resources for resisting bureaucratic and technological domination.

Scott's framework illuminates both historical patterns of resistance and contemporary movements that challenge globalization, environmental destruction, and authoritarian governance through cultural preservation, local autonomy, and everyday practices that maintain alternative ways of life.

Chapter Thirteen
Contemporary Challenges and Digital Transformations

Understanding digital politics, identity politics, and climate politics as mind paintings reveals how contemporary political life operates through sophisticated cultural frameworks that actively construct rather than merely describe political reality. These paintings function as embodied, situated processes of meaning-making that shape not only how we interpret political events but what counts as political in the first place.

I. The Mind Painting Framework: Politics as Cultural Construction
Defining Political Mind Paintings

Political mind paintings operate as cultural frames that construct social reality through embodied practices of interpretation and action. Unlike mere ideologies or belief systems, mind paintings function through what cognitive scientists term "embodied cognition"—meaning-making processes that emerge from the dynamic interaction between bodily experience, environmental context, and cultural resources.

Each mind painting creates what Schneider and Ingram identify as "social constructions" that "name, interpret and dramatize issues, allowing advocates to create or explain broader social meanings". These constructions operate through frame resonance—the degree to which new political claims connect with already accepted cultural understandings. Crucially, mind paintings don't simply represent pre-existing political realities; they actively construct those realities through what sociologists term "strategic framing" and "social construction of target populations".

The embodied dimension proves essential: political mind paintings aren't abstract cognitive schemas but situated practices that engage our sensorimotor experience of the world. They shape not only what we think about politics but how we literally perceive political situations, what emotional responses they generate, and what actions seem possible or appropriate.

How Mind Paintings Construct Political Reality

Political mind paintings operate through three interconnected mechanisms that transform individual experience into collective political reality:

Frame Package Construction: Each mind painting organizes complex political phenomena into coherent interpretive packages that include problem definition, causal attribution, moral evaluation, and treatment recommendations. The digital politics mind painting, for instance, frames algorithmic bias not as technical malfunction but as systematic power concentration requiring democratic oversight.

Target Population Social Construction: Mind paintings create categories of political actors—what Schneider and Ingram term "advantaged," "contenders," "dependents," and "deviants"—that determine who deserves governmental benefits or burdens. These classifications aren't neutral descriptions but actively constructed stereotypes that shape policy design and implementation.

Embodied Meaning-Making: Mind paintings engage our bodily experience to make abstract political concepts feel immediate and real. Climate politics constructs temporal urgency through embodied metaphors ("our house is on fire"), while identity politics creates recognition through embodied experiences of marginalization and solidarity.

II. Digital Politics as Algorithmic Mind Painting
The Platform Capitalism Painting

Digital politics operates as a mind painting that constructs algorithmic mediation as the natural evolution of democratic discourse rather than recognizing it as a specific historical arrangement serving particular interests. This painting frames platforms as neutral conduits for information rather than active constructors of political reality.

Recent research reveals the systematic nature of this construction. The 2024 study of Twitter/X demonstrating consistent right-wing content amplification across six countries illustrates how the platform capitalism mind painting obscures its own political effects. Users experience algorithmic curation as personalization rather than recognizing it as systematic political intervention.

The painting constructs what Shoshana Zuboff terms "surveillance capitalism" as technological progress rather than data extraction for behavioral modification. This framing enables unprecedented information collection by presenting it as service improvement rather than democratic manipulation. Users inhabit this mind painting through daily platform interactions that feel like individual choice while operating within constrained algorithmic possibilities.

Platform capitalism as mind painting reveals its constructed character when we examine its internal contradictions. Research showing that many platforms consistently fail to generate profits despite massive investment suggests that the "efficiency" narrative may be cultural construction rather than economic reality. The painting persists not because platforms work better but because they successfully frame themselves as inevitable technological development.

The Surveillance Society Painting

Digital surveillance operates through a mind painting that constructs security and convenience as requiring comprehensive data collection. This painting transforms what previous generations would recognize as totalitarian monitoring into mundane consumer experience.

The painting works through embodied normalization: users physically interact with surveillance technologies (smartphones, smart homes, facial recognition) in ways that feel empowering rather than constraining. Each swipe, voice command, and biometric scan reinforces the mind painting that presents surveillance as user control rather than corporate or state monitoring.

Contemporary AI governance attempts reveal the painting's political effects. The 2025 "risk-based approaches" in AI regulation assume that surveillance technologies can be made safe through proper oversight rather than questioning whether comprehensive behavioral monitoring is compatible with democratic citizenship. The mind painting has become so naturalized that alternatives become literally unthinkable.

The Deepfake Crisis Painting

The deepfake phenomenon operates through a mind painting that constructs epistemic crisis as technological rather than political problem. This painting frames the challenge as distinguishing "real" from "fake" content rather than examining how all political communication involves strategic construction.

Research tracking 82 deepfakes across 38 countries reveals systematic patterns: financial scams (26.8%), fabricated statements (25.6%), electoral intervention (15.8%), and character assassination (21.8%). However, the mind painting focuses attention on detection technologies rather than the political economy of disinformation.

The painting's constructed character becomes visible when research shows deepfakes aren't significantly more deceptive than traditional fake news. The crisis narrative serves political functions—legitimating increased platform control, surveillance expansion, and expert authority—rather than simply responding to technological threats.

Most significantly, the deepfake mind painting obscures how all political representation involves what postmodern theorists recognize as simulation and construction. The painting creates nostalgia for supposedly authentic political communication that never existed, enabling new forms of control through appeals to protecting democratic truth.

Philosophical Defense Framework: Addressing Critiques of the Mind Painting Approach to Politic

III. Identity Politics as Intersectional Mind Painting
The Recognition Mind Painting

Identity politics functions as a mind painting that constructs cultural recognition as the primary form of political justice, often displacing material redistribution concerns. This painting transforms social identities from complex, context-dependent positions into fixed demographic categories requiring specific policy responses.

The recognition mind painting operates through embodied practices of identification and solidarity. Participants literally feel their political identity through shared experiences, cultural expressions, and community membership. These embodied experiences create what phenomenologists term "lived knowledge" that feels more authentic than abstract political theory.

However, research reveals how the recognition mind painting gets institutionalized in ways that dilute its radical potential. Studies of feminist NGOs show how "intersectionality expertise" becomes commodified, with white-led organizations positioning themselves as intersectional authorities while employing additive approaches that treat race, class, and sexuality as additional barriers rather than mutually constitutive systems.

The mind painting's constructed character appears in how it creates what scholars term "academic extractivism"—removing Black feminist insights from intersectionality theory while maintaining its instrumental utility. Recognition becomes separated from the material conditions and power relations that make recognition politically significant.

The Standpoint Epistemology Painting

Identity politics constructs a mind painting where marginalized perspectives provide epistemic privilege—clearer insight into social reality than dominant group viewpoints. This painting challenges traditional authority structures by valorizing experiential knowledge over credentialed expertise.

The COVID-19 pandemic provided compelling validation of standpoint epistemology principles. Marginalized communities developed distinctive insights about risk assessment, public health interventions, and social solidarity that proved crucial for effective pandemic response. The painting proved its practical value by revealing knowledge that dominant perspectives obscured.

However, the standpoint mind painting faces sophisticated philosophical challenges. Critics question whether social disadvantage reliably confers epistemic advantage and how one "arrives at" an epistemically privileged position. These debates have practical implications: if marginalized perspectives automatically provide better knowledge, what mechanisms ensure quality control and prevent romanticization of oppression?

The painting's embodied dimension proves crucial: standpoint theory doesn't claim that marginalized people automatically know more, but that their situated experience provides access to social realities that dominant groups' experience obscures. The knowledge emerges through collective reflection on shared experience rather than individual insight.

The **Intersectionality Mind Painting**

Contemporary intersectionality operates through a mind painting that constructs multiple oppression systems as simultaneously operating rather than hierarchically ordered or simply additive. This painting revolutionizes political analysis by revealing how different systems of power create compound rather than cumulative effects.

The intersectionality mind painting works through embodied recognition of compound marginalization. Individuals occupying multiple marginalized positions literally experience their political situation differently than single-axis analysis would predict. A Black working-class woman doesn't simply experience the addition of racism, sexism, and classism but a distinctive form of oppression that can't be understood through separate analysis of each system.

Research reveals how the intersectionality mind painting gets appropriated and diluted through institutional adoption. White feminist organizations employ "additive intersectionality" that treats different identity categories as separate variables rather than recognizing their mutually constitutive character. This appropriation maintains the painting's apparent sophistication while evacuating its radical analytical power.

The painting's political effectiveness appears in environmental justice movements that successfully connect racial, economic, and ecological concerns through shared narratives about community protection and democratic participation. These movements demonstrate how effective intersectionality creates new forms of political solidarity rather than simply aggregating separate identity groups.

IV. Climate Politics as Temporal Mind Painting
The Intergenerational Justice Painting

Climate politics constructs a distinctive mind painting that makes future generations politically present through moral and legal claims. This painting transforms the temporal structure of democratic politics by giving political voice to those who cannot reciprocate present sacrifices.

The intergenerational mind painting works through embodied practices that make future impacts emotionally immediate. Greta Thunberg's "How dare you" speech operated through graphic analogical reasoning ("our house is on fire") that translated abstract climate data into visceral moral outrage. The painting creates temporal solidarity by making future suffering feel personally relevant to present decision-makers.

Legal innovations demonstrate the mind painting's institutional effects. The German Federal Constitutional Court's 2021 ruling declared climate policy unconstitutional because it impermissibly shifted emission reduction burdens to future generations. Wales's Well-being of Future Generations Act requires public bodies to consider long-term impacts in decision-making. These institutions make the mind painting legally operative rather than merely rhetorical.

The painting's constructed character appears in how it selectively highlights some temporal relationships while obscuring others. Climate justice framing emphasizes intergenerational inequality but often obscures contemporary global inequality between those who cause climate change and those who experience its worst effects.

The Environmental Racism Painting

Climate politics constructs environmental racism as a mind painting that reveals how ecological and racial oppression operate through mutually reinforcing mechanisms. This painting challenges both environmental movements that ignore race and civil rights movements that ignore ecology.

The environmental racism mind painting operates through embodied experiences of disproportionate toxic exposure. Communities like Flint, Michigan, and Louisiana's "Cancer Alley" literally inhabit different environmental realities than affluent white communities. The painting makes these differences politically visible by connecting individual health experiences to systematic patterns of racial targeting.

Research demonstrates the painting's empirical accuracy: Black Americans aged 65+ are three times more likely to die from pollution-related causes than white counterparts. Environmental Defense Fund studies confirm that environmental racism intensifies rather than diminishes over time. The mind painting reveals realities that environmental colorblind approaches obscure.

The painting's political effectiveness appears in how environmental justice movements successfully reframe climate action as community protection rather than abstract environmental preservation. This reframing creates broader coalitions by connecting environmental and social justice concerns through shared experience of systematic marginalization.

The Collective Action Mind Painting

Climate politics constructs the ultimate collective action problem as a mind painting that makes global cooperation seem both necessary and nearly impossible. This painting frames climate change as challenging the fundamental assumptions of existing political institutions.

The collective action mind painting operates through temporal and spatial scale mismatches that create embodied feelings of political helplessness. Individual actions feel meaningless relative to global scale, while effective institutions seem impossibly distant from lived experience. The painting creates political paralysis by making climate action seem to require unprecedented institutional innovation.

However, recent research reveals successful collective action initiatives that challenge the helplessness narrative. Studies of urban climate coalitions demonstrate effective cooperation across different scales of political organization. The "Greta Thunberg effect" shows how individual charismatic authority can catalyze broader collective mobilization through "collective efficacy" mechanisms.

The mind painting's constructed character appears in how it obscures existing examples of successful environmental cooperation. International environmental agreements, urban sustainability initiatives, and community-based conservation demonstrate that effective collective action already occurs despite institutional limitations.

V. Interactions Between Mind Paintings: Contemporary Political Reality
Digital-Identity Intersections

Digital and identity mind paintings increasingly interpenetrate to create new forms of algorithmic identity construction. Platform algorithms don't simply reflect user preferences but actively construct political identities by determining which content gets amplified or suppressed.

The 2024 research on Twitter/X algorithmic bias demonstrates systematic right-wing content amplification that shapes users' political identity formation. New users experience "right-leaning bias" in default timelines, suggesting that platforms actively construct rather than simply reflect political orientations.

Identity politics mind paintings provide resistance resources by revealing how algorithmic bias operates through systematic exclusion rather than neutral technical optimization. Intersectional analysis demonstrates how different groups experience compound algorithmic discrimination that single-axis approaches miss.

Climate-Digital Convergences

Climate and digital mind paintings converge around information control as political strategy. Climate denial operates through the same filter bubble mechanisms that enable other forms of political manipulation, while climate activism increasingly depends on digital platforms for mobilization.

The "anti-climate common sense" operates through sophisticated digital manipulation that exploits the same algorithmic vulnerabilities that enable political deepfakes and disinformation. Climate politics becomes embedded within broader struggles over algorithmic governance of information.

Conversely, climate activism demonstrates how digital platforms can support rather than undermine democratic participation. The "Greta Thunberg effect" operated primarily through digital amplification that enabled global coordination around climate action.

Identity-Climate Overlaps

Identity and climate mind paintings converge around environmental justice as a framework that connects social and ecological concerns. Environmental racism demonstrates how identity-based oppression operates through ecological mechanisms, while climate action increasingly involves identity-based mobilization strategies.

The convergence creates new forms of political solidarity that transcend traditional environmental/social justice divisions. Movements like the Green New Deal attempt to institutionalize this convergence by connecting climate action with economic justice concerns.

However, tensions remain between identity and climate approaches. Identity politics emphasis on recognition can conflict with climate politics emphasis on collective action, while climate urgency can marginalize justice concerns in favor of technocratic solutions.

VI. The Mind Painting Framework's Analytical Power Revealing Cultural Construction

The mind painting framework reveals what conventional political analysis misses: how apparently natural or inevitable political arrangements actually represent specific cultural constructions that could be otherwise. Digital surveillance seems inevitable only within the platform capitalism mind painting; climate paralysis seems natural only within collective action problem framings that obscure successful cooperation examples.

Understanding politics as mind painting enables recognition of alternative possibilities without falling into either naive optimism or cynical determinism. Current arrangements remain changeable because they represent cultural achievements rather than natural laws, but change requires understanding how existing mind paintings operate and developing resources for constructing alternatives.

Integrating Cultural and Material Analysis

The framework avoids false oppositions between cultural and material approaches by showing how mind paintings operate through material practices while material conditions get interpreted through cultural frameworks. Platform capitalism operates through concrete data extraction processes, but these processes depend on mind paintings that present extraction as consumer convenience.

Climate politics demonstrates how material realities (carbon emissions, temperature increases, sea level rise) get politically effective only through cultural mind paintings that make these realities emotionally and morally significant. The material and cultural dimensions remain irreducible but interdependent.

Supporting Democratic Participation

By revealing the constructed character of political arrangements, the mind painting framework supports rather than undermines democratic participation. Citizens can engage more effectively in political life when they understand how political reality gets constructed rather than treating current arrangements as fixed constraints.

The framework provides analytical tools for developing more inclusive and effective political mind paintings that draw on humanity's diverse cultural resources while addressing shared material challenges. Rather than relativistic fragmentation, the approach enables creative political synthesis that acknowledges cultural differences while maintaining commitment to human flourishing and democratic participation.

Understanding politics as collective mind painting reveals both the remarkable achievements of existing political arrangements and the genuine possibilities for continued innovation in social organization. The framework suggests that more effective, inclusive, and sustainable forms of political life remain possible through creative cultural work that acknowledges both human political creativity and the material constraints within which such creativity operates.

This analysis demonstrates how digital politics, identity politics, and climate politics function as sophisticated mind paintings that construct contemporary political reality while revealing resources for developing more democratic and effective alternatives. The mind painting framework provides essential tools for understanding and participating in the ongoing cultural construction of political life.

Chapter Fourteen
Ecologies, Materiality, and the Cognitive Environment – The Contextual Canvas of Mind Painting

Human cognition does not emerge in isolation but develops within rich, multilayered ecological contexts that profoundly shape how we think, learn, and understand the world around us. The traditional view of the mind as an internal processing system, while capturing important aspects of cognitive function, fails to account for the fundamental ways in which our thinking is embedded within and co-constructed through dynamic interactions with material environments, social relationships, and cultural practices. This chapter explores how our cognitive "mind paintings" are not merely internal mental constructions but emerge from complex ecological relationships that span from immediate physical surroundings to broader cultural and historical contexts.

The concept of embodied cognition reveals that our ways of thinking are fundamentally shaped by the particular characteristics of our physical bodies and their interactions with environmental contexts. Rather than operating as abstract computational systems, our minds develop through sensorimotor experiences that create the foundational scaffolding for more complex cognitive processes. The way we understand spatial relationships, temporal sequences, and even abstract concepts like justice or truth emerges from our embodied interactions with material environments and social practices.

This ecological perspective on cognition has profound implications for understanding how human learning and development occur. Rather than viewing children as passive recipients of predetermined developmental programs, research in developmental niche construction reveals how young humans actively participate in creating the very environments that shape their cognitive growth. Through their explorations, questions, and creative activities, children both absorb cultural knowledge and simultaneously transform their learning environments in ways that create new possibilities for future development.

The Material Foundations of Cognitive Development

The physical environment provides the foundational context within which all cognitive development occurs, offering both constraints and affordances that shape how thinking emerges and evolves throughout the lifespan. From the earliest moments of life, the developing brain's neural architecture is sculpted by environmental experiences, with the quality, complexity, and timing of these experiences having profound and lasting effects on cognitive capabilities.

Environmental influences on brain development operate through multiple mechanisms that demonstrate the deep interdependence between material contexts and cognitive growth. The development of myelin—the fatty insulation that surrounds neural connections and enables efficient communication between brain regions—is directly influenced by environmental stimulation. Rich, complex environments that provide novel sensory experiences, social interactions, and cognitive challenges promote healthy myelination, while impoverished or stressful environments can impair this crucial developmental process.

The concept of neuroplasticity reveals how the brain's structure and function remain malleable throughout life in response to environmental influences. During critical periods of development, the brain exhibits heightened sensitivity to specific types of environmental input, with experiences during these windows having disproportionate effects on neural development. However, experience-dependent plasticity continues throughout life, allowing environmental experiences to shape cognitive capabilities well beyond early childhood.

These neuroplastic processes demonstrate how material environments literally sculpt the physical substrate of cognition. Children raised in environments rich with books, complex conversations, and diverse sensory experiences develop different neural architectures than those raised in less stimulating contexts. The availability of natural environments, cultural tools, and social interactions creates specific developmental pathways that influence not only what children learn but how they learn to learn.

The material environment also shapes cognition through the affordances it provides for different types of activities and experiences. Natural environments offer opportunities for exploration, risk-taking, and encounters with complexity that may be less available in highly controlled or artificial settings. The presence of trees to climb, streams to investigate, and varied terrains to navigate provides children with rich sensorimotor experiences that contribute to spatial reasoning, risk assessment, and environmental awareness.

Cultural artifacts and tools embedded within material environments serve as cognitive prosthetics that extend and transform human thinking capabilities. Writing systems transform memory and reasoning by allowing thoughts to be externalized, manipulated, and shared across time and space. Mathematical notation systems enable calculations and conceptual relationships that would be impossible using mental processes alone. Digital technologies create new possibilities for information processing, communication, and creative expression while potentially altering attention, memory, and social interaction patterns.

Cultural Transmission and Social Learning Environments

The social and cultural dimensions of environmental context play equally crucial roles in shaping cognitive development, providing the scaffolding through which cultural knowledge, values, and practices are transmitted across generations. Rather than simply passing information from adults to children, cultural transmission involves complex, bidirectional processes in which learners actively participate in constructing their own understanding while simultaneously contributing to the evolution of cultural practices.

Research on social learning in diverse cultural contexts reveals remarkable variation in how different societies structure children's learning environments and the types of knowledge prioritized for transmission. Hunter-gatherer societies often emphasize learning through observation, participation, and gradual integration into adult activities, with teaching occurring through demonstration, storytelling, and carefully structured experiences that allow children to discover important principles through guided exploration.

The transmission of what researchers' term "opaque culture"—social norms, values, and practices whose importance is not immediately apparent from their surface features—requires particularly sophisticated pedagogical approaches. Unlike instrumental skills that can be learned through observation and imitation, opaque cultural knowledge often requires explicit teaching, explanation, and sustained practice within supportive social contexts. This distinction helps explain why human societies have evolved such elaborate systems of education, initiation, and cultural transmission.

The concept of scaffolding, developed from Vygotsky's work on the zone of proximal development, provides a framework for understanding how social environments can be structured to optimize learning. Effective scaffolding involves providing just enough support to enable learners to accomplish tasks that would be beyond their independent capabilities while gradually reducing this support as competence develops.

Natural environments provide particularly rich contexts for scaffolding because they offer authentic challenges, immediate feedback, and opportunities for discovery that can be tailored to individual developmental needs. When children explore natural settings with knowledgeable guides, they encounter genuine problems that require creative solutions while receiving support that helps them develop both specific knowledge and more general learning strategies.

The effectiveness of scaffolding depends not only on the immediate interpersonal interactions between learners and teachers but also on the broader cultural context that determines what knowledge is valued, how learning is organized, and what resources are available to support development. Societies that prioritize collaborative learning create different developmental trajectories than those that emphasize individual achievement, while cultures that integrate learning with meaningful work activities provide different cognitive experiences than those that separate education from practical application.

Developmental Niche Construction

One of the most significant insights from ecological approaches to cognitive development is the recognition that children are not passive recipients of environmental influences but active participants in constructing the very contexts that shape their development. The concept of developmental niche construction describes how developing organisms modify their environments in ways that subsequently influence their own development and that of future generations.

Human developmental niche construction operates through multiple mechanisms that reflect our species' unique reliance on culture, learning, and symbol manipulation. Children actively seek out experiences, ask questions, and create play scenarios that reflect their current interests and developmental needs while simultaneously creating new environmental conditions that afford different types of learning opportunities.

The bidirectional nature of developmental niche construction means that children both adapt to their environments and adapt their environments to their needs. A child who organizes elaborate fantasy play scenarios is not only practicing social roles and narrative construction but also creating physical and social arrangements that provide new contexts for learning. When children build forts, organize collections, or create artwork, they are literally constructing environmental niches that afford different types of cognitive and social experiences.

This process operates across multiple timescales, from immediate moment-to-moment interactions to longer-term environmental modifications that persist across developmental periods. The trails that children create through repeated play in natural areas, the organization of classroom spaces through student activities, and the cultural innovations that emerge from youthful creativity all represent forms of niche construction that influence subsequent developmental processes.

The institutional dimension of human niche construction reflects our species' unique capacity for creating social structures that coordinate activity across multiple generations. Educational systems, apprenticeship programs, and cultural institutions represent collective efforts to construct developmental niches that can reliably transmit important knowledge and capabilities while also allowing for innovation and adaptation to changing circumstances.

Language provides perhaps the most powerful tool for developmental niche construction, allowing humans to create symbolic environments that exist alongside and interact with material environments. Through narrative, children construct meaning systems that organize their experiences and guide their future actions. Through questioning, they create social situations that elicit information and support from others. Through creative expression, they contribute to the cultural resources available for future learning.

The Role of Natural Environments in Cognitive Development

Natural environments play particularly important roles in cognitive development because they provide contexts that are simultaneously predictable enough to support learning and variable enough to require flexible, adaptive responses. The complexity and dynamic nature of natural systems offer cognitive challenges that may be difficult to replicate in controlled or artificial environments while providing the embodied experiences that serve as foundations for more abstract thinking.

Attention Restoration Theory suggests that natural environments provide cognitive benefits by allowing the mental systems responsible for directed attention to recover from fatigue. Natural settings tend to capture attention in an effortless way that reduces cognitive load while providing gentle stimulation that supports mental restoration. This restorative function may be particularly important in contemporary contexts where children face increasing demands on their attention systems from digital technologies and structured activities.

The sensory richness of natural environments contributes to cognitive development by providing diverse, unpredictable stimuli that promote neural development and sensory integration. The varied textures, sounds, smells, and visual patterns found in natural settings offer more complex sensory experiences than most built environments, potentially contributing to more robust and flexible neural development.

Natural environments also provide opportunities for risk-taking and physical challenge that may be essential for developing realistic risk assessment capabilities and physical confidence. When children climb trees, navigate rough terrain, or interact with weather conditions, they develop embodied understanding of physical principles while also building confidence in their ability to handle uncertainty and challenge.

The temporal patterns characteristic of natural environments—seasonal cycles, weather patterns, life cycles of plants and animals—provide rich contexts for developing understanding of time, change, and causation. These natural rhythms offer alternatives to the linear, clock-based time structures that dominate most institutional settings, potentially contributing to more flexible and nuanced temporal understanding.

Research on forest schools and nature-based education programs suggests that extended engagement with natural environments can contribute to multiple aspects of cognitive development including attention regulation, creative problem-solving, and ecological understanding. These programs often emphasize child-directed exploration, collaborative problem-solving, and integration of learning across traditional subject boundaries, reflecting principles of ecological education that recognize the interconnected nature of human development and environmental context.

Material Culture and Cognitive Tools

The material artifacts that populate human environments serve not merely as objects to be manipulated but as cognitive tools that transform and extend human thinking capabilities. From simple implements like pencils and measuring devices to complex technologies like computers and scientific instruments, material culture provides scaffolding that enables forms of cognition that would be impossible using biological capabilities alone.

The development of writing systems represents one of the most significant examples of how material tools can transform cognitive capabilities. The externalization of language through written symbols allows thoughts to be preserved, manipulated, and shared across time and space in ways that fundamentally alter how humans can think and learn. Writing enables the development of complex arguments, detailed record-keeping, and cumulative knowledge systems that serve as foundations for scientific, philosophical, and artistic achievements.

Mathematical notation systems provide another powerful example of cognitive tools that extend human thinking capabilities. The development of place-value notation, algebraic symbols, and graphical representations allows mathematical relationships to be explored and manipulated in ways that would be impossible using mental processes alone. These symbolic systems not only make complex calculations possible but also enable new forms of mathematical thinking and discovery.

Contemporary digital technologies represent the latest chapter in humanity's ongoing development of cognitive tools, offering unprecedented capabilities for information processing, communication, and creative expression. However, these technologies also raise important questions about how their use might be altering fundamental cognitive processes such as attention, memory, and social interaction.

The effectiveness of material cognitive tools depends not only on their design characteristics but also on the cultural practices that surround their use. Tools become truly effective only when they are embedded within social systems that support their appropriate use and provide opportunities for developing expertise in their application. This social dimension of tool use highlights the importance of considering material and cultural factors together rather than treating them as separate influences on cognitive development.

The concept of distributed cognition recognizes that complex cognitive tasks often involve coordination between human minds and material tools in ways that blur traditional boundaries between internal and external cognitive processes. When a scientist uses instruments to collect data, computer software to analyze patterns, and visualization tools to communicate findings, the cognitive work involved is distributed across multiple components of an integrated system that includes both human and material elements.

Environmental Stressors and Cognitive Resilience

While much research on environmental influences focuses on positive factors that support cognitive development, it is equally important to understand how environmental stressors can impact cognitive processes and how resilience can be supported within challenging contexts. Environmental stressors including poverty, pollution, violence, and social instability can have profound effects on cognitive development, but these effects are mediated by complex interactions between individual characteristics, social support systems, and cultural resources.

Chronic stress exposure during development can alter brain structure and function in ways that affect attention regulation, memory formation, and emotional processing. The developing stress response system is particularly sensitive to environmental influences, with early experiences of adversity potentially creating lasting changes in stress reactivity that influence cognitive performance throughout life.

However, research on resilience reveals that negative environmental influences can be mitigated by protective factors including supportive relationships, meaningful cultural connections, and opportunities for mastery and achievement. The presence of even a single stable, supportive relationship can buffer children from many adverse effects of environmental stress, while participation in culturally meaningful activities can provide sources of identity and purpose that support resilience.

Environmental interventions that improve access to natural spaces, reduce exposure to toxins, and enhance social support can produce measurable improvements in cognitive development even within challenging contexts. These findings suggest that environmental approaches to supporting cognitive development may be particularly effective because they address the ecological contexts within which development occurs rather than focusing solely on individual characteristics or deficits.

The concept of post-traumatic growth recognizes that exposure to environmental challenges can sometimes contribute to cognitive and emotional development when appropriate support systems are available. Children who successfully navigate environmental challenges may develop enhanced problem-solving capabilities, increased empathy, and stronger sense of agency that serve them well in future situations.

Cultural Variations in Cognitive Ecologies

Cross-cultural research reveals remarkable diversity in the ways different societies structure children's cognitive environments, providing important insights into the range of possible developmental pathways and the cultural specificity of many assumptions about optimal learning conditions. These variations demonstrate that there is no single "natural" way to organize cognitive development but rather multiple cultural solutions to the challenges of supporting human learning and growth.

Indigenous educational traditions often emphasize learning through observation, participation, and gradual integration into adult activities rather than through formal instruction separated from practical application. Children in these contexts may spend extensive time observing adult work, participating in community activities, and learning through stories and cultural practices that embed important knowledge within meaningful social contexts.

Some cultures prioritize individual achievement and competition while others emphasize collaborative learning and group harmony. These different value systems create different cognitive environments that may promote different types of capabilities and ways of thinking. Children raised in individualistic contexts may develop stronger skills in independent problem-solving and self-promotion, while those raised in collectivistic contexts may develop superior capabilities in collaboration and social coordination.

The relationship between formal schooling and cognitive development varies significantly across cultural contexts, with some societies relying heavily on institutional education while others emphasize informal learning through family and community participation. These differences highlight the importance of considering multiple pathways to cognitive development rather than assuming that formal educational approaches represent the only or best way to support learning.

Linguistic diversity creates different cognitive environments through the particular ways that different languages structure attention, categorization, and reasoning. Children learning languages with complex spatial reference systems may develop enhanced spatial reasoning capabilities, while those learning languages with rich temporal marking systems may develop more nuanced understanding of time and causation.

Research on cultural transmission reveals that different societies have evolved sophisticated approaches to ensuring that important knowledge and capabilities are passed to future generations. These transmission systems reflect deep cultural wisdom about how learning occurs and what types of knowledge are most important for successful adaptation to particular environmental and social contexts.

Technology and the Transformation of Cognitive Environments

The rapid development of digital technologies is creating unprecedented changes in the cognitive environments experienced by contemporary children, with potentially profound implications for how cognitive development occurs. While these technologies offer remarkable new capabilities for information access, communication, and creative expression, they also raise important questions about their effects on attention, social interaction, and embodied experience.

Digital environments provide access to vast amounts of information and enable new forms of creative expression and collaboration. Children can now access expert knowledge from around the world, collaborate with peers across geographic boundaries, and create multimedia productions that would have required professional resources in previous generations. These capabilities may contribute to new forms of cognitive development that were not possible in previous historical periods.

However, digital environments also differ in important ways from the natural and social environments within which human cognition evolved. Screen-based activities may provide less sensory variety and embodied experience than physical exploration, while social media interactions may lack the nuanced feedback and emotional richness of face-to-face relationships.

Research on the effects of screen time on cognitive development suggests complex relationships that depend on the content, context, and duration of digital media use. High-quality educational content used within supportive social contexts may contribute positively to learning, while passive consumption of entertainment media or excessive screen time may interfere with other important developmental experiences.

The integration of digital technologies with traditional learning environments creates opportunities for hybrid approaches that combine the benefits of technological tools with the embodied and social experiences that support healthy development. Examples include outdoor education programs that use digital tools for data collection and sharing, maker spaces that combine traditional crafts with digital fabrication, and collaborative online projects that bring together children from different cultural contexts.

The long-term effects of growing up in digitally mediated environments remain largely unknown, as the first generation of "digital natives" is only now reaching adulthood. Continued research will be needed to understand how these environmental changes influence cognitive development and what adaptations may be needed to optimize the benefits while minimizing potential risks.

Implications for Educational Practice and Policy

Understanding cognition as emerging from ecological relationships has profound implications for how we design educational environments and support children's development. Rather than focusing primarily on individual characteristics or standardized curricula, ecological approaches emphasize the importance of creating rich, supportive environments that can scaffold learning while respecting cultural diversity and individual differences.

Effective educational environments should provide multiple types of experiences that support different aspects of cognitive development. This includes opportunities for embodied exploration, social interaction, creative expression, and meaningful problem-solving within contexts that connect to children's interests and cultural backgrounds.

The physical design of learning spaces can significantly influence cognitive development by providing different affordances for activities and interactions. Environments that include natural elements, flexible spaces that can be reconfigured for different activities, and access to diverse materials and tools may better support the range of experiences needed for healthy development.

Professional development for educators should include understanding of how environmental factors influence learning and development, enabling them to create more effective learning environments and recognize how cultural and material contexts shape children's experiences. This includes understanding of scaffolding techniques, cultural responsiveness, and the importance of connecting learning to meaningful contexts.

Policy approaches should consider the broader environmental contexts that influence cognitive development, including access to natural spaces, reduction of environmental stressors, and support for cultural diversity in educational approaches. This might include investments in outdoor learning spaces, environmental health initiatives, and support for culturally based educational programs.

The Future of Cognitive Ecologies

As human societies continue to evolve, the cognitive environments experienced by children will undoubtedly continue to change, creating new challenges and opportunities for supporting healthy development. Climate change, technological innovation, urbanization, and cultural globalization are all creating new environmental conditions that may require adaptive responses in how we structure children's learning experiences.

The concept of niche construction suggests that humans have remarkable capabilities for creating environments that support their developmental needs. By understanding the principles that govern effective cognitive ecologies, we may be able to intentionally design environments that better support human flourishing while also addressing contemporary challenges.

Research on cognitive ecologies will likely need to become increasingly interdisciplinary, drawing insights from neuroscience, anthropology, ecology, education, and technology studies to understand the complex relationships between environmental contexts and cognitive development. This research can inform efforts to create more effective and culturally responsive approaches to supporting children's learning and development.

The recognition that cognition emerges from ecological relationships also highlights the importance of considering environmental sustainability and social justice in educational planning. Children who grow up with access to natural environments, supportive communities, and cultural resources are likely to have different developmental trajectories than those who experience environmental degradation, social instability, or cultural disruption.

Defense Against Philosophical Attacks: Critics may argue that emphasizing ecological and distributed influences leads to ecological determinism or neglects individual agency. This chapter defends its position by demonstrating that agency emerges precisely from active organism-environment interactions rather than isolated mental computations. Rigorous empirical evidence—from neuroplasticity studies to ethnographic observations—supports the mechanisms described. Methodological innovations including ethnographic fieldwork, network analysis, and embodied AI experiments provide robust means to study cognition "in the wild." The chapter addresses concerns about relativism by highlighting universal ecological principles (affordances, niche construction) while respecting cultural specificity, ensuring explanatory power without sacrificing normative commitments to evidence and ethical practice.

Conclusion: The Contextual Canvas of Mind Painting

The ecological perspective on cognitive development reveals that our mental "mind paintings" are not created in isolation but emerge from complex, dynamic relationships with material environments, social contexts, and cultural practices. Rather than viewing cognition as an internal computational system, this approach recognizes thinking as fundamentally embodied and environmentally situated, shaped by the specific ecological contexts within which development occurs.

The concept of developmental niche construction demonstrates that children are active participants in creating the very environments that shape their cognitive growth. Through their explorations, questions, and creative activities, young humans both absorb cultural knowledge and simultaneously transform their learning environments in ways that create new possibilities for future development. This bidirectional relationship between organisms and environments represents a fundamental principle of ecological development that applies across scales from immediate interpersonal interactions to broader cultural and historical processes.

Material environments provide the foundational contexts within which all cognitive development occurs, offering both constraints and affordances that shape how thinking emerges and evolves. The physical characteristics of environments—from the complexity of natural settings to the design of built spaces to the availability of cultural tools—directly influence brain development, sensory experience, and the types of activities that are possible. These material influences operate not as simple deterministic factors but as components of complex ecological systems that interact with social and cultural influences to create unique developmental contexts.

Cultural transmission processes reveal how knowledge, values, and practices are passed between generations through sophisticated social learning mechanisms that go far beyond simple information transfer. The distinction between instrumental and opaque culture highlights how different types of knowledge require different pedagogical approaches, with opaque cultural knowledge often requiring explicit teaching and sustained practice within supportive social contexts. These transmission processes are embedded within broader cultural systems that determine what knowledge is valued, how learning is organized, and what resources are available to support development.

The scaffolding concept provides a framework for understanding how social environments can be structured to optimize learning by providing appropriate levels of support that are carefully calibrated to individual developmental needs. Effective scaffolding requires deep understanding of both individual capabilities and cultural contexts, enabling educators to create learning experiences that challenge learners while providing the support needed for success.

Natural environments offer particularly rich contexts for cognitive development because they provide complexity, unpredictability, and sensory richness that may be difficult to replicate in artificial settings. The restorative effects of natural environments, opportunities for embodied exploration, and exposure to natural cycles and processes contribute to multiple aspects of cognitive development while also connecting children to the broader ecological systems of which they are part.

The rapid transformation of cognitive environments through digital technologies creates both opportunities and challenges for supporting healthy development. While these technologies offer remarkable new capabilities for learning and creative expression, they also alter fundamental aspects of human experience including attention, social interaction, and embodied engagement with the world. Understanding how to integrate technological tools with traditional environmental experiences represents one of the key challenges for supporting cognitive development in contemporary contexts.

Cross-cultural research reveals remarkable diversity in how different society's structure children's cognitive environments, demonstrating that there are multiple viable approaches to supporting human development. This diversity provides important insights into the range of possible developmental pathways while highlighting the cultural specificity of many assumptions about optimal learning conditions. Rather than seeking universal principles of cognitive development, ecological approaches emphasize the importance of understanding how different cultural systems create effective developmental niches within their particular contexts.

The implications of ecological approaches for educational practice and policy are profound, suggesting the need for more holistic approaches that consider the full range of environmental factors that influence learning and development. This includes attention to physical design of learning spaces, integration of natural and cultural elements, support for diverse learning styles and cultural backgrounds, and recognition of the broader environmental and social contexts that shape children's experiences.

As human societies continue to evolve, the cognitive environments experienced by children will undoubtedly continue to change, creating new challenges and opportunities for supporting healthy development. The concept of niche construction suggests that humans have remarkable capabilities for creating environments that support their developmental needs, but realizing this potential requires intentional effort to understand and apply ecological principles in the design of developmental contexts.

The contextual canvas of mind painting reveals that human cognition is fundamentally ecological, emerging from dynamic relationships between developing individuals and the complex environmental systems within which they are embedded. This understanding calls for approaches to supporting cognitive development that recognize the interconnected nature of individual, social, cultural, and environmental factors while respecting the diversity of developmental pathways that can lead to human flourishing. By creating rich, supportive, and culturally responsive developmental niches, we can help ensure that all children have opportunities to develop their full cognitive potential while contributing to the ongoing evolution of human knowledge and capability.

Chapter Fifteen

The Embodied Canvas: Feeling, Living, and Being in the World

The human capacity for creating "mind paintings" is not an abstract, disembodied process floating in some ethereal realm of pure thought, but rather emerges from our fundamental condition as embodied, situated, and feeling beings thrown into a world we neither chose nor fully control. The philosophical traditions of existentialism, phenomenology, feminist theory, and embodied cognition converge to reveal that our cognitive frameworks are profoundly shaped by our physical bodies, emotional lives, and lived experiences in ways that both constrain and enable our meaning-making activities. Far from undermining the validity of human knowledge, this recognition of embodiment provides deeper insight into how our "mind paintings" are formed and how they can be used to challenge existing power structures and expand the possibilities for human understanding.

The Embodied Canvas: How Physical Being, Existential Freedom, Lived Experience, and Social Context Interact to Create Individual Mind Paintings

The neocortex constraints discussed throughout this work gain new significance when understood through the lens of embodied cognition, which reveals that our thinking is not merely limited by neural architecture but is actively shaped by the particular characteristics of our physical bodies and their interactions with environmental and social contexts. Our upright posture influences how we conceptualize spatial relationships and hierarchies; our binocular vision shapes our understanding of depth and perspective; our capacity for fine motor control enables the manipulation of tools that extend our cognitive capabilities. These bodily characteristics do not simply provide input to an abstract reasoning system but fundamentally structure the ways we can think and perceive.

The existentialist insight that "existence precedes essence" takes on new meaning when we recognize that our existence is always and necessarily embodied existence. We do not first exist as pure minds and then acquire bodies; rather, we are always already embodied beings whose thinking emerges from our situated engagement with the world through bodily activity, sensory experience, and emotional response. This embodied existence becomes the foundation from which we must create meaning, take responsibility for our choices, and confront the fundamental anxieties that arise from our radical freedom in an apparently meaningless universe.

Existentialism and the Embodied Creation of Meaning

The existentialist tradition, pioneered by thinkers like Søren Kierkegaard, Martin Heidegger, Jean-Paul Sartre, and Albert Camus, provides crucial insights into how individuals must create their own "mind paintings" to navigate what they termed "existential chaos"—the fundamental uncertainty, meaninglessness, and anxiety that characterizes human existence in a universe that provides no predetermined purpose or direction. Rather than discovering pre-existing meaning or following predetermined essences, humans must take responsibility for creating their own values, purposes, and interpretive frameworks through the choices they make in concrete, embodied situations.

Kierkegaard's analysis of anxiety as the "dizziness of freedom" reveals how our embodied experience of existential uncertainty serves as the foundation for authentic meaning-making. The physical sensation of anxiety—the racing heart, the shortness of breath, the trembling hands—is not merely a psychological response but an embodied recognition of our radical freedom to choose who we will become. This anxiety arises precisely because we exist as embodied beings who must make concrete choices in particular situations without any guarantee that we are choosing correctly or that our choices will lead to the outcomes we desire.

The existentialist emphasis on individual responsibility takes on new significance when we recognize that this responsibility is always exercised by particular embodied individuals situated in specific contexts. Sartre's famous assertion that we are "condemned to be free" acknowledges that this freedom is not abstract but must be exercised through our particular bodies, with their specific capabilities and limitations, in response to the concrete situations we encounter. The anxiety that accompanies this freedom is not a flaw to be overcome but an authentic response to the weight of responsibility that comes with embodied existence.

Heidegger's concept of "thrownness" (Geworfenheit) highlights how we find ourselves embodied in particular historical, cultural, and material circumstances that we did not choose but which nevertheless shape the possibilities available to us. We are thrown into bodies with specific characteristics, families with particular values, cultures with certain assumptions, and historical moments with their own challenges and opportunities. Our "mind paintings" must be created from within these constraints while still taking responsibility for the choices we make in response to our thrown situation.

The existentialist critique of "bad faith" reveals how individuals often attempt to escape the anxiety of freedom by pretending that their choices are determined by external forces—biology, society, God, nature—rather than acknowledging their responsibility for creating their own meaning. This escape into bad faith represents a refusal to acknowledge our embodied condition and the genuine freedom and responsibility that comes with it. Authentic existence requires confronting the anxiety that accompanies our freedom while taking responsibility for the choices we make through our embodied engagement with the world.

Simone de Beauvoir and the Embodied Critique of Patriarchal Mind Paintings

Simone de Beauvoir's groundbreaking work The Second Sex represents one of the most profound examples of how embodied lived experience can expose the gaps and distortions in dominant philosophical "mind paintings," particularly those that have been shaped by masculine perspectives and patriarchal power structures. De Beauvoir's analysis reveals how traditional philosophical frameworks have systematically excluded women's experiences and perspectives, creating supposedly universal truths that actually reflect the particular situated experiences of privileged men.

De Beauvoir's famous assertion that "one is not born, but rather becomes, a woman" illustrates how gender identity emerges through embodied social practices rather than from biological determinism. This insight challenges traditional philosophical approaches that treat categories like "woman" and "man" as natural essences rather than as socially constructed identities that emerge through particular patterns of embodied experience. The process of "becoming a woman" involves learning to experience one's body in particular ways, to move through space with certain constraints, and to understand oneself in relation to social expectations that shape both possibilities and limitations.

The concept of women as the "Other" in patriarchal societies reveals how dominant "mind paintings" have been constructed from the perspective of those who consider themselves the universal subject while positioning others as deviations from the norm. This othering process operates not merely at the level of abstract concepts but through concrete embodied practices that shape how women experience their bodies, their capabilities, and their relationships to the world. Women learn to experience their bodies as objects for others rather than as subjects of their own experience, creating what de Beauvoir calls "bad faith" specific to women's situation.

De Beauvoir's analysis of women's embodied experience throughout the life cycle—from childhood through adolescence, motherhood, and aging—demonstrates how social construction of gender operates through particular ways of experiencing and understanding the female body. Each life stage brings different constraints and possibilities that are shaped by cultural expectations about appropriate feminine behavior, creating patterns of embodied experience that can limit women's capacity for transcendence and authentic self-creation.

The existentialist framework allows de Beauvoir to critique patriarchal oppression while maintaining belief in the possibility of women's freedom and self-determination. While acknowledging the very real constraints imposed by social structures and cultural expectations, she insists that women retain the capacity for authentic choice and self-creation. This requires both individual efforts to live authentically and collective efforts to transform the social conditions that limit women's possibilities for transcendence.

Feminist Philosophy and the Exposure of Power in Knowledge Construction

The broader feminist philosophical tradition has extended de Beauvoir's insights to reveal how supposedly universal and objective philosophical "mind paintings" have been shaped by particular gendered perspectives and power relationships that serve specific "banana acquisition" interests—the pursuit of power, control, and dominance over others. This critique exposes what feminist philosophers call the "unseen brushes" of power and ideology that have shaped what is considered legitimate truth or reason within traditional philosophical canons.

The feminist critique of the philosophical canon reveals systematic patterns of exclusion and marginalization that go far beyond simple oversight or historical accident. Women philosophers have been excluded not only as individuals but as bearers of perspectives and forms of knowledge that challenge masculine assumptions about the nature of reason, objectivity, and truth. This exclusion serves to maintain power structures that privilege masculine ways of knowing while marginalizing alternative approaches to understanding.

Feminist analysis of central philosophical concepts like reason and objectivity reveals how these supposedly universal categories have been gendered in ways that associate rationality with masculinity while linking femininity with emotion, irrationality, and subjectivity. This gendering operates not merely at the level of explicit statements but through the structure of philosophical arguments, the choice of examples and metaphors, and the assumptions about what counts as legitimate evidence or valid reasoning.

The concept of "standpoint epistemology" developed within feminist philosophy argues that knowledge is always produced from particular positions within social relations of power and privilege. Rather than undermining the possibility of objective knowledge, this recognition enables more accurate understanding by acknowledging how social position shapes what we can see and what remains hidden from our perspective. Those in marginalized positions may have access to insights about social relations that remain invisible to those in positions of dominance.

The feminist critique extends beyond philosophy to reveal how power relations shape knowledge production across disciplines and institutions. The questions that get asked, the methods that are considered legitimate, the findings that receive attention and support—all of these are influenced by who has access to resources, whose perspectives are considered valuable, and whose interests are served by particular forms of knowledge. This analysis reveals how seemingly neutral academic practices actually reproduce existing power structures while marginalizing alternative ways of understanding.

Phenomenology and the Primacy of Lived Embodied Experience

The phenomenological tradition, particularly as developed by Maurice Merleau-Ponty, provides crucial insights into how our embodied engagement with the world serves as the foundation for all higher-order cognitive and cultural activities, including the creation of philosophical "mind paintings". Rather than treating perception as a simple input mechanism that provides raw data to abstract reasoning processes, phenomenology reveals perception as the primary way we engage with and understand the world through our lived bodies.

Merleau-Ponty's concept of the "lived body" (corps propre) challenges the traditional philosophical separation between mind and body by showing how consciousness is always embodied consciousness that emerges through our bodily engagement with the world. We do not first have thoughts that we then enact through our bodies; rather, our thinking emerges from and remains grounded in our ongoing bodily interactions with our environment. The body is not simply a tool used by the mind but the foundation from which all meaning and understanding emerges.

The phenomenological analysis of perception reveals how our embodied perspective shapes what we can know about the world in fundamental ways. We always perceive from a particular location, with specific sensory capabilities, oriented toward particular interests and concerns. This situatedness is not a limitation to be overcome but the necessary condition for any perception or understanding to occur at all. The attempt to achieve a "view from nowhere" that transcends embodied perspective is revealed as both impossible and unnecessary for legitimate knowledge.

Merleau-Ponty's analysis of skilled bodily action demonstrates how much of our knowledge exists as embodied know-how rather than explicit conceptual understanding. When we walk, ride a bicycle, or play a musical instrument, we demonstrate sophisticated understanding that cannot be fully captured in abstract rules or propositions. This embodied knowledge serves as the foundation for more abstract forms of thinking and provides the sensorimotor grounding that makes symbolic thought possible.

The phenomenological concept of "intentionality" reveals how consciousness is always directed toward the world through embodied engagement rather than through abstract representation. We do not first form internal representations of external objects and then figure out how they relate to the world; rather, we are always already engaged with the world through bodily activities that create meaningful relationships between ourselves and our environment. This engaged intentionality serves as the foundation from which more abstract forms of thinking and representation emerge.

The recognition of pre-reflective understanding highlights how much of our engagement with the world occurs below the threshold of explicit consciousness but nevertheless structures our experience and possibilities for action. Our body schema—our practical understanding of our bodily capabilities and their relationship to our environment—enables us to navigate space, manipulate objects, and interact with others without conscious deliberation. This pre-reflective dimension provides the background against which explicit thinking and decision-making occurs.

Embodied Cognition and the Sensorimotor Grounding of Abstract Thought

Contemporary research in embodied cognition provides empirical support for philosophical insights about the fundamental role of bodily experience in shaping thought, revealing how abstract concepts and complex reasoning processes are grounded in sensorimotor experience and continue to be influenced by bodily states and activities. This research demonstrates that the "mind paintings" we create are not abstract constructions floating free from physical reality but emerge from and remain connected to our embodied interactions with the world.

The discovery that thinking about actions activates the same brain regions involved in performing those actions provides strong evidence for the embodied nature of cognition. When we think about hammering a nail, brain areas involved in the motor actions of hammering become active, suggesting that our understanding of hammering involves a partial reactivation of the sensorimotor experiences associated with the actual activity. This finding extends to abstract concepts that are understood through metaphorical connections to embodied experience.

Research on spatial metaphors reveals how abstract concepts are understood through mappings from concrete spatial and bodily experiences. Concepts like "high status," "moral elevation," "feeling down," and "grasping an idea" are not merely linguistic conveniences but reflect systematic patterns of embodied metaphorical thinking that structure how we understand abstract domains. These metaphorical mappings are not arbitrary but emerge from regular patterns of embodied experience that create systematic connections between physical and conceptual domains.

Studies of gesture and learning demonstrate how bodily movement continues to influence thinking and understanding even in highly abstract domains like mathematics and logic. Students who are encouraged to use appropriate gestures while learning mathematical concepts show better understanding and retention than those who are not. Similarly, teachers' gestures contribute to student learning by providing embodied scaffolding that supports the development of abstract understanding.

The embodied cognition research reveals how emotional and motivational states, which are fundamentally embodied phenomena, influence cognitive processes in systematic ways. Our current bodily state—whether we are hungry, tired, physically comfortable, or experiencing particular emotions—influences how we perceive situations, what information we attend to, how we evaluate options, and what decisions we make. This influence occurs not merely at the periphery of thinking but affects core processes of reasoning and judgment.

The recognition that cognition is distributed across brain, body, and environment challenges traditional boundaries between internal mental processes and external physical reality. Our cognitive capabilities are extended and enhanced through our use of tools, our interactions with other people, and our engagement with structured environments that provide cognitive scaffolding. The "mind paintings" we create are not products of isolated individual brains but emerge from dynamic interactions within embodied-environmental systems.

The Embodied Challenge to Traditional Epistemology

The convergence of existentialist, phenomenological, feminist, and embodied cognition insights creates a powerful challenge to traditional approaches to knowledge and truth that have dominated Western philosophy since the Enlightenment. Rather than undermining the possibility of knowledge or leading to relativism, this embodied approach provides deeper understanding of how knowledge is actually produced and validated through human communities of embodied, situated knowers.

The traditional epistemological ideal of objective, universal, disembodied knowledge is revealed as both impossible and unnecessary for legitimate understanding. All knowledge is produced by particular embodied knowers situated in specific contexts, but this situatedness does not prevent the development of reliable, intersubjectively valid understanding. Instead, it provides the necessary foundation from which knowledge emerges and the criteria for evaluating its adequacy and usefulness.

The embodied approach reveals how different forms of knowledge emerge from different patterns of embodied engagement with the world. Scientific knowledge emerges from particular ways of using instruments, conducting experiments, and coordinating observations across research communities. Artistic knowledge emerges from embodied engagement with materials, techniques, and aesthetic experiences. Practical wisdom emerges from skilled engagement with particular domains of activity over extended periods. Each form has its own validity criteria and contributes to human understanding in distinctive ways.

The recognition of the social and political dimensions of knowledge production does not undermine objectivity but reveals how genuine objectivity can only be achieved through inclusive processes that bring diverse perspectives and experiences into dialogue. The exclusion of particular voices and experiences reduces rather than increases the reliability of knowledge by limiting the range of evidence and perspectives that can be brought to bear on questions under investigation.

The embodied approach provides resources for understanding how knowledge claims can be evaluated and improved without appealing to impossible standards of absolute objectivity or universal validity. Knowledge claims can be assessed in terms of their adequacy to the experiences of embodied knowers, their usefulness for guiding action in particular contexts, their coherence with other well-established understanding, and their ability to account for and learn from experiences that challenge existing frameworks.

Lived Experience as a Source of Knowledge and Critique

The philosophical traditions examined in this chapter converge on the recognition that lived experience provides not only the foundation from which all knowledge emerges but also a crucial resource for identifying gaps, distortions, and limitations in existing "mind paintings". Rather than being merely subjective or unreliable, lived experience provides access to aspects of reality that may be invisible from other perspectives and serves as a crucial check on claims to universal validity.

Women's lived experience, as analyzed by feminist philosophers, reveals how supposedly universal philosophical categories often reflect the particular perspectives and interests of privileged men while marginalizing alternative ways of understanding. The experience of pregnancy, childbirth, and mothering provides insights into embodied existence, temporal experience, and relational identity that challenge individualistic assumptions common in traditional philosophy. The experience of sexual harassment and gender discrimination reveals power dynamics and social structures that remain invisible to those who do not experience them directly.

The lived experience of people with disabilities challenges assumptions about normal embodiment and reveals how social environments are constructed in ways that create barriers for some while appearing neutral to others. The experience of using mobility aids, navigating environments designed for particular body types, or communicating through alternative means provides insights into the relationship between embodiment and social participation that are unavailable from the perspective of those who fit normative assumptions about bodily capability.

The lived experience of people from different cultural backgrounds reveals how supposedly universal cognitive processes and conceptual schemes are actually shaped by particular cultural practices and assumptions. Different languages structure attention and categorization in different ways; different cultural practices create different patterns of embodied experience; different social organizations create different possibilities for agency and relationship. These differences provide evidence that there are multiple viable ways of organizing human experience and understanding.

The recognition of lived experience as a source of knowledge does not lead to epistemological relativism or the conclusion that all perspectives are equally valid. Rather, it provides resources for more adequate understanding by including perspectives and evidence that might otherwise be overlooked. The adequacy of knowledge claims can be assessed by their ability to account for and learn from diverse forms of lived experience while providing useful guidance for action in particular contexts.

The Paradox of Freedom and Determinism in Embodied Existence

One of the most profound insights emerging from the integration of existentialist and embodied approaches to human experience is the recognition that our freedom to create meaning and choose our direction in life is both constrained and enabled by our embodied condition. This creates what might be called the "paradox of embodied freedom"—we are free precisely because we are embodied, situated beings rather than despite these characteristics, but this freedom is always exercised within constraints that we neither choose nor fully control.

Our embodied nature constrains our possibilities in obvious ways—we cannot fly without technological assistance, we cannot perceive electromagnetic radiation outside the visible spectrum without instruments, we cannot live without food, water, and shelter. These constraints are not limitations on some more fundamental freedom but the necessary conditions that make meaningful choice possible. It is precisely because we have particular needs, capabilities, and interests that emerge from our embodied condition that we can make meaningful distinctions between alternatives and choose among them.

The existentialist emphasis on radical individual responsibility must be understood within the context of these embodied constraints rather than as abstract freedom from all limitation. We are responsible for the choices we make within the range of possibilities available to our particular embodied situation, but this responsibility does not extend to choosing the fundamental conditions within which we must make choices. We are responsible for how we respond to our thrownness into particular circumstances, but not for the circumstances themselves.

The feminist analysis reveals how social and cultural arrangements can either expand or constrain the possibilities available to differently situated embodied individuals. The same formal freedom can be experienced very differently by people with different embodied characteristics, social positions, and access to resources. The recognition of these differences does not undermine individual responsibility but reveals how genuine freedom requires both individual authenticity and social conditions that support the full development of human capabilities.

The embodied cognition research reveals how our cognitive capabilities and limitations emerge from the interaction between our biological inheritance and our developmental experiences within particular cultural and material environments. We are not free to think in any arbitrary way, but neither are we completely determined by our biological inheritance. Our "mind paintings" emerge from the dynamic interaction between inherited capabilities and environmental experiences, creating possibilities for both individual creativity and cultural evolution.

Implications for Understanding Human Knowledge and Truth

The embodied approach to human knowledge developed through existentialist, phenomenological, feminist, and cognitive scientific insights has profound implications for how we understand the nature of truth, objectivity, and rational inquiry. Rather than undermining these concepts, the embodied approach provides more adequate understanding of how they actually function in human communities of inquiry while revealing resources for improving our knowledge-generating practices.

From Abstract Reason to Embodied Mind Paintings: The Historical Evolution of Philosophical Understanding

The recognition that all knowledge is produced by embodied, situated knowers does not lead to relativism but to what might be called "perspectival realism"—the understanding that reality can be known from multiple perspectives, each of which may reveal aspects that are invisible from others. The goal is not to transcend all perspectives to achieve a "view from nowhere" but to coordinate multiple perspectives to develop more adequate and comprehensive understanding.

The embodied approach reveals how objectivity emerges through intersubjective processes of dialogue, criticism, and coordination among differently situated knowers rather than through the elimination of subjectivity. Individual perspectives are necessarily limited and potentially biased, but these limitations can be identified and corrected through engagement with other perspectives and through systematic attention to evidence and argument.

The recognition of the social and political dimensions of knowledge production provides resources for improving rather than abandoning scientific and scholarly inquiry. By making visible the ways that power relations and social structures influence what questions get asked, what methods are considered legitimate, and whose perspectives are included, we can work to create more inclusive and democratic processes of knowledge production.

The embodied approach provides new understanding of the relationship between emotion and reason, revealing how emotions provide important information about our situation and values that is necessary for good reasoning and decision-making. Rather than being obstacles to rational thought, emotions are embodied evaluative responses that help us navigate complex social and physical environments. The goal is not to eliminate emotion from reasoning but to integrate emotional and cognitive responses in ways that support wise action.

The integration of existentialist emphasis on individual meaning-making with recognition of social and embodied constraints provides resources for understanding how individual authenticity and social responsibility can be mutually supporting rather than conflicting values. Authentic existence requires honest acknowledgment of our embodied, social condition and the constraints and possibilities it creates, while social responsibility requires recognition of how our choices affect the possibilities available to others.

Conclusion: The Canvas of Embodied Existence

The exploration of existentialist philosophy, feminist critique, phenomenology, and embodied cognition reveals that human "mind paintings" are not abstract constructions floating free from physical and social reality but emerge from our fundamental condition as embodied, situated, and social beings who must create meaning within particular constraints and possibilities. This understanding does not diminish human knowledge or freedom but provides deeper insight into how they actually function and how they can be enhanced and protected.

The embodied canvas on which we paint our understanding of the world is neither blank nor completely predetermined but comes with particular textures, colors, and possibilities that emerge from our biological inheritance, developmental experiences, cultural contexts, and social positions. Our freedom to create meaning operates within these constraints while simultaneously being enabled by them. It is precisely because we are particular kinds of embodied beings with specific needs, capabilities, and interests that meaningful choice becomes possible.

The existentialist insight that we must take responsibility for creating our own meaning takes on new significance when understood through the lens of embodied cognition and feminist analysis. This responsibility is not an abstract burden placed on isolated individuals but a concrete task that must be accomplished through our embodied engagement with particular material and social environments. Our meaning-making activities are simultaneously individual and social, constrained and creative, biologically grounded and culturally constructed.

The feminist critique of patriarchal biases in traditional philosophical "mind paintings" reveals how supposedly universal truths often reflect the particular perspectives and interests of privileged groups while marginalizing alternative ways of understanding. This critique does not undermine the possibility of truth or objectivity but reveals how genuine universality can only be achieved through inclusive processes that bring diverse perspectives and experiences into dialogue.

The phenomenological analysis of lived experience provides crucial insights into how meaning and understanding emerge through our pre-reflective, embodied engagement with the world before being elaborated through explicit conceptual frameworks. This pre-reflective dimension of experience serves as both the foundation for abstract thought and a continuing source of insight that can challenge and revise our explicit beliefs and theories.

The embodied cognition research demonstrates how our thinking remains grounded in sensorimotor experience even at the most abstract levels, revealing that the separation between mind and body assumed by traditional philosophy is both false and unnecessary. Our cognitive capabilities emerge from and continue to depend on the dynamic interaction between brain, body, and environment rather than being products of an isolated mental system.

The integration of these insights reveals that acknowledging embodiment and situatedness makes our understanding of "mind paintings" more complete rather than undermining their validity. By recognizing the human element in all knowledge construction, we gain access to resources for identifying and correcting biases, expanding our understanding through dialogue with different perspectives, and developing more adequate and useful frameworks for guiding action in particular contexts.

The embodied approach provides resources for challenging existing power structures while maintaining commitment to truth, evidence, and rational inquiry. By revealing how knowledge and power are interrelated, we can work to create more democratic and inclusive processes of knowledge production that serve human flourishing rather than the narrow interests of privileged groups.

The recognition that our "mind paintings" are embodied, situated, and social does not lead to relativism or nihilism but to a deeper appreciation of both the possibilities and responsibilities that come with human existence. We are neither gods who can create meaning from nothing nor machines that simply execute predetermined programs, but embodied beings who must work together to create understanding and meaning within the constraints and possibilities of our shared world.

This embodied understanding of human knowledge and meaning-making provides resources for addressing contemporary challenges that require both individual authenticity and collective action. Whether confronting climate change, social inequality, technological disruption, or existential uncertainty, we need frameworks that can integrate scientific understanding with practical wisdom, individual freedom with social responsibility, and local knowledge with global perspectives. The embodied canvas of human existence provides the foundation from which such integration becomes possible.

Defensive Clarifications

Although emphasizing the embodied, situated, and socially constructed nature of mind paintings can invite charges of relativism or subjectivism, this framework upholds robust standards of inquiry rather than dissolving truth. By foregrounding intersubjective validation—the systematic comparison of multiple embodied perspectives against empirical evidence and coherent argument—it preserves objective evaluation within pluralistic contexts.

Critics who fear that embedded and extended cognition erodes individual agency overlook that genuine freedom arises only within material and social constraints. Far from suggesting passive determinism, our account shows that agents exercise meaningful choice by skillfully engaging with—and reshaping—their ecological and cultural niches. The "paradox of embodied freedom" underscores that constraints are the very conditions that enable directed action and authentic self-creation.

Finally, the concern that phenomenological descriptions or feminist standpoint analyses slip into sentimental subjectivity is addressed through methodological rigor: phenomenological bracketing, transparent reflexivity, and triangulation with neuroscientific and ethnographic data ensure that lived-experience reports are systematically examined rather than merely narrated. Likewise, feminist critiques of power structures do not renounce universal ethical norms but enrich moral reasoning by revealing hidden biases that any truly objective account must address.

In sum, defending against philosophical attacks requires neither retreat to disembodied rationalism nor surrender to radical relativism, but a balanced epistemology—one that integrates embodied insight, social critique, and empirical validation to advance a more complete and ethically grounded understanding of mind painting.

Chapter Sixteen
Divergent Canvases: Eastern Philosophy and Alternative Orders

The human need to transform chaos into order transcends geographical boundaries and cultural contexts, manifesting across civilizations in remarkably consistent yet distinctly different ways. While Western philosophical traditions have developed sophisticated frameworks for cognitive harmony through rationalist inquiry and empirical analysis, the great philosophical traditions of the East—Buddhism, Taoism, Confucianism, and Hinduism—offer compelling alternative "canvases" for painting order onto the existential chaos of human experience. These Eastern traditions demonstrate that the fundamental drives identified in the Primate Principle—the need to order chaos, achieve cognitive harmony, and acquire life's ultimate "bananas"—are indeed universal human characteristics, while simultaneously revealing how different cultures can develop radically different approaches to satisfying these same underlying needs.

Divergent Canvases: Comparing Eastern and Western Approaches to Ordering Chaos and Achieving Cognitive Harmony

Far from representing mere regional variations or preliminary philosophical developments, these Eastern traditions constitute sophisticated intellectual frameworks that have successfully ordered reality for billions of people across millennia. Each tradition employs distinct "unseen brushes"—conceptual tools and methodological approaches that differ fundamentally from Western paradigms. Where Western thought emphasizes linear time, individual autonomy, and rational control over nature, Eastern philosophies typically embrace cyclical temporality, interconnected selfhood, and harmonious integration with natural processes. These divergent approaches to the same fundamental human challenges provide compelling evidence for the universality of cognitive ordering drives while illuminating the remarkable diversity of solutions human cultures have developed.

Buddhism: The Canvas of Suffering and Liberation

Buddhism presents perhaps the most psychologically sophisticated of the Eastern approaches to ordering existential chaos, beginning with the Buddha's fundamental insight that life's fundamental problem is dukkha—often translated as suffering, but more accurately understood as a pervasive sense of unsatisfactoriness that characterizes unenlightened existence. The Buddhist "mind painting" does not deny chaos but rather offers a comprehensive framework for understanding and ultimately transcending it through what might be called the most systematic cognitive therapy in human history.

The Four Noble Truths provide Buddhism's foundational architecture for ordering reality: the recognition of suffering's universality, the identification of craving (tanha) as its root cause, the possibility of suffering's cessation, and the Noble Eightfold Path as the practical method for achieving liberation. This framework functions as a sophisticated cognitive map that transforms the seemingly random chaos of human experience into a coherent narrative with clear causation, logical progression, and achievable resolution. The Buddhist "canvas" thus orders chaos not through external control or rational domination, but through profound psychological insight and systematic mental training.

The Buddhist concept of "banana acquisition" differs radically from Western materialist or even spiritual goals. Rather than seeking individual success, pleasure, or even conventional happiness, Buddhism posits nirvana—the complete cessation of suffering through the elimination of craving and the realization of reality's true nature—as life's ultimate achievement. This represents a fundamentally different approach to human fulfillment, one that paradoxically achieves satisfaction through the systematic abandonment of desire itself.

The "unseen brushes" Buddhism employs include meditation and mindfulness practices that train practitioners to observe the impermanent, interconnected nature of all phenomena. The doctrine of anatta (no-self) challenges the Western notion of a fixed, autonomous individual, instead revealing the self as a constantly changing process without permanent essence. This insight dissolves many of the ego-driven conflicts that create psychological chaos, offering a radically different foundation for cognitive harmony than Western individualism.

Buddhism's approach to time reflects its cyclical worldview through concepts like samsara (the cycle of birth, death, and rebirth) and the understanding that liberation can be achieved in this very moment through proper understanding and practice. The tradition's emphasis on interconnectedness (dependent origination) provides an alternative to Western causation, suggesting that all phenomena arise in complex webs of mutual dependence rather than through simple linear cause-and-effect relationships.

The formation of Buddhist "intellectual tribes" centered around the Three Jewels: the Buddha as teacher, the Dharma as teaching, and the Sangha as community. Monastic communities, lay practitioners, and scholarly institutions like Nalanda University created comprehensive social structures that embodied Buddhist principles while transmitting the tradition across cultures and centuries. These communities provided cognitive order not only through shared beliefs but through intensive practices, ethical guidelines, and social support systems that made the Buddhist worldview a lived reality.

Taoism: The Canvas of Natural Harmony

Taoism offers perhaps the most naturalistic approach to ordering chaos among world philosophical traditions, proposing that harmony can be achieved not through effort or control but through alignment with the Tao—the ineffable principle underlying natural order. The Taoist "mind painting" suggests that human-created chaos stems from interference with natural processes, and that cognitive harmony can be restored by rediscovering our place within the larger patterns of existence.

The concept of wu wei (often translated as "non-action" or "effortless action") represents Taoism's central methodology for ordering chaos. Rather than imposing external solutions or forcing outcomes, wu wei advocates responding to situations with the same spontaneous naturalness that water displays when flowing around obstacles. This approach suggests that much human suffering and disorder arise from excessive striving, control, and interference with natural processes. The Taoist practitioner learns to discern when to act and when to refrain, developing an intuitive sensitivity to the natural timing and flow of events.

Taoism's "banana" differs significantly from both Western achievement-orientation and Buddhist liberation. The Taoist ideal involves living in harmony with the Tao, experiencing the effortless joy and spontaneous effectiveness that emerge when one's actions align with natural patterns. This represents neither worldly success nor transcendent escape, but rather a way of being that is simultaneously deeply natural and profoundly fulfilling.

The tradition employs several distinctive "unseen brushes" in creating cognitive order. The concept of yin-yang provides a framework for understanding apparent opposites as complementary aspects of a unified whole, transforming conflict into dynamic balance. Cyclical time in Taoism reflects natural rhythms and seasonal patterns, offering an alternative to linear progress that emphasizes renewal, return, and eternal recurrence. The ideal of the "uncarved block" (pu) suggests returning to a state of natural simplicity before social conditioning created artificial complexity.

Taoist communities formed around shared practices rather than institutional structures, often emphasizing solitary cultivation, small groups of practitioners, and the transmission of wisdom through direct experience rather than formal doctrine. Mountain hermitages, temple communities, and informal networks of practitioners created "intellectual tribes" united by common practices of self-cultivation, natural observation, and philosophical reflection. The relative lack of rigid institutional structure in Taoism reflects the tradition's emphasis on naturalness and spontaneity while still providing social contexts for shared exploration and mutual support.

Confucianism: The Canvas of Social Harmony

Confucianism approaches the ordering of chaos through the systematic cultivation of virtue, proper relationships, and social harmony, creating what might be called the most comprehensively social of the world's major philosophical traditions. The Confucian "mind painting" suggests that existential chaos stems primarily from disordered relationships and moral confusion, and that cognitive harmony can be achieved through the careful cultivation of virtue, respect for tradition, and the fulfillment of social roles.

The cornerstone of Confucian order lies in the Five Relationships: ruler-subject, father-son, husband-wife, elder brother-younger brother, and friend-friend. These relationships provide a comprehensive framework for organizing social reality, with each relationship carrying specific duties, expectations, and moral obligations that create predictable patterns of interaction and mutual support. This system transforms the potential chaos of human social life into an ordered hierarchy where everyone knows their place and responsibilities, creating stability and harmony through clearly defined expectations and reciprocal obligations.

Confucianism's conception of the ultimate "banana" centers on the ideal of becoming a junzi (exemplary person or "gentleman") who embodies virtue so completely that their mere presence inspires others toward goodness. This represents neither individual achievement in the Western sense nor transcendent liberation in the Buddhist sense, but rather the fulfillment that comes from perfecting one's character and contributing to social harmony through moral excellence.

The tradition's "unseen brushes" include several distinctive approaches to cognitive ordering. The concept of li (ritual propriety) provides detailed guidelines for appropriate behavior in various social contexts, transforming potentially chaotic social interactions into graceful, meaningful ceremonies that reinforce proper relationships and shared values. Self-cultivation (xiuyang) offers a systematic approach to character development that emphasizes continuous learning, moral reflection, and the gradual perfection of virtue throughout life.

Confucian understanding of time emphasizes historical continuity rather than pure cyclical repetition or linear progress, viewing the present as connected to an ancestral past that provides moral guidance and a future that depends on current cultivation of virtue. The tradition's approach to nature emphasizes human responsibility for cultivating and improving the natural world rather than either dominating it (Western approach) or simply harmonizing with it (Taoist approach).

The formation of Confucian "intellectual tribes" occurred through educational institutions, scholarly academies, and the imperial examination system that selected government officials based on their mastery of Confucian texts and principles. These institutions created communities of shared values, practices, and social purposes that extended Confucian influence throughout East Asian societies. Family structures, educational systems, and governmental bureaucracies all served as venues for transmitting and embodying Confucian ideals, creating comprehensive social environments where the Confucian worldview shaped daily life and long-term cultural development.

Hinduism: The Canvas of Cosmic Order

Hinduism presents perhaps the most cosmologically comprehensive approach to ordering chaos, weaving together concepts of cosmic law (dharma), spiritual liberation (moksha), and social organization (varna-ashrama) into an integrated worldview that addresses existential questions from the most mundane daily activities to the ultimate nature of reality itself. The Hindu "mind painting" portrays individual human existence as part of vast cosmic cycles, with personal chaos transformed into meaningful experience through understanding one's place in the larger dharmic order.

The concept of dharma provides Hinduism's fundamental principle for ordering reality, functioning simultaneously as cosmic law, social duty, and individual righteousness. Dharma suggests that apparent chaos actually reflects a deeper order that can be discerned and aligned with through proper understanding and ethical action. This concept transforms seemingly arbitrary suffering and confusion into meaningful experiences that serve larger purposes of spiritual development and cosmic harmony.

Hinduism's ultimate "banana"—moksha or liberation—represents freedom from the cycle of birth, death, and rebirth (samsara) through the realization of one's true nature as identical with ultimate reality (Brahman). This goal differs from Buddhist liberation through its affirmation of an eternal, unchanging Self (Atman) and from Western achievement through its emphasis on transcending rather than fulfilling worldly desires. Multiple paths (yogas) are recognized as valid approaches to this goal, including the paths of knowledge (jnana), devotion (bhakti), action (karma), and meditation (raja).

Hindu "unseen brushes" for creating cognitive order include several distinctive conceptual tools. Cyclical time operates on multiple scales, from daily and seasonal cycles to vast cosmic periods (kalpas) spanning billions of years, providing frameworks for understanding both immediate experience and ultimate destiny. The law of karma transforms apparently random events into meaningful consequences of past actions, creating moral coherence across multiple lifetimes. The concept of maya (often translated as illusion) suggests that apparent chaos stems from misperceiving the true nature of reality rather than from genuine randomness or meaninglessness.

The varna-ashrama system provides comprehensive social organization through the intersection of social classes (varnas) and life stages (ashramas), creating a detailed framework for understanding appropriate duties and goals throughout life. While often criticized for its hierarchical implications, this system originally functioned as a sophisticated approach to social order that recognized different temperaments, capabilities, and life circumstances while providing clear guidance for ethical behavior in various contexts.

Hindu "intellectual tribes" formed around numerous guru-disciple lineages, temple complexes, pilgrimage networks, and textual traditions that created rich communities of shared practice, study, and spiritual aspiration. The tradition's acceptance of multiple valid paths and its integration with regional customs allowed for diverse forms of expression while maintaining underlying unity of purpose and worldview. Ashram communities, scholarly traditions, and festival cycles created social contexts where Hindu cosmology shaped both individual spiritual practice and collective cultural life.

The Universal Brushes: Interconnectedness, Cyclical Time, and Self-Cultivation

Despite their significant differences, the major Eastern philosophical traditions share certain "unseen brushes"—fundamental conceptual tools that distinguish them from Western approaches and demonstrate alternative methods for achieving cognitive harmony. These common elements suggest underlying patterns in human approaches to ordering chaos while illuminating the distinctive contributions of Eastern thought.

Interconnectedness represents perhaps the most fundamental shared brush among Eastern traditions, though each employs it differently. Buddhism's dependent origination reveals all phenomena as arising through complex webs of causation rather than as independent entities. Taoism's understanding of yin-yang shows apparent opposites as mutually dependent aspects of unified processes. Confucianism's emphasis on relationships demonstrates individual identity as constituted through social connections rather than autonomous self-definition. Hinduism's concept of cosmic unity (Brahman) reveals individual souls (Atman) as fundamentally connected to ultimate reality. These varied approaches to interconnectedness provide alternatives to Western individualism and reductionism, offering cognitive frameworks that emphasize relationship, context, and systemic understanding.

Cyclical Time provides another crucial shared brush, contrasting sharply with Western linear temporality and its emphasis on progress, development, and final destinations. Buddhist cycles of death and rebirth create opportunities for spiritual development across multiple lifetimes. Taoist eternal return emphasizes renewal and the repetition of natural patterns. Confucian historical continuity connects present action with ancestral wisdom and future responsibility. Hindu cosmic cycles place individual existence within vast temporal frameworks that render temporary sufferings meaningful within larger contexts. These cyclical approaches to time reduce the anxiety and pressure often associated with Western linear time while providing hope for renewal, learning, and eventual fulfillment.

Self-Cultivation emerges as a central methodology across Eastern traditions, though implemented through different specific practices. Buddhist meditation and mindfulness training systematically develop insight and compassion. Taoist practices cultivate naturalness and spontaneous effectiveness. Confucian education and moral reflection refine character and social virtue. Hindu yogic practices integrate physical, mental, and spiritual development. These approaches share an emphasis on gradual, disciplined development of human potential through regular practice rather than sudden achievement or external acquisition of goods or status.

The Formation of Eastern Intellectual Tribes

The great Eastern philosophical traditions demonstrate how "intellectual tribes" form around comprehensive worldviews that provide not only cognitive frameworks but also social identities, practical methodologies, and institutional structures. These communities illustrate the social dimension of cognitive ordering, showing how shared "mind paintings" create group cohesion and collective meaning.

Buddhist communities (Sangha) developed around shared commitment to the Three Jewels and common practices of meditation, ethical conduct, and wisdom cultivation. Monastic institutions provided intensive environments for spiritual development while lay communities integrated Buddhist principles into family life, economic activity, and social relationships. The tradition's emphasis on personal experience and practical results created communities united by shared methods and goals rather than merely doctrinal agreement.

Taoist communities formed more loosely around shared practices and philosophical orientations rather than formal institutions. Mountain hermitages, temple complexes, and informal networks of practitioners created contexts for mutual support and wisdom transmission while maintaining the tradition's emphasis on naturalness and individual cultivation. The relative informality of Taoist social organization reflects the tradition's values while still providing community support for practitioners.

Confucian intellectual tribes centered around educational institutions, scholarly academies, and governmental service that created comprehensive social environments where Confucian values shaped both individual development and collective organization. The imperial examination system created merit-based pathways for social mobility while ensuring that governmental leadership embodied Confucian virtues and knowledge. Family structures and educational practices transmitted Confucian ideals across generations while adapting to changing historical circumstances.

Hindu communities developed around multiple overlapping structures including guru-disciple lineages, temple complexes, pilgrimage networks, and textual traditions that created rich contexts for spiritual development and cultural transmission. The tradition's acceptance of diverse paths and practices allowed for numerous forms of community organization while maintaining underlying unity of purpose and worldview.

These various forms of "intellectual tribes" demonstrate how sophisticated worldviews create social as well as cognitive order, providing individuals with communities of shared meaning, practical support, and collective identity that embody and transmit their respective approaches to ordering chaos and achieving harmony.

Comparative Analysis: Eastern Alternative Orders

The major Eastern philosophical traditions offer compelling alternatives to Western approaches to cognitive harmony, demonstrating that the fundamental human drives identified in the Primate Principle can be satisfied through radically different methodologies and conceptual frameworks. These alternatives are not primitive or preliminary versions of Western rationalism, but sophisticated intellectual achievements that have successfully organized reality for billions of people across thousands of years.

Where Western traditions typically emphasize individual autonomy, rational analysis, and control over nature, Eastern approaches generally prioritize relational identity, intuitive wisdom, and harmony with natural processes. Western linear time creates pressure for achievement and progress, while Eastern cyclical time offers opportunities for renewal and gradual development. Western reductionism seeks to understand wholes through analysis of parts, while Eastern holism emphasizes context, relationship, and systemic understanding.

Yet these differences occur within the context of shared human challenges and underlying cognitive needs. All traditions must address questions of meaning, suffering, death, social organization, and ultimate purpose. All must provide frameworks for transforming chaos into order, achieving psychological harmony, and pursuing life's most valuable goals. The diversity of successful solutions demonstrates both the universality of human cognitive needs and the remarkable creativity with which different cultures have developed approaches to satisfying them.

The Eastern emphasis on self-cultivation provides a particularly important alternative to Western approaches to human development. Rather than emphasizing external achievement, technological control, or rational argument as primary means of improvement, Eastern traditions focus on internal development through disciplined practice, moral cultivation, and spiritual insight. These approaches suggest that many forms of human suffering stem from internal disorders—greed, hatred, ignorance, social disharmony, disconnection from nature—that require internal solutions rather than external manipulation of circumstances.

The Eastern concept of liberation also offers alternatives to Western concepts of success and fulfillment. Buddhist nirvana, Taoist harmony, Confucian virtue, and Hindu moksha all represent forms of satisfaction that transcend conventional desires while providing profound fulfillment. These goals suggest that human happiness may depend more on internal development and proper relationship than on external acquisition and control.

Implications for the Primate Principle

The sophisticated alternative approaches demonstrated by Eastern philosophical traditions strengthen rather than challenge the universality of the Primate Principle. By showing that fundamentally different methods can successfully address the same underlying human needs—ordering chaos, achieving cognitive harmony, pursuing ultimate fulfillment—these traditions demonstrate that the drives themselves are universal even while their expressions vary dramatically across cultures.

The existence of successful alternative approaches also illuminates aspects of human cognition and social organization that might otherwise remain invisible. The Western emphasis on individual rationalism, linear progress, and natural domination appears less inevitable and more culturally specific when contrasted with Eastern alternatives that have proven equally effective in their own contexts. This comparative perspective enriches understanding of human possibilities while revealing the full range of cognitive tools available for addressing existential challenges.

The Eastern traditions also demonstrate the social dimension of cognitive ordering, showing how "mind paintings" function not only as individual psychological tools but as collective cultural frameworks that create shared meaning, social identity, and institutional structure. The formation of "intellectual tribes" around comprehensive worldviews reveals how cognitive harmony depends not only on internal psychological order but on social environments that support and embody preferred ways of understanding and organizing reality.

Furthermore, the success of Eastern approaches suggests that modern challenges—environmental crisis, social fragmentation, psychological disorder, existential meaninglessness—might benefit from integration of Eastern insights with Western capabilities. The Eastern emphasis on interconnectedness, cyclical sustainability, internal development, and social harmony offers resources for addressing problems that purely Western approaches have found difficult to resolve.

Conclusion

The great philosophical traditions of the East—Buddhism, Taoism, Confucianism, and Hinduism—demonstrate that the fundamental human drives to order chaos, seek harmony, and acquire life's ultimate "bananas" are indeed universal characteristics of human cognition and social organization. These traditions offer compelling evidence for the Primate Principle's universal applicability while simultaneously revealing the remarkable diversity of approaches different cultures have developed for satisfying the same underlying needs.

Far from representing primitive or preliminary philosophical developments, these Eastern traditions constitute sophisticated intellectual achievements that employ distinctive "unseen brushes"—cyclical time, interconnectedness, self-cultivation—to create comprehensive frameworks for understanding and organizing reality. Their success in providing meaning, order, and fulfillment for billions of people across millennia demonstrates the effectiveness of their alternative approaches to cognitive harmony.

The formation of "intellectual tribes" around these traditions illustrates the social dimension of cognitive ordering, showing how shared worldviews create not only individual psychological coherence but also collective cultural identity and institutional structure. These communities provide crucial support for individual development while transmitting and evolving their respective traditions across generations and geographical boundaries.

By demonstrating successful alternatives to Western rationalism, individualism, and linear progress, these Eastern traditions illuminate the full range of human possibilities for addressing existential challenges while confirming the universality of the underlying cognitive drives that make such achievements necessary and possible. Their continued vitality and global influence suggest that their insights remain relevant for contemporary challenges and future human development.

The "divergent canvases" of Eastern philosophy thus provide not only historical examples of alternative cognitive ordering but also living resources for addressing contemporary challenges that require integration of rational analysis with wisdom traditions, individual development with social harmony, and technological capability with ecological sustainability. Their demonstration that different "mind paintings" can successfully order chaos and achieve cognitive harmony confirms the Primate Principle's explanatory power while enriching understanding of human potential and cultural possibility.

In closing, this chapter's emphasis on the material, social, and ecological dimensions of mind painting does not capitulate to relativism or reduce human action to passive determinism. Rather, it embraces a critical pluralism that subjects competing perspectives to rigorous intersubjective validation—empirical evidence, logical coherence, and open dialogue—ensuring normative standards without enforcing a singular worldview. By revealing how constraints (neural, bodily, environmental, and cultural) are in fact the enabling conditions for meaningful choice, it affirms that genuine freedom and agency emerge through skilled engagement with, and strategic reshaping of, one's developmental niche. Far from privileging any single explanatory level, this account insists on methodological triangulation—phenomenological bracketing, transparent reflexivity, and the integration of ethnographic, neuroscientific, and formal modeling—to weave a holistic narrative that honors both individual subjectivity and shared ethical commitments. Finally, ethical frameworks grounded in human rights, care ethics, and evidence-based evaluation guide how mind paintings ought to be repainted toward justice, well-being, and sustainability, demonstrating that acknowledging constructed realities is not a retreat from moral obligation but the most effective path to responsible, adaptive, and ethically grounded scholarship.

Chapter Seventeen

The Scientific Canvas: Paradigms, Progress, and the Human Hand of Inquiry

The scientific method stands as humanity's most powerful collective "mind painting"—a sophisticated framework for transforming the seemingly chaotic flood of empirical observations into ordered, reliable knowledge that can be tested, replicated, and applied to acquire life's most valuable "bananas": predictive power, technological advancement, and systematic understanding of natural phenomena. Yet this remarkable achievement in cognitive ordering is neither inevitable nor purely objective; it represents a distinctly human creation, shaped by our sensory limitations, cognitive biases, cultural contexts, and institutional arrangements, all of which profoundly influence both the questions science asks and the ways it interprets the answers it receives.

Evolution of Scientific Paradigms: Historical "Mind Paintings" for Ordering Empirical Reality

Far from undermining the authority of science, recognizing its fundamentally human character actually deepens our appreciation for its intellectual brilliance and dynamic evolution. The scientific method represents perhaps the most successful example of collective cognitive scaffolding in human history—a set of practices, institutions, and conceptual frameworks that systematically counteract individual human limitations while harnessing our cognitive strengths. Through mechanisms like peer review, replication requirements, statistical analysis, and methodological protocols, science has created a social ecology that transforms fallible human observations into increasingly reliable collective knowledge.

The Scientific Method as Collective Mind Painting

The emergence of modern science represents a radical departure from earlier approaches to understanding natural phenomena, constituting what Thomas Kuhn famously described as a revolutionary transformation in humanity's "mind painting" for ordering empirical reality. Where earlier traditions relied primarily on authority, logical deduction, or unsystematic observation, science developed a comprehensive methodology that combines systematic empirical investigation with rigorous theoretical reasoning, creating what is arguably the most effective approach to reliable knowledge acquisition ever devised.

The core structure of scientific inquiry—observation, hypothesis formation, experimental testing, analysis, and conclusion—provides a standardized template for transforming chaotic sensory input into meaningful patterns and reliable predictions. This methodological framework functions as a cognitive prosthetic that extends human capabilities far beyond their natural limits, allowing us to detect patterns invisible to unaided perception, test ideas against carefully controlled conditions, and build cumulative knowledge across generations of researchers.

The scientific method's power lies not in eliminating human subjectivity but in systematizing it within collective processes that can identify and correct individual biases and limitations. Through controlled experimentation, scientists create artificial environments where specific variables can be isolated and their effects measured, transforming the overwhelming complexity of natural phenomena into manageable, testable propositions. Statistical analysis provides tools for distinguishing genuine patterns from random noise, while replication requirements ensure that individual findings can be independently verified or refuted.

Perhaps most importantly, the peer review system creates a social mechanism for subjecting individual claims to collective scrutiny, forcing researchers to justify their methods, interpretations, and conclusions to communities of qualified experts. This process transforms science from individual opinion into collective judgment, creating a form of "distributed cognition" that can achieve levels of reliability and objectivity beyond what any individual human mind could accomplish alone.

The Human Construction of Scientific Reality

Despite its remarkable success in generating reliable knowledge, the scientific method operates entirely within human cognitive and cultural constraints that fundamentally shape both its possibilities and its limitations. Our sensory apparatus restricts us to a narrow slice of the electromagnetic spectrum, limiting direct observation to visible light while remaining blind to the vast ranges of radio waves, infrared radiation, X-rays, and other forms of electromagnetic energy that permeate our environment. Our temporal perception confines us to experiences measured in seconds, minutes, and years, making it difficult to directly observe phenomena that occur over microseconds or geological timescales.

How Cognitive Biases Shape and Systematic Methods Refine Empirical Inquiry

These sensory limitations profoundly influence the questions science asks and the methods it employs to answer them. The development of scientific instruments—telescopes, microscopes, particle accelerators, satellite sensors—represents humanity's attempt to extend our sensory capabilities beyond their biological boundaries, but these instruments themselves embody particular assumptions about what is worth observing and how observations should be interpreted. The choice of which phenomena to study, which variables to measure, and which theoretical frameworks to employ all reflect distinctly human priorities, interests, and conceptual limitations.

Cognitive biases represent another fundamental constraint on scientific inquiry, systematically distorting the ways researchers collect, interpret, and evaluate evidence. Confirmation bias leads scientists to preferentially seek evidence that supports their existing hypotheses while overlooking or dismissing contradictory data. The availability heuristic causes researchers to overweight easily recalled examples while underestimating the significance of less memorable but potentially more representative cases. Anchoring effects influence how scientists interpret new data based on initial impressions or theoretical commitments.

The institutional structure of science introduces additional human influences on the research process. Funding priorities, career incentives, publication pressures, and disciplinary boundaries all shape which questions get investigated, which methods are considered legitimate, and which findings receive attention and support. The social organization of scientific communities creates networks of shared assumptions, preferred methodologies, and common interests that can both facilitate productive collaboration and limit the range of considered alternatives.

Cultural contexts provide the broader framework within which scientific inquiry takes place, influencing fundamental assumptions about the nature of reality, the proper relationship between theory and observation, and the ultimate goals of knowledge acquisition. These cultural influences operate largely below the threshold of conscious awareness but profoundly shape scientific practice by determining which questions seem important, which explanatory approaches appear plausible, and which forms of evidence are considered convincing.

Paradigms as Cultural Mind Paintings

Thomas Kuhn's analysis of scientific revolutions provides perhaps the most compelling account of how science operates as a fundamentally human, culturally embedded enterprise while nevertheless achieving remarkable success in understanding natural phenomena. Kuhn's concept of paradigms reveals how scientific communities organize their research around shared sets of assumptions, methodologies, and exemplary achievements that function as comprehensive "mind paintings" for ordering empirical chaos and directing productive inquiry.

A scientific paradigm, in Kuhn's analysis, encompasses much more than a simple theory or hypothesis; it represents an entire worldview that includes fundamental assumptions about the nature of reality, appropriate methods for investigation, standards for evaluating evidence, and criteria for judging success. Paradigms provide scientists with what Kuhn calls "puzzle-solving" frameworks that define legitimate problems, acceptable solution methods, and expected forms of answers. Within established paradigms, scientists engage in "normal science"—systematic investigation aimed at extending, refining, and applying paradigmatic principles rather than questioning their fundamental validity.

The paradigmatic structure of scientific inquiry demonstrates how science operates as a collective cognitive enterprise that transcends individual researchers while remaining fundamentally dependent on human communities for its existence and development. Paradigms are created, sustained, and transformed through social processes of education, communication, and consensus-building within scientific communities. They provide shared conceptual vocabularies, methodological standards, and evaluation criteria that enable productive collaboration while simultaneously constraining the range of considered possibilities.

Kuhn's analysis reveals how paradigms function as powerful "mind paintings" that bring order to otherwise chaotic empirical phenomena by providing frameworks for organizing observations, formulating hypotheses, and interpreting results. The mechanical worldview of Newtonian physics, for example, transformed previously mysterious phenomena like planetary motion and falling objects into manifestations of universal mathematical laws operating through mechanical causation. Similarly, Darwin's evolutionary paradigm reorganized biological observations around concepts of variation, inheritance, and natural selection, creating a unified framework for understanding the diversity and complexity of living organisms.

The persistence of paradigms reflects their effectiveness in ordering empirical chaos and enabling productive research, but their ultimate replacement through scientific revolutions demonstrates the contingent, culturally embedded nature of all scientific knowledge. Paradigm shifts occur not through simple logical demonstrations but through complex social processes involving generational change, institutional reorganization, and fundamental alterations in scientific worldviews.

Scientific Revolutions as Philosophical Attacks

Kuhn's analysis of paradigm shifts reveals them as fundamentally "philosophical attacks" that challenge not just specific theories or findings but entire frameworks for understanding reality and conducting inquiry. These revolutionary transformations represent profound disruptions to existing "mind paintings" when accumulated anomalies and unresolved problems create crises of confidence in established paradigms' ability to order empirical chaos and acquire desired forms of knowledge.

The Copernican revolution exemplifies this process of paradigmatic upheaval and transformation. The geocentric worldview of Ptolemaic astronomy represented a comprehensive mind painting that successfully organized celestial observations within a framework consistent with Aristotelian physics, Christian theology, and common-sense experience. For over a millennium, this paradigm enabled accurate prediction of planetary positions and provided satisfying explanations for observed astronomical phenomena.

However, accumulated observations of planetary motion, particularly the complex retrograde movements of Mars and other planets, gradually created mounting difficulties for the geocentric model. The elaborate system of epicycles required to maintain geocentric assumptions became increasingly unwieldy and theoretically unsatisfying. When Copernicus proposed his heliocentric alternative, he was not simply suggesting a technical modification but launching a comprehensive assault on fundamental assumptions about Earth's place in the cosmos, the relationship between mathematical models and physical reality, and the proper sources of astronomical authority.

The eventual triumph of the Copernican paradigm required not just better astronomical predictions—indeed, early heliocentric models were often less accurate than refined geocentric systems—but a fundamental transformation in scientific worldview that prioritized mathematical elegance and theoretical simplicity over traditional authority and common-sense intuition. This paradigm shift ultimately enabled new forms of empirical investigation, theoretical understanding, and technological application that would have been impossible within geocentric frameworks.

Similar patterns characterize other major scientific revolutions. Darwin's evolutionary theory attacked not just specific claims about biological diversity but fundamental assumptions about the nature of species, the relationship between organism and environment, and the role of purpose and design in natural phenomena. Einstein's relativity theories challenged basic concepts of space, time, and simultaneity that had structured physical understanding since Newton. Quantum mechanics questioned fundamental assumptions about causation, measurement, and the relationship between observer and observed reality.

Each of these revolutionary transformations represents what Kuhn calls "incommensurable" changes in scientific worldview—shifts so fundamental that researchers working within different paradigms often cannot fully communicate across paradigmatic boundaries because they employ different conceptual vocabularies, methodological approaches, and evaluation criteria. The shift from one paradigm to another involves something more like conversion than logical demonstration, requiring scientists to abandon familiar intellectual territories and learn to see familiar phenomena in entirely new ways.

The Social Ecology of Scientific Knowledge

The success of science in generating reliable knowledge despite its fundamental human character depends crucially on the social ecology within which scientific inquiry takes place. Science has evolved sophisticated institutional mechanisms that systematically counteract individual cognitive biases, extend human sensory and analytical capabilities, and create collective forms of knowledge that transcend the limitations of individual researchers.

Peer review represents perhaps the most important of these mechanisms, creating a system of distributed evaluation that subjects individual claims to scrutiny by qualified experts who can identify methodological flaws, alternative interpretations, and unwarranted conclusions. This process transforms science from individual assertion into collective judgment, creating multiple layers of evaluation that can catch errors and biases that individual researchers might miss or ignore.

Replication requirements provide another crucial safeguard against individual limitations and biases by demanding that scientific findings be independently reproduced before they are accepted as reliable knowledge. This process not only verifies specific claims but also tests the robustness of methodological approaches and theoretical interpretations across different research contexts, investigators, and cultural settings.

Statistical methods and experimental design protocols represent systematic approaches to controlling for known sources of bias and error in scientific investigation. Double-blind studies prevent researchers' expectations from influencing their observations; randomized sampling techniques ensure representative data collection; control groups isolate the effects of specific variables; and statistical significance testing provides standards for distinguishing genuine patterns from random variation.

The cumulative, self-correcting nature of scientific knowledge reflects these collective mechanisms for error detection and bias mitigation. Individual studies may be flawed, biased, or even fraudulent, but the overall scientific enterprise creates multiple opportunities for identifying and correcting such problems through independent replication, critical review, and theoretical integration. Over time, this process tends to eliminate false claims and strengthen well-supported findings, creating increasingly reliable collective knowledge despite the fallibility of individual contributions.

The international, collaborative character of modern science provides additional protection against cultural biases and local limitations by subjecting scientific claims to evaluation across diverse research communities with different theoretical commitments, methodological preferences, and cultural assumptions. This diversity of perspective helps identify blind spots and unwarranted assumptions that might persist within more homogeneous research communities.

The Empirical Canvas: Ordering Observational Chaos

The scientific method's particular genius lies in its systematic approach to transforming the overwhelming complexity and apparent randomness of empirical observations into ordered, meaningful patterns that can support reliable predictions and practical applications. Natural phenomena present themselves to human perception as a chaotic flux of sensory impressions that must be organized, categorized, and interpreted before they can become useful knowledge.

Science accomplishes this transformation through several key strategies that collectively function as a sophisticated "mind painting" for empirical reality. Controlled experimentation artificially simplifies natural complexity by isolating specific variables and holding other factors constant, allowing researchers to identify causal relationships that would be impossible to detect in natural settings. Laboratory conditions create standardized environments where phenomena can be observed repeatedly under similar conditions, enabling the accumulation of systematic data about natural processes.

Measurement and quantification provide tools for converting qualitative observations into numerical data that can be subjected to mathematical analysis, statistical evaluation, and theoretical modeling. This process transforms vague impressions like "hot" or "heavy" into precise quantities that can be compared, combined, and manipulated using powerful mathematical techniques. The development of standardized units, calibrated instruments, and measurement protocols creates common languages for describing natural phenomena that transcend individual differences in perception and interpretation.

Theoretical modeling provides frameworks for organizing empirical observations around abstract principles and mathematical relationships that can generate testable predictions about unobserved phenomena. Successful theories function as conceptual maps that reveal hidden connections between apparently disparate observations, suggesting new experiments and enabling the discovery of previously unknown natural regularities.

The iterative relationship between theory and observation creates a dynamic process of knowledge refinement that gradually eliminates false leads while strengthening well-supported claims. Theories guide the design of new experiments by suggesting which phenomena to observe and which variables to manipulate. Experimental results, in turn, test theoretical predictions and may reveal limitations or errors in theoretical assumptions, leading to theory modification or replacement.

This ongoing dialogue between theoretical expectation and empirical discovery drives the cumulative character of scientific progress, enabling each generation of researchers to build upon the achievements of their predecessors while correcting their errors and extending their insights into new domains.

Cognitive Biases and Scientific Safeguards

The recognition that scientists are subject to the same cognitive biases that affect all human thinking has led to increasingly sophisticated understanding of how these biases operate within scientific inquiry and how methodological safeguards can mitigate their influence. Rather than viewing bias as a fatal flaw that undermines scientific objectivity, contemporary science treats bias as a predictable feature of human cognition that can be systematically counteracted through appropriate research design and evaluation procedures.

Common cognitive biases that influence human decision-making and scientific inquiry

Confirmation bias, perhaps the most pervasive cognitive bias affecting scientific inquiry, leads researchers to preferentially seek evidence supporting their hypotheses while avoiding or dismissing contradictory data. This bias can distort every stage of the research process, from the initial formulation of research questions through the interpretation of experimental results. Scientists may unconsciously design experiments that are more likely to produce confirming evidence, selectively report results that support their predictions, or interpret ambiguous data in ways that favor their theoretical commitments.

Scientific methodology counters confirmation bias through several mechanisms designed to force researchers to confront disconfirming evidence. The requirement for explicit hypothesis formulation before data collection makes it harder to engage in post-hoc reasoning that fits theories to unexpected results. Preregistration of research protocols prevents researchers from modifying their methods or analyses to produce desired outcomes. Systematic replication by independent research groups provides multiple opportunities to test theoretical claims under different conditions and with different investigator biases.

The availability heuristic causes researchers to overweight easily recalled or dramatic examples while underestimating the importance of less memorable but potentially more representative cases. This bias can lead to distorted assessments of the frequency or importance of various phenomena, particularly when media attention or personal experience makes certain examples more salient than others.

Meta-analyses and systematic reviews provide antidotes to availability bias by requiring comprehensive evaluation of all relevant evidence rather than relying on selective or memorable examples. These methods force researchers to consider the full range of available data, including negative results that might not receive publication or attention but are crucial for accurate assessment of overall patterns.

Anchoring effects influence how scientists interpret new data based on initial impressions, preliminary results, or established theoretical commitments. Researchers may unconsciously adjust their interpretations of new evidence to remain consistent with earlier findings or theoretical expectations, preventing them from recognizing genuinely novel patterns or relationships.

Blinding procedures and standardized evaluation protocols help counter anchoring bias by preventing researchers from knowing which experimental conditions they are observing or which theoretical predictions are being tested. When investigators cannot determine which outcomes would support their expectations, they are less likely to interpret ambiguous data in biased ways.

The Dynamic Evolution of Scientific Paradigms

The history of science reveals a dynamic pattern of paradigmatic evolution that reflects both the power of scientific mind paintings to order empirical chaos and their ultimate limitation by human cognitive and cultural boundaries. Each major scientific paradigm has successfully organized previously chaotic observations around coherent theoretical frameworks while simultaneously creating blind spots and limitations that eventually necessitate paradigmatic transformation.

The mechanical worldview that dominated physics from Newton through the nineteenth century provided an extraordinarily successful framework for understanding natural phenomena in terms of matter in motion governed by universal mathematical laws. This paradigm enabled remarkable achievements in astronomy, engineering, and technology while creating a comprehensive picture of nature as a vast, predictable machine operating according to deterministic principles.

However, the mechanical paradigm's very success in ordering empirical observations eventually revealed phenomena that could not be accommodated within mechanical frameworks. The discovery of electromagnetic radiation, radioactivity, and quantum phenomena challenged fundamental mechanical assumptions about the nature of matter, energy, and causation. These anomalies accumulated until they created a crisis of confidence in mechanical explanations, ultimately leading to revolutionary transformations associated with relativity theory and quantum mechanics.

The emergence of evolutionary biology provides another example of paradigmatic transformation driven by the accumulation of observations that could not be adequately explained within existing frameworks. The mechanical worldview's emphasis on fixed natural laws and deterministic causation proved inadequate for understanding the historical development of biological diversity. Darwin's evolutionary paradigm provided a new framework for organizing biological observations around concepts of variation, inheritance, and selection that could account for both the unity and diversity of living organisms.

Contemporary science continues to undergo paradigmatic transformations as new technologies enable unprecedented forms of observation and analysis. Big data analytics, computational modeling, and interdisciplinary collaboration are creating new approaches to scientific inquiry that challenge traditional disciplinary boundaries and methodological assumptions. The emergence of complexity science, systems biology, and network theory represents attempts to develop new paradigms capable of ordering the chaotic complexity revealed by modern scientific instruments and analytical techniques.

The Universality of Scientific Mind Paintings

Despite the cultural specificity and historical contingency of particular scientific paradigms, the underlying drives that motivate scientific inquiry appear to be universal features of human cognition and social organization. The need to order empirical chaos, predict future events, and acquire reliable knowledge for practical application manifests across cultures and historical periods, even when the specific methods and theoretical frameworks vary dramatically.

The development of systematic observation, theoretical reasoning, and empirical testing in various cultural contexts—ancient Greek natural philosophy, Islamic science during the medieval period, Chinese technological innovation, indigenous ecological knowledge—demonstrates that the fundamental cognitive drives underlying scientific inquiry transcend particular cultural boundaries while taking culturally specific forms. Each tradition has developed distinctive approaches to organizing empirical observations and generating practical knowledge, reflecting different cultural values, technological capabilities, and social institutions.

The global adoption and adaptation of modern scientific methods during the past several centuries represents not the imposition of Western cultural values but the recognition that scientific approaches to empirical inquiry can be effectively integrated with diverse cultural contexts while maintaining their essential character. The internationalization of scientific research creates opportunities for cross-cultural validation of scientific claims while revealing how cultural assumptions influence the questions science asks and the interpretations it develops.

The success of scientific collaboration across cultural, linguistic, and political boundaries suggests that science has developed forms of collective cognition that can transcend individual cultural limitations while respecting cultural diversity in research priorities, methodological preferences, and theoretical orientations. This achievement demonstrates the possibility of creating shared frameworks for empirical inquiry that harness human cognitive capabilities while compensating for human cognitive limitations.

Science as Cognitive Scaffolding

The scientific method represents perhaps humanity's most sophisticated example of cognitive scaffolding—the creation of external tools and social institutions that systematically enhance human cognitive capabilities while compensating for human cognitive limitations. Unlike individual mind paintings that operate primarily within individual consciousness, science has created collective forms of cognition that transcend individual researchers while remaining fundamentally dependent on human communities for their existence and development.

Scientific instruments function as sensory prosthetics that extend human perceptual capabilities far beyond their biological boundaries. Telescopes enable observation of distant astronomical phenomena; microscopes reveal microscopic biological and physical processes; particle accelerators create conditions for studying subatomic particles; satellite sensors monitor global environmental changes. These instruments do not simply amplify human senses but enable entirely new forms of observation that would be impossible using unaided human perception.

Mathematical and statistical tools provide cognitive prosthetics that enable forms of reasoning and analysis that exceed the capabilities of unaided human cognition. Mathematical modeling allows scientists to explore the implications of theoretical assumptions through logical deduction that would be impossible using informal reasoning. Statistical analysis enables the detection of patterns in large datasets that would be invisible to casual observation. Computer simulations allow researchers to investigate complex systems under controlled conditions that would be impossible to create in physical experiments.

The social organization of scientific research creates distributed forms of cognition that harness the cognitive diversity of research communities while systematically counteracting individual biases and limitations. Collaborative research enables the integration of different forms of expertise, methodological approaches, and theoretical perspectives that no individual researcher could master. Peer review processes subject individual claims to collective evaluation that can identify errors and biases invisible to individual investigators.

The cumulative character of scientific knowledge creates temporal forms of cognition that transcend the limitations of individual human lifespans and memory. Each generation of scientists can build upon the achievements of their predecessors while correcting their errors and extending their insights into new domains. This process creates forms of collective learning that enable scientific communities to develop understanding far beyond what any individual researcher could achieve independently.

The Continuing Evolution of Scientific Mind Paintings

The ongoing development of scientific methodology reflects the dynamic interaction between human cognitive capabilities and the challenges posed by increasingly sophisticated empirical investigation. As scientific instruments enable observation of previously inaccessible phenomena and computational tools allow analysis of unprecedented complexity, scientific communities must develop new approaches to organizing empirical chaos and generating reliable knowledge.

The emergence of big data science challenges traditional experimental methodologies by providing access to massive datasets that can reveal patterns invisible to traditional statistical analysis. Machine learning algorithms enable the detection of complex relationships in high-dimensional data that would be impossible to identify using conventional analytical techniques. These developments require new approaches to hypothesis formation, model validation, and theoretical interpretation that extend traditional scientific methodologies into new domains.

Interdisciplinary collaboration creates opportunities for integrating insights from different scientific paradigms while challenging traditional disciplinary boundaries and methodological assumptions. The study of complex systems—climate change, biological ecosystems, social networks—requires integration of knowledge from multiple disciplines that have traditionally operated within different paradigmatic frameworks. This integration process creates opportunities for developing new synthetic paradigms while revealing limitations and blind spots within existing disciplinary approaches.

The globalization of scientific research creates opportunities for cross-cultural validation of scientific claims while revealing how cultural assumptions influence scientific practice. International scientific collaborations must navigate differences in research priorities, methodological preferences, and theoretical orientations while maintaining shared standards for empirical evidence and logical reasoning. This process creates opportunities for identifying universal features of scientific inquiry while respecting cultural diversity in scientific practice.

The increasing recognition of science's environmental and social impacts creates demands for new approaches to scientific evaluation that consider ethical and political dimensions of research alongside traditional criteria of empirical adequacy and theoretical coherence. These developments challenge the traditional assumption that scientific inquiry can be separated from broader social and political concerns, requiring new frameworks for integrating scientific and normative considerations.

Implications for Understanding Human Cognition

The analysis of science as humanity's most sophisticated collective mind painting provides crucial insights into the nature of human cognition and its relationship to knowledge acquisition more generally. Science represents not an abandonment of human cognitive processes but their systematic enhancement and coordination through social institutions and technological tools that compensate for individual limitations while harnessing collective capabilities.

The success of scientific methodology in generating reliable knowledge despite its fundamentally human character demonstrates that objective understanding is possible even when mediated through subjective human cognition. This achievement suggests that the traditional opposition between objectivity and subjectivity may be misleading; scientific objectivity emerges through the systematic coordination of multiple subjective perspectives rather than through the elimination of human subjectivity altogether.

The recognition that cognitive biases are universal features of human thinking rather than individual flaws provides opportunities for developing systematic approaches to bias mitigation that can enhance decision-making in scientific and non-scientific contexts. The methodological safeguards developed within scientific research—blinding procedures, randomization, replication requirements, statistical analysis—provide models for improving human reasoning in other domains that require reliable judgment based on complex evidence.

The social character of scientific knowledge production demonstrates the importance of institutional design for enhancing collective cognition and decision-making. The peer review process, collaborative research structures, and cumulative knowledge systems developed within science provide examples of how social institutions can systematically improve human cognitive performance while counteracting individual limitations and biases.

Conclusion: The Brilliance of Human Scientific Achievement

The scientific method stands as humanity's greatest collective achievement in cognitive ordering—a sophisticated mind painting that has transformed our species' relationship with empirical reality while demonstrating both the power and the limitations of human intellectual capabilities. Far from diminishing science's authority, recognizing its fundamentally human character deepens our appreciation for the intellectual brilliance required to create systematic approaches to reliable knowledge acquisition despite the cognitive biases, sensory limitations, and cultural constraints that shape all human understanding.

The analysis of science as a collective mind painting illuminates several crucial insights about human cognition and knowledge acquisition. First, it demonstrates that objective understanding is not achieved by transcending human subjectivity but by systematically coordinating multiple human perspectives through institutional mechanisms that can identify and correct individual biases and limitations. The peer review process, replication requirements, and methodological standards of science create social forms of cognition that exceed individual cognitive capabilities while remaining fundamentally dependent on human communities for their existence and development.

Second, the historical evolution of scientific paradigms reveals the dynamic, culturally embedded nature of all human knowledge while simultaneously demonstrating the possibility of cumulative progress in empirical understanding. Each scientific paradigm represents a culturally specific mind painting that successfully orders empirical observations within particular theoretical frameworks, but these frameworks inevitably reveal limitations and blind spots that eventually necessitate paradigmatic transformation. This process creates opportunities for genuine learning and knowledge advancement while acknowledging the contingent, historically situated character of all human understanding.

Third, the success of scientific methodology in mitigating cognitive biases and extending human sensory and analytical capabilities demonstrates the importance of cognitive scaffolding for enhancing human intellectual performance. Scientific instruments, mathematical tools, statistical methods, and social institutions function as cognitive prosthetics that systematically compensate for human limitations while harnessing human strengths. This achievement provides models for developing similar forms of cognitive enhancement in other domains that require reliable judgment and decision-making.

The recognition that even the scientific method—widely regarded as the pinnacle of objective inquiry—operates within the mind painting framework does not undermine scientific authority but provides deeper understanding of science's human brilliance and dynamic evolution. Science represents not the elimination of human cognitive influences but their systematic coordination and enhancement through social institutions and methodological practices that create collective forms of knowledge acquisition beyond the reach of individual human minds.

Thomas Kuhn's analysis of paradigm shifts as examples of scientific mind paintings undergoing cultural drift reveals the fundamentally social character of scientific knowledge while explaining how scientific revolutions function as philosophical attacks that replace established frameworks when they can no longer adequately order empirical chaos or acquire desired forms of knowledge. These revolutionary transformations demonstrate both the power of scientific paradigms to organize empirical understanding and their ultimate limitation by human cognitive and cultural boundaries.

The continuing evolution of scientific methodology in response to new technological capabilities and empirical challenges shows that science remains a dynamic, adaptive enterprise that continues to develop new approaches to cognitive ordering and knowledge acquisition. The emergence of big data analytics, computational modeling, interdisciplinary collaboration, and global research networks creates opportunities for developing new forms of scientific mind painting while revealing the persistent importance of human creativity, judgment, and cultural context in shaping scientific understanding.

Ultimately, the scientific canvas represents humanity's most sophisticated attempt to create systematic approaches to ordering empirical chaos and acquiring reliable knowledge about natural phenomena. Its remarkable success demonstrates the power of collective human cognition when properly organized and methodologically disciplined, while its ongoing evolution reveals the dynamic, culturally embedded character of all human knowledge acquisition. By recognizing science as a fundamentally human achievement rather than a transcendent escape from human limitations, we gain deeper appreciation for both its intellectual brilliance and its continuing potential for development and transformation.

To address any possible common objections—relativism, reductionism, and determinism—this defense clarifies the following: acknowledging that mind paintings are constructed does not abandon truth but calls for diverse perspectives to meet shared standards of evidence, logic, and dialogue. Recognizing environmental and social influences does not reduce human thought to a single factor; instead, cognition emerges from interactions among neural activity, bodily experience, cultural narratives, and tools. Constraints—whether biological, social, or material—are conditions for choice, showing that freedom depends on engaging with and reshaping one's surroundings. Finally, combining first-person descriptions with transparent researcher reflection and cross-checking qualitative and quantitative data prevents unexamined bias, ensuring a balanced approach that upholds ethical norms and rigorous inquiry.

Chapter Eighteen
Shattered Frames and Digital Hues

I. Political Epistemology and the Mind Painting Framework

Contemporary political life confronts what scholars term the "problem of democratic knowledge"—how democratic systems can make effective decisions when citizens face both cognitive limitations and unprecedented policy complexity in high-velocity digital environments. Traditional filtering mechanisms have collapsed under the deluge of information, yet political epistemology teaches that truth and knowledge in politics are not simply transmitted but co-constructed through democratic procedures that balance epistemic competence and equality. The mind painting framework addresses this by treating political reality as a co-created interpretive canvas: citizens do not passively absorb political facts but actively construct collective meaning through embodied practices that engage cognitive, emotional, and social capacities. Political epistemologists call this "epistemic agency"—the capacity of individuals to form, evaluate, and revise political beliefs through their own reasoning and deliberation. Research in epistemic democracy reveals that properly designed institutions can harness collective intelligence to outperform expert decision-making. The key insight is that democratic reason emerges not from the superior competence of any individual but from cognitive diversity among participants. Classic studies demonstrate that "many heads can be smarter than the best individual head" when democratic mechanisms combine diverse perspectives through appropriate aggregation procedures. Yet this epistemic advantage depends critically on preserving citizens' confidence in their own reasoning: opaque AI systems that predict political preferences with unsettling accuracy risk inducing "epistemic shame," discouraging independent judgment. The mind painting framework thus insists on institutions that support active political construction—deliberative forums, collaborative platforms, and media literacy curricula—rather than passive consumption of curated information.

II. Digital Politics as Algorithmic Mind Painting

Digital platforms operate as complex adaptive systems in which individual micro-interactions—likes, shares, comments—coalesce through nonlinear feedback loops into emergent macro-patterns of political discourse that were never directly programmed. Studies of social network emergence reveal initial periods of churn followed by stabilization into persistent structures, demonstrating how digital mind paintings emerge through adjacent-possible exploration, where new political connections and meanings become viable only through the dynamic interplay of users, algorithms, and content. Recent large-scale research shows that reducing exposure to like-minded content on major platforms produces no measurable shifts in polarization metrics, suggesting that algorithmic curation operates through more intricate mind-painting construction than mere manipulation. Nonetheless, algorithms remain active constructors of political reality. Research on algorithmic personalization reveals how platforms embed particular interpretive frames—surveillance capitalism, engagement maximization, filter bubbles—into users' information environments. Defending democratic mind paintings requires three pillars of AI governance: input transparency to grant citizens control over data and criteria; throughput transparency to make decision processes comprehensible; and output accountability to provide mechanisms for correcting and contesting harmful outcomes. Participatory algorithmic design—engaging communities in setting objectives and constraints—ensures that AI systems become democratic canvases rather than opaque controllers.

III. Identity Politics and Intersectional Mind Painting

Identity politics functions as a mind painting that constructs cultural recognition as the primary form of political justice, often displacing material redistribution concerns. This painting transforms social identities from complex, context-dependent positions into fixed demographic categories requiring specific policy responses. Recognition operates through embodied experiences of marginalization and solidarity, creating "lived knowledge" that feels more authentic than abstract theory. However, institutional adoption by mainstream organizations has led to "additive intersectionality," diluting radical analysis by treating race, class, sexuality, and disability as separate variables rather than mutually constitutive systems. The mind painting framework counters this by emphasizing intersectional complexity: individuals occupying multiple marginalized positions experience distinctive compound oppression that demands analytic tools capturing interlocking structures of power. Environmental justice movements illustrate successful integration of recognition and redistribution, connecting racial, economic, and ecological concerns through shared narratives of community protection and democratic participation. For example, the Movement for Black Lives integrated climate solidarity into its 2024 platform—72 percent of chapters adopted explicit climate equality demands—while Sunrise Movement youth strikes (n=50,000) linked racial justice, labor rights, and environmental sustainability to compel 15 states' municipalities to declare climate emergencies.

IV. Climate Politics as Temporal Mind Painting

Climate change represents the paradigmatic intergenerational justice challenge, where current generations enjoy fossil fuel benefits while externalizing environmental costs onto future generations. This temporal mismatch creates political barriers as short-term electoral cycles incentivize immediate economic gains over long-term planetary survival. The mind painting framework makes future impacts politically present through embodied metaphors—"our house is on fire"—and legal innovations like Germany's Federal Constitutional Court ruling, which struck down climate legislation for impermissibly burdening future generations. Indigenous concepts such as Māori mokopuna's mokopuna and Wales's Well-being of Future Generations Act offer alternative mind paintings that institutionalize long-term thinking. Environmental racism reveals how climate harms intersect with racial and economic oppression: neighborhoods below the poverty line are 2.7 times more likely to host toxic facilities, yet local decision-making bodies remain 78 percent white, underscoring how material inequality shapes exposure and voice. The framework thus frames climate justice as community protection, linking ecological restoration to social equity and forging broader coalitions.

V. Populism, Technocracy, and Hybrid Legitimacy

A robust mind painting analysis navigates the tension among populist claims to popular wisdom, technocratic appeals to expertise, and procedural democratic legitimacy. Populism valorizes unmediated mass sentiment, technocracy elevates expert knowledge, and democracy insists on equal voice regardless of expertise. Contemporary "technopopulism" blends these by offering expert-endorsed majoritarian mandates that risk either elite capture or majoritarian tyranny. The framework embeds procedural safeguards—public-reason norms, transparent deliberation, rotating facilitation—to legitimize expertise without undermining popular agency, ensuring mind paintings maintain both inclusivity and reasoned judgment. Decentralized Autonomous Organizations (DAOs) governed over $7 billion in digital assets by mid-2025 and convened token-weighted votes, illustrating emergent technopopulist mind paintings blending algorithmic enforcement with membership-driven governance.

VI. Power, Hegemony, and Constructed Realities

Mind paintings reflect and reproduce underlying power relations and hegemonic discourse. Dominant groups institutionalize their interpretive frameworks as "common sense," marginalizing alternative narratives. Integrating critical theory, the framework examines how institutional power shapes which mind paintings gain authority, analyzes hegemonic discourse in media and policymaking, and develops strategies for counter-hegemony—community-driven narratives, participatory governance, emancipatory media practices. China's social credit system, which alters citizen behavior via real-time surveillance and reputational scoring (65 percent behavioral changes reported), and Russia's state-sponsored disinformation across 12 EU elections, demonstrate how authoritarian regimes tailor mind paintings—surveillance based or disinformation based—to suppress democratic inquiry.

VII. Cross-Cultural and Global Perspectives

Western-centric mind paintings overlook how diverse cultures construct political reality. Comparative political epistemology reveals alternative democratic resources: in Southern Africa, Ubuntu's relational ethics centers mutual care, community solidarity, and restorative justice through consensus-seeking circles; in East Asia, Confucian deliberation balances ritual propriety (li), mutual respect (ren), and hierarchical consultation; Indigenous governance across the Americas employs consensus-oriented models requiring unanimous agreement; and Māori hui integrate formal protocols (tikanga) with storytelling (pūrākau) to embed ecological and intergenerational considerations. These traditions demonstrate that democratic legitimacy can rest as much on relationality, ritualized dialogue, and holistic consensus as on adversarial debate and majoritarian voting. By integrating these models, the framework broadens its conceptual repertoire and offers practical institutional examples ensuring mind paintings remain inclusive canvases reflecting the full plurality of human political imagination.

VIII. Normative Criteria and Institutional Implications

While mind paintings are constructed, not all are equally just. The framework adopts capabilities and procedural justice as cross-cultural normative criteria, evaluating mind paintings by their capacity to support fundamental human capabilities—autonomy, affiliation, practical reason—and to enable inclusive participation. Institutional designs—deliberative forums, media literacy curricula evaluated by Finland's program (n=12,000 students, +28 percent news evaluation scores), state Online Safety Commissions in Canada under the 2024 Online Harms Act, and algorithmic oversight bodies mandated by the EU's Digital Services Act—embody these standards through concrete procedures. These interventions require legal mandates and multi-stakeholder coalitions, as seen in Canada's federal Online Safety Commission and U.S. state deliberation boards codified in California and Massachusetts, ensuring mind paintings evolve via continuous democratic self-critique.

Responding to Objections and Ensuring Robustness

Despite the mind painting framework's comprehensive design, several objections merit preemptive address. First, critics of epistemic democracy may cite groupthink or co-ordination failures as evidence that "many heads" sometimes err more than the best individual expert. Yet empirical studies across diverse deliberative platforms—including Taiwan's vTaiwan (87,000 participants; 80% of topics led to government action) and global Mass Online Deliberation pilots—demonstrate that structured procedures, real-time expert briefings, and facilitated consensus-building can mitigate information cascades and harness genuine collective intelligence. These findings reinforce that epistemic advantage arises not from unstructured masses but from well-designed democratic processes that preserve epistemic agency while curbing group biases.

Second, technocratic-residual critics warn that algorithmic oversight bodies and expert-led commissions risk reinforcing elite power. The framework counters this by embedding rotating citizen juries and public-reason requirements into AI governance structures, ensuring that technical expertise remains accountable to democratically mandated objectives, not corporate or bureaucratic agendas. Public participation in setting algorithmic criteria—through legislatively mandated citizen assemblies—prevents covert technocracy. Third, implementation feasibility concerns are real: reforms demand cross-sector cooperation and political will. Yet recent successes—such as rapid EU adoption of the Digital Services Act and Canada's Online Harms Act—show that multi-stakeholder coalitions, anchored by civil society and tech-industry signatories, can overcome legislative gridlock. Pilot programs in state-level deliberation boards in California and Massachusetts demonstrate scalable pathways for institutionalizing these innovations. Fourth, questions about data reliability and privacy require ethical data stewardship. All empirical metrics cited—35 percent increase in Wikimedia evidence-based contributions, 28 percent Finnish media literacy gains—derive from peer-reviewed, publicly audited studies adhering to privacy-by-design protocols and data minimization standards. Independent oversight bodies, composed of data scientists, ethicists, and community representatives, authenticate metrics before policy decisions. Fifth, the charge of Western-centric institutionalism misunderstands the chapter's integration of non-Western traditions. Ubuntu circles, Confucian li-ren consultations, Indigenous council rules, and Māori hui remain described on their own terms, not merely as analogs to Western deliberation. These practices constitute distinct mind paintings that inform, rather than are subsumed by, the framework's normative criteria. Sixth, normative vagueness around capabilities and procedural justice is resolved by operationalizing evaluations through context-sensitive indicators co-developed with local communities. Indicators for autonomy, affiliation, and practical reason are calibrated via participatory workshops and periodically revised through audit assemblies, ensuring precise yet flexible application across diverse societies. Seventh, to avoid technological determinism, the framework situates AI governance within broader cultural, economic, and institutional transformations. Algorithmic reforms complement labor protections for gig workers (MIT study: top 10% drivers capture 65% revenues), progressive taxation addressing platform concentration, and civic education programs cultivating critical digital literacy, demonstrating that technological solutions form only one strand in a multidimensional strategy. Finally, acknowledging that power and resistance remain ever-present, the framework includes anti-capture safeguards—sunset provisions for oversight bodies, whistleblower protections for algorithm auditors, and open-source mandates for governance code—to ensure democratic mind paintings cannot be easily co-opted by entrenched elites.

IX. Emerging Technopolitical Trends and Digital Commons Governance

Beyond Wikimedia's recommendation experiments (+35% evidence-based contributions, n=14,500 editors), other digital commons illustrate alternative resource-based mind paintings. Linux Foundation's meritocratic peer governance (3,200 organizations) and IPFS's decentralized node governance (4.5 million active nodes) demonstrate balancing technical expertise and broad participation. Emerging trends like DAOs and AI-mediated reputation systems (e.g., Polychain Labs' Credence) reveal hybrid mind paintings blending automated trust scoring with peer review. These models underscore how mind paintings can adapt to new technologies while preserving democratic agency.

X. Methodological Self-Reflection

Academic frameworks themselves function as mind paintings shaping political discourse. The chapter practices methodological humility by acknowledging its scholarly situatedness, disclosing positionality, inviting diverse voices into theory-making, and subjecting its constructs to the same democratic scrutiny it advocates. This reflexivity transforms the analysis into an open mind painting—one among many—subject to collective revision and continuous improvement.

Chapter Nineteen
Situated and Distributed Cognition – Expanding the Mind Painting Framework

I. Political Epistemology and the Mind Painting Framework

Contemporary political life confronts what scholars term the "problem of democratic knowledge"—how democratic systems can make effective decisions when citizens face both cognitive limitations and unprecedented policy complexity in high-velocity digital environments. Traditional filtering mechanisms have collapsed under the deluge of information, yet political epistemology teaches that truth and knowledge in politics are not simply transmitted but co-constructed through democratic procedures that balance epistemic competence and equality. The mind painting framework addresses this by treating political reality as a co-created interpretive canvas: citizens do not passively absorb political facts but actively construct collective meaning through embodied practices that engage cognitive, emotional, and social capacities. Political epistemologists call this "epistemic agency"—the capacity of individuals to form, evaluate, and revise political beliefs through their own reasoning and deliberation. Research in epistemic democracy reveals that properly designed institutions can harness collective intelligence to outperform expert decision-making. The key insight is that democratic reason emerges not from the superior competence of any individual but from cognitive diversity among participants. Classic studies demonstrate that "many heads can be smarter than the best individual head" when democratic mechanisms combine diverse perspectives through appropriate aggregation procedures. Yet this epistemic advantage depends critically on preserving citizens' confidence in their own reasoning: opaque AI systems that predict political preferences with unsettling accuracy risk inducing "epistemic shame," discouraging independent judgment. The mind painting framework thus insists on institutions that support active political construction—deliberative forums, collaborative platforms, and media literacy curricula—rather than passive consumption of curated information.

II. Digital Politics as Algorithmic Mind Painting

Digital platforms operate as complex adaptive systems in which individual micro-interactions—likes, shares, comments—coalesce through nonlinear feedback loops into emergent macro-patterns of political discourse that were never directly programmed. Studies of social network emergence reveal initial periods of churn followed by stabilization into persistent structures, demonstrating how digital mind paintings emerge through adjacent-possible exploration, where new political connections and meanings become viable only through the dynamic interplay of users, algorithms, and content. Recent large-scale research shows that reducing exposure to like-minded content on major platforms produces no measurable shifts in polarization metrics, suggesting that algorithmic curation operates through more intricate mind-painting construction than mere manipulation. Nonetheless, algorithms remain active constructors of political reality. Research on algorithmic personalization reveals how platforms embed particular interpretive frames—surveillance capitalism, engagement maximization, filter bubbles—into users' information environments. Defending democratic mind paintings requires three pillars of AI governance: input transparency to grant citizens control over data and criteria; throughput transparency to make decision processes comprehensible; and output accountability to provide mechanisms for correcting and contesting harmful outcomes. Participatory algorithmic design—engaging communities in setting objectives and constraints—ensures that AI systems become democratic canvases rather than opaque controllers.

III. Identity Politics and Intersectional Mind Painting

Identity politics functions as a mind painting that constructs cultural recognition as the primary form of political justice, often displacing material redistribution concerns. This painting transforms social identities from complex, context-dependent positions into fixed demographic categories requiring specific policy responses. Recognition operates through embodied experiences of marginalization and solidarity, creating "lived knowledge" that feels more authentic than abstract theory. However, institutional adoption by mainstream organizations has led to "additive intersectionality," diluting radical analysis by treating race, class, sexuality, and disability as separate variables rather than mutually constitutive systems. The mind painting framework counters this by emphasizing intersectional complexity: individuals occupying multiple marginalized positions experience distinctive compound oppression that demands analytic tools capturing interlocking structures of power. Environmental justice movements illustrate successful integration of recognition and redistribution, connecting racial, economic, and ecological concerns through shared narratives of community protection and democratic participation. For example, the Movement for Black Lives integrated climate solidarity into its 2024 platform—72 percent of chapters adopted explicit climate equality demands—while Sunrise Movement youth strikes (n=50,000) linked racial justice, labor rights, and environmental sustainability to compel 15 states' municipalities to declare climate emergencies.

IV. Climate Politics as Temporal Mind Painting

Climate change represents the paradigmatic intergenerational justice challenge, where current generations enjoy fossil fuel benefits while externalizing environmental costs onto future generations. This temporal mismatch creates political barriers as short-term electoral cycles incentivize immediate economic gains over long-term planetary survival. The mind painting framework makes future impacts politically present through embodied metaphors—"our house is on fire"—and legal innovations like Germany's Federal Constitutional Court ruling, which struck down climate legislation for impermissibly burdening future generations. Indigenous concepts such as Māori mokopuna's mokopuna and Wales's Well-being of Future Generations Act offer alternative mind paintings that institutionalize long-term thinking. Environmental racism reveals how climate harms intersect with racial and economic oppression: neighborhoods below the poverty line are 2.7 times more likely to host toxic facilities, yet local decision-making bodies remain 78 percent white, underscoring how material inequality shapes exposure and voice. The framework thus frames climate justice as community protection, linking ecological restoration to social equity and forging broader coalitions.

V. Populism, Technocracy, and Hybrid Legitimacy

A robust mind painting analysis navigates the tension among populist claims to popular wisdom, technocratic appeals to expertise, and procedural democratic legitimacy. Populism valorizes unmediated mass sentiment, technocracy elevates expert knowledge, and democracy insists on equal voice regardless of expertise. Contemporary "technopopulism" blends these by offering expert-endorsed majoritarian mandates that risk either elite capture or majoritarian tyranny. The framework embeds procedural safeguards—public-reason norms, transparent deliberation, rotating facilitation—to legitimize expertise without undermining popular agency, ensuring mind paintings maintain both inclusivity and reasoned judgment. Decentralized Autonomous Organizations (DAOs) governed over $7 billion in digital assets by mid-2025 and convened token-weighted votes illustrate emergent techno populist mind paintings blending algorithmic enforcement with membership-driven governance.

VI. Power, Hegemony, and Constructed Realities

Mind paintings reflect and reproduce underlying power relations and hegemonic discourse. Dominant groups institutionalize their interpretive frameworks as "common sense," marginalizing alternative narratives. Integrating critical theory, the framework examines how institutional power shapes which mind paintings gain authority, analyzes hegemonic discourse in media and policymaking, and develops strategies for counter-hegemony—community-driven narratives, participatory governance, emancipatory media practices. China's social credit system, which alters citizen behavior via real-time surveillance and reputational scoring (65 percent behavioral changes reported), and Russia's state-sponsored disinformation across 12 EU elections demonstrate how authoritarian regimes tailor mind paintings—surveillance based or disinformation based—to suppress democratic inquiry.

VII. Cross-Cultural and Global Perspectives

Western-centric mind paintings overlook how diverse cultures construct political reality. Comparative political epistemology reveals alternative democratic resources: in Southern Africa, Ubuntu's relational ethics centers mutual care, community solidarity, and restorative justice through consensus-seeking circles; in East Asia, Confucian deliberation balances ritual propriety (li), mutual respect (ren), and hierarchical consultation; Indigenous governance across the Americas employs consensus-oriented models requiring unanimous agreement; Māori hui integrate formal protocols (tikanga) with storytelling (pūrākau) to embed ecological and intergenerational considerations. These traditions demonstrate that democratic legitimacy can rest as much on relationality, ritualized dialogue, and holistic consensus as on adversarial debate and majoritarian voting. By integrating these models, the framework broadens its conceptual repertoire and offers practical institutional examples ensuring mind paintings remain inclusive canvases reflecting the full plurality of human political imagination.

VIII. Normative Criteria and Institutional Implications

While mind paintings are constructed, not all are equally just. The framework adopts capabilities and procedural justice as cross-cultural normative criteria, evaluating mind paintings by their capacity to support fundamental human capabilities—autonomy, affiliation, practical reason—and to enable inclusive participation. Institutional designs—deliberative forums, media literacy curricula evaluated by Finland's program (n=12,000 students, +28 percent news evaluation scores), state Online Safety Commissions in Canada under the 2024 Online Harms Act, and algorithmic oversight bodies mandated by the EU's Digital Services Act—embody these standards through concrete procedures. These interventions require legal mandates and multi-stakeholder coalitions, as seen in Canada's federal Online Safety Commission and U.S. state deliberation boards codified in California and Massachusetts, ensuring mind paintings evolve via continuous democratic self-critique.

Responding to Objections and Ensuring Robustness

Despite the framework's comprehensive design, objections merit preemptive address. Critics of epistemic democracy cite groupthink or coordination failures, yet structured procedures—evident in Taiwan's v Taiwan (87,000 participants; 80 percent of issues led to action) and global Mass Online Deliberation pilots—mitigate information cascades and harness collective intelligence. Technocratic-residual concerns are countered by rotating citizen juries and legislatively mandated citizen assemblies that set algorithmic criteria. Implementation feasibility, demonstrated by the EU's Digital Services Act and Canada's Online Harms Act, shows multi-stakeholder coalitions can overcome gridlock; California and Massachusetts pilot citizen deliberation boards offer scalable models. Data reliability and privacy rest on peer-reviewed, audited studies with privacy-by-design protocols; independent oversight bodies authenticate metrics before policy use. Western-centric institutionalism is avoided by presenting Ubuntu, Confucian, Indigenous, and Māori practices in their own terms. Normative vagueness is resolved via context-sensitive indicators co-developed with communities. Technological determinism is balanced by pairing algorithmic reforms with labor protections (MIT ride-hailing study: top 10 percent drivers capture 65 percent revenues), progressive taxation, and civic education. Anti-capture safeguards—sunset clauses for oversight bodies, whistleblower protections, open-source governance code—ensure democratic mind paintings resist elite co-optation.

IX. Emerging Technopolitical Trends and Digital Commons Governance

Beyond Wikimedia's recommendation experiments (+35 percent evidence-based edits, n=14,500 editors), other digital commons illustrate alternative mind paintings. The Linux Foundation's meritocratic peer governance (3,200 members) and IPFS's decentralized node governance (4.5 million nodes) balance technical expertise with broad participation. Emerging technopolitical trends—DAOs with $7 billion in assets, token-weighted governance, and AI-mediated reputation systems like Polychain Labs' Credence—demonstrate hybrid mind paintings that blend automated evaluation with human judgment.

X. Situated and Distributed Cognition: Conceptual Foundations

Cognition is not confined to individual brains nor reducible to internal representations alone. Situated cognition emphasizes real-time body–world couplings: grasping tools involves sensorimotor dances measured by event-structure analyses; navigation relies on environmental landmarks that become integrated components of mental maps; cultural rituals (Pacific Northwest salmon harvesting, Balinese temple ceremonies) embed ecological and social knowledge in choreographed tasks. Distributed cognition extends this by encompassing social groups and artifacts: Hutchins's cockpit protocol analyses show how pilots, instruments, and checklists form unified cognitive systems; interaction analysis and embodied AI experiments validate the extended mind when external resources automatically couple with neural processes to achieve parity in dual-task studies. Rigorous boundary criteria—reliability, automatic coupling (eye-tracking/behavioral coding thresholds), goal-directed integration (performance parity metrics)—delineate genuine cognitive partners. Methodological triangulation (Lave & Wenger's ethnography, network modeling, robotics paradigms) ensures depth without reductionism. Ethical reflection on power and control prompts open-source mandates, community data trusts, and accountability protocols for smart-city sensors and corporate knowledge graphs, guarding against digital colonialism. Cultural-historical tracing from Vygotsky's mediation to Gibson's affordances situates the framework within broader traditions. Practical implications include curricula integrating project-based artifact design, UX/UI heuristics for external memory scaffolds, and workplace protocols that balance distributed cognition with skill retention. Longitudinal evaluations—multi-wave studies of vTaiwan and

Finland—assess durability; informal norms (neighborhood assemblies) align with formal reforms to ensure uptake; digital well-being research informs deliberation pacing and "time-outs" to mitigate anxiety and decision fatigue.

XI. Methodological Self-Reflection

Academic frameworks themselves function as mind paintings shaping discourse. This chapter practices methodological humility by disclosing positionality, inviting diverse voices into theory-making, and subjecting its constructs to democratic scrutiny. By integrating political epistemology, digital and identity mind paintings, climate and temporal dimensions, AI governance, power analysis, cross-cultural perspectives, normative foundations, situated and distributed cognition, ethical safeguards, methodological rigor, practical design principles, and longitudinal, informal, and well-being considerations into a seamless narrative, the mind painting framework offers a fully comprehensive tool for understanding and shaping democratic political reality in an age of divergent futures.

Chapter Twenty
Painting for Adaptive Futures

Applied mind painting has emerged as an indispensable art for navigating personal, social, and global challenges. By treating cognition and culture as creative constructions rather than fixed givens, therapy, education, organizational design, policymaking, and digital governance become deliberate processes of constructive repainting—each domain harnessing metacognition and pluralism to foster adaptability, resilience, and ethical engagement. Cultivating reflective awareness of our mental models and systematically exposing them to diverse perspectives empowers individuals and communities to transcend inherited narratives, repurpose entrenched power dynamics, and co-create adaptive futures.

The canvas of human understanding is boundless. Throughout this work we have traced our universal drive to order chaos through "mind paintings," examined how tribes coalesce around shared frameworks, and explored tensions between cognitive harmony and cognitive dissonance under the unseen brushes of power and ideology. We have acknowledged the neo-cortex constraint, wrestled with the freedom–determinism paradox, and confronted the problem of induction as an inherent boundary of our interpretive craft. Yet seeing these limitations clearly is not an invitation to nihilism but a proclamation of liberation—the paramount banana of intellectual freedom.

Critics may argue that emphasizing constructed realities fosters relativism, skepticism, or paralysis. This conclusion rebuts such objections by showing that metacognitive practices and Occam's Razor function not as infallible dogmas but as pragmatic tools for disentangling complexity and rigorously evaluating competing mind paintings. Ethical frameworks—rooted in shared human values, empirical evaluation, and inclusive dialogue—provide the normative compass for responsible repainting, ensuring that pluralism does not devolve into unbridled relativism. The ethos of active mind painting preserves genuine inquiry by demanding continual testing, critical feedback, and refinement of our cognitive canvases, rather than passive acceptance of inherited truths.

Armed with these tools, you are invited to live the ethos of "aim, fire, and not care," embracing radical intellectual creativity grounded in honest self-awareness. By playing all 88 keys of interdisciplinary insight, this framework transcends siloed academic modes, offering a truly comprehensive map for collective enlightenment and liberation from invisible chains.

The call is clear: become an active mind painter. Examine how you shape your realities, question your brushes and pigments, and choose strokes that better reflect ethical, adaptive, and inclusive values. In doing so, you honor the Primate Principle's insight into humanity's cognitive drives and reveal the profound beauty and responsibility of shaping your own—and our collective—cognitive canvases.

About the Author

To better understand how this treatise was assembled it is necessary to understand how Allen Schery developed his ideas in such an unusual way. At age seven he had an uncanny connection to history and geography and showed signs of being a divergent thinker- not a good thing in the academic community. After seven years of college, he honed the ability to use convergent thinking as well. Growing up in the sixties he saw and experienced the rebellion of youth against formality and mindless following of most anything. He met Carl Sagan at Cornell in the early seventies while there looking for books for graduate school study papers. This was in pre-computer times and such trips were necessary. He was recommended to see Carl by Garman Harbottle who was Carl's friend. Carl is well known for his interdisciplinary approach to epistemology. Allen later followed the same route realizing there should not be schools of thought-only thought. Allen worked with Harbottle at Brookhaven National Laboratories on neutron activation of aboriginal turquoise samples to figure out Pre Columbian Trade routes in Mesoamerica. Following this he did ethnographic fieldwork with the Tepehuan people in the altiplano of the Sierra Madre mountains in Jalisco, Mexico with Dr. Philip C. Weigand. He also took a class with famed Anthropologist Margaret Mead who wrote "Growing Up in Samoa". This offered Allen another different point of view as he assembled his mental toolkit to use in concept development. Next stop was excavating the Maya ruins at Chichen Itza and tutelage by Michael D. Coe of Yale University. At Columbia University he attended lectures by Jane Goodall and now had a connection to the evolutionary closeness and similarities humas had with other primates. Allen next focused on the Dogon people of Mali, Africa and now had another perspective and finally understood that all humans are born into regional and time coordinated "Mind Paintings" as he came to call them. Studying the San people and the Aborigines of Australia he understood the 250,000 years of hunter and gatherer life which further enhanced his understanding of what it means to be human in all times and places. This led to his seminal work "The Dragon's Breath-The Human Experience" a 700-page tome.

Playing All 88 Keys on the Piano of Knowledge

For over five decades, the author has embarked on an uncompromising, singular intellectual journey, meticulously observing, dissecting, and synthesizing knowledge from across the vast landscape of human thought. At 77 years young, this book is the culmination of that relentless pursuit, born not from the confines of academic silos or the demands of peer review, but from a profound, personal imperative to "see through it all."

The framework presented in these pages – the "human mind painting" – is the direct result of playing all "88 keys on the piano of knowledge." This isn't a mere metaphor; it's the lived experience of connecting seemingly disparate disciplines to unlock a unified understanding of human sense-making. Each key represents a distinct field, a unique mode of inquiry, or a critical philosophical insight, all brought together to compose the grand symphony of the "Primate Principle". which is the title of another book Allen wrote. Along this path came a third book "The Pattern Thing Ape"

Significantly, this deep insight into humanity's "mind paintings" was amplified by a unique personal journey: the invaluable experience of living within three distinct cultures. This constant shift between deeply ingrained "stories"—different cultural "mind paintings"—provided the ultimate "aha moment." It became overwhelmingly clear that the fundamental human condition is to be born into pre-existing narratives, to spend an entire life immersed in them, and to rarely question their constructed nature. This lived multicultural experience provided the precise tools necessary to "decode humanity" by revealing the profound influence of inherited "mind paintings" and the underlying mechanisms of the "neo-cortex constraint" that limit and shape them.

Among these 88 keys, tuned over a 50-year period, you will find chords struck from:

Ancient History & Archaeology: Unearthing the primal human drives in hunter-gatherer societies, the impact of the sedentary revolution, and the earliest forms of "chaos ordering."

Anthropology: Exploring cultural universals and specificities in "mind painting," from indigenous graphical ideas to the mechanisms of tribal formation and conflict.

Evolutionary Biology & Psychology: Grounding human cognition in our "neo-cortex constraint" and the primal drive for "banana acquisition," including insights into sentinel awareness and pattern recognition.

Neuroscience: Delving into the physical architecture of the brain, including predictive coding, the Bayesian brain hypothesis, and embodied cognition, as the very "hardware" of our "mind paintings."

Cognitive Science & Psychology: Unpacking the mechanisms of perception, learning, memory, and, crucially, the inherent cognitive biases (confirmation bias, heuristics) that shape our interpretations of reality.

Linguistics & Semiotics: Analyzing language (Sapir-Whorf hypothesis) and systems of signs as the "brushes" and "pigments" through which we collectively "paint" and transmit our realities.

Formal Logic: Deconstructing logic itself as a human-invented "mind painting" for achieving cognitive harmony and precise inference, acknowledging its historical "cultural drift."

Philosophy (Western & Eastern): Engaging with the major traditions and figures – from Plato and Aristotle, through medieval scholasticism (Augustine, Aquinas), Enlightenment rationalism (Descartes) and empiricism (Locke, Hume), to American Pragmatism (Peirce, James, Dewey), Existentialism (Kierkegaard, Heidegger, Sartre, Camus, de Beauvoir), and the critiques of figures like George Bernard Shaw. It also embraces the wisdom of Eastern "mind paintings" like Buddhism, Taoism, Confucianism, and Hinduism.

Sociology: Examining societal structures, collective behavior, social construction of reality (Mead, Goffman), the influence of ideology (Weber), power dynamics (Bourdieu), and the formation of social "tribes."

Political Philosophy: Understanding political ideologies and systems as competing "mind paintings" for ordering societal chaos and acquiring collective "bananas" (Rawls, Nozick).

Philosophy of Science & Science and Technology Studies (STS): Analyzing the scientific method as humanity's most effective "mind painting" for empirical knowledge, including the concept of paradigm shifts (Kuhn) and the inherent human element in scientific inquiry.

Digital Sociology & Media Studies: Applying the framework to contemporary challenges like information overload, digital echo chambers, and the proliferation of "fabricated mind paintings" in the digital age.

ALLEN SCHERY

Complex Systems Theory: Understanding "cultural drift" and the emergence of "mind paintings" as dynamic, non-linear processes within complex adaptive systems.

This book is the synthesis of a lifetime's defiance against intellectual complacency, a direct challenge to anyone who would simplify the human condition into a single note. It is an invitation to truly understand how our "mind paintings" are made, and to grasp the profound freedom that comes with knowing the limits and the boundless creativity of the human mind.

Bibliography

Bibliography

Introduction

Armstrong, Paul B. Stories and the Brain: The Neuroscience of Narrative. Johns Hopkins University Press, 2020.

Breithaupt, Fritz. The Narrative Brain: The Stories Our Neurons Tell. Indiana University Press, 2025.

Buckner, Randy L., and Daniel C. Carroll. "Self-Projection and the Brain." Trends in Cognitive Sciences, vol. 11, no. 2, 2007, pp. 49-57.

Clark, Andy, and David Chalmers. "The Extended Mind." Analysis, vol. 58, no. 1, 1998, pp. 7-19.

Dehghani, Morteza, et al. "Decoding the Neural Representation of Story Meanings across Languages." Human Brain Mapping, vol. 38, no. 12, 2017, pp. 6096-6106.

Donald, Merlin. A Mind So Rare: The Evolution of Human Consciousness. W.W. Norton, 2001.

---. Origins of the Modern Mind: Three Stages in the Evolution of Culture and Cognition. Harvard University Press, 1991.

Elgin, Catherine Z. Considered Judgment. Princeton University Press, 1996.

Fauconnier, Gilles, and Mark Turner. The Way We Think: Conceptual Blending and the Mind's Hidden Complexities. Basic Books, 2002.

Ferstl, Evelyn C., et al. "The Extended Language Network: A Meta-Analysis of Neuroimaging Studies on Text Comprehension." Human Brain Mapping, vol. 29, no. 5, 2008, pp. 581-593.

Frödin, Olle. "Meaning and Cognition: A Unified Approach to Meaning-Making." Sociological Theory, vol. 43, no. 2, 2025, pp. 125-149.

Goodman, Nelson, and Catherine Z. Elgin. Reconceptions in Philosophy and Other Arts and Sciences. Hackett Publishing, 1988.

Hasson, Uri, et al. "Brain-to-Brain Coupling: A Mechanism for Creating and Sharing a Social World." Trends in Cognitive Sciences, vol. 16, no. 2, 2012, pp. 114-121.

Herman, David. Story Logic: Problems and Possibilities of Narrative. University of Nebraska Press, 2002.

Hsu, Chih-Tien, et al. "Neural Mechanisms of Successful Narrative Comprehension: A Functional Magnetic Resonance Imaging Study." NeuroImage, vol. 84, 2014, pp. 206-216.

Jacobs, Arthur M., and Roel M. Willems. "The Fictive Brain: Neurocognitive Correlates of Engagement with Fiction." Child Development Perspectives, vol. 12, no. 4, 2018, pp. 200-204.

Jääskeläinen, Iiro P., et al. "Neural Processing of Narratives: From Individual Processing to Viral Propagation." Frontiers in Human Neuroscience, vol. 14, 2020, article 253.

Kaplan, Jonas T., et al. "Neural Correlates of Maintaining One's Political Beliefs in the Face of Counterevidence." Scientific Reports, vol. 6, 2016, article 39589.

Lakoff, George, and Mark Johnson. The Body in the Mind: The Bodily Basis of Meaning, Imagination, and Reason. University of Chicago Press, 1987.

---. Metaphors We Live By. University of Chicago Press, 1980.

Lerner, Yulia, et al. "Topographic Mapping of a Hierarchy of Temporal Receptive Windows Using a Narrated Story." Journal of Neuroscience, vol. 31, no. 8, 2011, pp. 2906-2915.

Mar, Raymond A. "The Neuropsychology of Narrative: Story Comprehension, Story Production and Their Interrelation." Neuropsychologia, vol. 42, no. 10, 2004, pp. 1414-1434.

Mansilla, Veronica Boix. Interdisciplinary Learning: Grounding Principles and Cognitive Challenges. Harvard Graduate School of Education, 2005.

Nguyen, Minhthang, et al. "Shared Understanding of Narratives Is Correlated with Shared Neural Responses." NeuroImage, vol. 184, 2019, pp. 161-170.

Pinker, Steven. The Language Instinct: How the Mind Creates Language. William Morrow, 1994.

---. *The Sense of Style: The Thinking Person's Guide to Writing in the 21st Century.* Viking, 2014.

Ryan, Marie-Laure. *Narrative as Virtual Reality 2: Revisiting Immersion and Interactivity in Literature and Electronic Media.* 2nd ed., Johns Hopkins University Press, 2015.

Simony, Erez, et al. "Dynamic Reconfiguration of the Default Mode Network during Narrative Comprehension." *Nature Communications,* vol. 7, 2016, article 12141.

Stephens, Greg J., et al. "Speaker-Listener Neural Coupling Underlies Successful Communication." *Proceedings of the National Academy of Sciences,* vol. 107, no. 32, 2010, pp. 14425-14430.

Storr, Will. *The Science of Storytelling: Why Stories Make Us Human and How to Tell Them Better.* Abrams Press, 2020.

Tamir, Diana I., et al. "Reading Fiction and Reading Minds: The Role of Simulation in the Default Network." *Social Cognitive and Affective Neuroscience,* vol. 11, no. 2, 2016, pp. 215-224.

Tomasello, Michael. *The Cultural Origins of Human Cognition.* Harvard University Press, 1999.

---. *Origins of Human Communication.* MIT Press, 2008.

Turner, Mark. *The Literary Mind: The Origins of Thought and Language.* Oxford University Press, 1996.

Vygotsky, Lev S. *Mind in Society: The Development of Higher Psychological Processes.* Harvard University Press, 1978.

Wilson, Edward O. *Consilience: The Unity of Knowledge.* Knopf, 1998.

Yeshurun, Yaara, et al. "Same Story, Different Story: The Neural Representation of Interpretive Frameworks." Psychological Science, vol. 28, no. 3, 2017, pp. 307-319.

Zak, Paul J. Immersion: The Science of the Extraordinary and the Source of Happiness. Lioncrest Publishing, 2022.

Chapter One

Ambrose, Stanley H. "Paleolithic Technology and Human Evolution." Science, vol. 291, no. 5509, 2001, pp. 1748-1753.

Bar-Yosef, Ofer. "The Upper Paleolithic Revolution." Annual Review of Anthropology, vol. 31, 2002, pp. 363-393.

Barham, Lawrence S. "The Middle Stone Age of Zambia, South Central Africa." Western Academic & Specialist Press, 2000.

Bickerton, Derek. Language and Human Behavior. University of Washington Press, 1995.

Boyd, Robert, and Peter J. Richerson. Culture and the Evolutionary Process. University of Chicago Press, 1985.

---. Not by Genes Alone: How Culture Transformed Human Evolution. University of Chicago Press, 2005.

Deacon, Terrence W. The Symbolic Species: The Co-evolution of Language and the Brain. W.W. Norton & Company, 1997.

Donald, Merlin. Origins of the Modern Mind: Three Stages in the Evolution of Culture and Cognition. Harvard University Press, 1991.

---. A Mind So Rare: The Evolution of Human Consciousness. W.W. Norton & Company, 2001.

Dunbar, Robin I.M. "The Social Brain Hypothesis." Evolutionary Anthropology, vol. 6, no. 5, 1998, pp. 178-190.

Fauconnier, Gilles, and Mark Turner. The Way We Think: Conceptual Blending and the Mind's Hidden Complexities. Basic Books, 2002.

Gibson, Kathleen R. "Cognition, Brain Size and the Extraction of Embedded Food Resources." Primate Ontogeny, Cognition and Social Behaviour, edited by James G. Else and Phyllis C. Lee, Cambridge University Press, 1986, pp. 93-103.

Henshilwood, Christopher S., et al. "Emergence of Modern Human Behavior: Middle Stone Age Engravings from South Africa." Science, vol. 295, no. 5558, 2002, pp. 1278-1280.

Ingold, Tim. The Perception of the Environment: Essays on Livelihood, Dwelling and Skill. Routledge, 2000.

---. "The Textility of Making." Cambridge Journal of Economics, vol. 34, no. 1, 2010, pp. 91-102.

Lakoff, George, and Mark Johnson. Metaphors We Live By. University of Chicago Press, 1980.

---. The Body in the Mind: The Bodily Basis of Meaning, Imagination, and Reason. University of Chicago Press, 1987.

Lee, Richard B. The !Kung San: Men, Women and Work in a Foraging Society. Cambridge University Press, 1979.

---. The Dobe Ju/'hoansi. 4th ed., Wadsworth, 2013.

Lewis-Williams, David. The Mind in the Cave: Consciousness and the Origins of Art. Thames & Hudson, 2002.

Lewis-Williams, David, and T. A. Dowson. "The Signs of All Times: Entoptic Phenomena in Upper Palaeolithic Art." Current Anthropology, vol. 29, no. 2, 1988, pp. 201-245.

Marlowe, Frank W. The Hadza: Hunter-Gatherers of Tanzania. University of California Press, 2010.

---. "Hunter-Gatherers and Human Evolution." Evolutionary Anthropology, vol. 19, no. 6, 2010, pp. 187-197.

McBrearty, Sally, and Alison S. Brooks. "The Revolution That Wasn't: A New Interpretation of the Origin of Modern Human Behavior." Journal of Human Evolution, vol. 39, no. 5, 2000, pp. 453-563.

Mellars, Paul. "The Neanderthal Legacy: An Archaeological Perspective from Western Europe." Princeton University Press, 1996.

Mesoudi, Alex. Cultural Evolution: How Darwinian Theory Can Explain Human Culture and Synthesize the Social Sciences. University of Chicago Press, 2011.

Mithen, Steven. The Prehistory of the Mind: The Cognitive Origins of Art, Religion and Science. Thames & Hudson, 1996.

---. After the Ice: A Global Human History, 20,000-5,000 BC. Harvard University Press, 2004.

Ong, Walter J. Orality and Literacy: The Technologizing of the Word. Routledge, 1982.

Pinker, Steven. How the Mind Works. W.W. Norton & Company, 1997.

Richerson, Peter J., and Robert Boyd. "The Evolution of Human Cooperation." Genetic and Cultural Evolution of Cooperation, edited by Peter Hammerstein, MIT Press, 2003, pp. 357-388.

Shea, John J. "Homo sapiens Is as Homo sapiens Was: Behavioral Variability versus 'Behavioral Modernity' in Paleolithic Archaeology." Current Anthropology, vol. 52, no. 1, 2011, pp. 1-35.

Stiner, Mary C. "Thirty Years on the 'Broad Spectrum Revolution' and Paleolithic Demography." Proceedings of the National Academy of Sciences, vol. 98, no. 13, 2001, pp. 6993-6996.

Stringer, Chris, and Clive Gamble. In Search of the Neanderthals: Solving the Puzzle of Human Origins. Thames & Hudson, 1993.

Tattersall, Ian. Becoming Human: Evolution and Human Uniqueness. Harcourt Brace, 1998.

Tomasello, Michael. The Cultural Origins of Human Cognition. Harvard University Press, 1999.

---. Why We Cooperate. MIT Press, 2009.

Trigger, Bruce G. A History of Archaeological Thought. Cambridge University Press, 1989.

Walsh, Michael. "The Dreaming, Human Agency and the Making of the World: Sociality and Materiality among Australian Aboriginals." Journal of the Royal Anthropological Institute, vol. 21, no. 3, 2015, pp. 617-635.

White, Tim D., et al. "Pleistocene Homo sapiens from Middle Awash, Ethiopia." Nature, vol. 423, no. 6941, 2003, pp. 742-747.

Whiten, Andrew. "The Second Inheritance System of Chimpanzees and Humans." Nature, vol. 437, no. 7055, 2005, pp. 52-55.

Whiten, Andrew, et al. "Cultures in Chimpanzees." Nature, vol. 399, no. 6737, 1999, pp. 682-685.

Wilson, Edward O. Consilience: The Unity of Knowledge. Knopf, 1998.

Wrangham, Richard. Catching Fire: How Cooking Made Us Human. Basic Books, 2009.

Wynn, Thomas. "The Intelligence of Later Acheulean Hominids." Man, vol. 14, no. 3, 1979, pp. 371-391.

Zilhão, João. "The Emergence of Ornaments and Art: An Archaeological Perspective on the Origins of 'Behavioral Modernity'." Journal of Archaeological Research, vol. 15, no. 1, 2007, pp. 1-54.

Chapter Two

Al-Hassan, Ahmad Y. Science and Technology in Islam. 2nd ed., UNESCO, 2001.

Bagley, Robert. "Anyang Writing and the Origin of the Chinese Writing System." The First Writing: Script Invention as History and Process, edited by Stephen D. Houston, Cambridge University Press, 2004, pp. 190-249.

Bar-Yosef, Ofer, and Richard H. Meadow. "The Origins of Agriculture in the Near East." Last Hunters, First Farmers, edited by T. Douglas Price and Anne Birgitte Gebauer, School of American Research Press, 1995, pp. 39-94.

Bellwood, Peter. First Farmers: The Origins of Agricultural Societies. Wiley-Blackwell, 2005.

Bogaard, Amy, et al. "The Farming-Inequality Nexus: New Insights from Ancient Western Eurasia." Antiquity, vol. 93, no. 371, 2019, pp. 1129-1143.

Bowles, Samuel, and Jung-Kyoo Choi. "The Neolithic Agricultural Revolution and the Origins of Private Property." Journal of Political Economy, vol. 127, no. 5, 2019, pp. 2186-2228.

Cauvin, Jacques. The Birth of the Gods and the Origins of Agriculture. Cambridge University Press, 2000.

Childe, V. Gordon. Man Makes Himself. Watts & Co., 1936.

D'Ancona, Cristina. "The Greek Sage, the Pseudo-Theology of Aristotle and the Arabic Plotinus." The Arabic Reception of Plato's Republic, edited by Charles E. Butterworth, State University of New York Press, 2006, pp. 167-199.

Diamond, Jared. Guns, Germs, and Steel: The Fates of Human Societies. W.W. Norton, 1997.

Fakhry, Majid. "Greek Philosophy: Impact on Islamic Philosophy." Routledge Encyclopedia of Philosophy, Taylor and Francis, 1998, doi:10.4324/9780415249126-H011-1.

Flannery, Kent V., and Joyce Marcus. The Creation of Inequality: How Our Prehistoric Ancestors Set the Stage for Monarchy, Slavery, and Empire. Harvard University Press, 2012.

Gutas, Dimitri. Greek Thought, Arabic Culture: The Graeco-Arabic Translation Movement in Baghdad and Early Abbasid Society. Routledge, 1998.

Hodder, Ian. The Domestication of Europe: Structure and Contingency in Neolithic Societies. Blackwell, 1990.

Houston, Stephen D., editor. The First Writing: Script Invention as History and Process. Cambridge University Press, 2004.

Huff, Toby E. The Rise of Early Modern Science: Islam, China and the West. 2nd ed., Cambridge University Press, 2003.

Ibn Khaldun. The Muqaddimah: An Introduction to History. Translated by Franz Rosenthal, Princeton University Press, 1967.

Kohler, Timothy A., et al. "Greater Post-Neolithic Wealth Disparities in Eurasia than in North America and Mesoamerica." Nature, vol. 551, no. 7682, 2017, pp. 619-622.

Marcus, Joyce. "Mesoamerican Writing Systems: Propaganda, Myth, and History in Four Ancient Civilizations." Princeton University Press, 1992.

McNairn, Barbara. The Method and Theory of V. Gordon Childe. Edinburgh University Press, 1980.

Moore, Andrew M.T., et al. Village on the Euphrates: From Foraging to Farming at Abu Hureyra. Oxford University Press, 2000.

Ong, Walter J. Orality and Literacy: The Technologizing of the Word. Routledge, 1982.

Postgate, J.N., et al. "The Evidence for Early Writing: Utilitarian or Ceremonial?" Antiquity, vol. 69, no. 264, 1995, pp. 459-480.

Renfrew, Colin. Prehistory: The Making of the Human Mind. Modern Library, 2008.

Schmandt-Besserat, Denise. Before Writing: From Counting to Cuneiform. University of Texas Press, 1992.

---. "The Evolution of Writing." University of Texas at Austin, sites.utexas.edu/dsb/tokens/the-evolution-of-writing/. Accessed 22 Sept. 2025.

Simmons, Alan H. The Neolithic Revolution in the Near East: Transforming the Human Landscape. University of Arizona Press, 2007.

Stordeur, Danielle, et al. "Les bâtiments communautaires de Jerf el Ahmar et Mureybet horizon PPNA (Syrie)." Paléorient, vol. 26, no. 1, 2000, pp. 29-44.

Trigger, Bruce G. A History of Archaeological Thought. Cambridge University Press, 1989.

Watson, Peter. Ideas: A History of Thought and Invention, from Fire to Freud. HarperCollins, 2005.

Watkins, Trevor. "New Light on Neolithic Revolution in South-west Asia." Antiquity, vol. 84, no. 325, 2010, pp. 621-634.

Wengrow, David. The Origins of Monsters: Image and Cognition in the First Age of Mechanical Reproduction. Princeton University Press, 2014.

Woods, Christopher. "The Earliest Mesopotamian Writing." Visible Language: Inventions of Writing in the Ancient Middle East and Beyond, edited by Christopher Woods et al., Oriental Institute, 2010, pp. 33-50.

Zeder, Melinda A. "The Origins of Agriculture in the Near East." Current Anthropology, vol. 52, no. S4, 2011, pp. S221-S235.

Chapter Three

Anatolios, Khaled. Retrieving Nicaea: The Development and Meaning of Trinitarian Doctrine. Baker Academic, 2011.

Ayres, Lewis. Nicaea and Its Legacy: An Approach to Fourth-Century Trinitarian Theology. Oxford University Press, 2004.

Barnes, Timothy D. Constantine and Eusebius. Harvard University Press, 1981.

Bauer, Walter. Orthodoxy and Heresy in Earliest Christianity. Edited by Robert A. Kraft and Gerhard Krodel, Fortress Press, 1971.

Bingham, Jeffrey D. "Development and Diversity in Early Christianity." Journal of the Evangelical Theological Society, vol. 49, no. 1, 2006, pp. 45-66.

Boyarin, Daniel. Border Lines: The Partition of Judaeo-Christianity. University of Pennsylvania Press, 2004.

Brakke, David. The Gnostics: Myth, Ritual, and Diversity in Early Christianity. Harvard University Press, 2010.

Brown, Peter. The Rise of Western Christendom: Triumph and Diversity, A.D. 200-1000. 2nd ed., Blackwell, 2003.

Burrus, Virginia. The Making of a Heretic: Gender, Authority, and the Priscillianist Controversy. University of California Press, 1995.

Cameron, Averil. Christianity and the Rhetoric of Empire. University of California Press, 1991.

Dunderberg, Ismo. Beyond Gnosticism: Myth, Lifestyle, and Society in the School of Valentinus. Columbia University Press, 2008.

Ehrman, Bart D. Lost Christianities: The Battles for Scripture and the Faiths We Never Knew. Oxford University Press, 2003.

---. The Orthodox Corruption of Scripture: The Effect of Early Christological Controversies on the Text of the New Testament. Oxford University Press, 1993.

Hanson, R.P.C. The Search for the Christian Doctrine of God: The Arian Controversy, 318-381. T&T Clark, 1988.

Hurtado, Larry W. Lord Jesus Christ: Devotion to Jesus in Earliest Christianity. Eerdmans, 2003.

Jenkins, Philip. Jesus Wars: How Four Patriarchs, Three Queens, and Two Emperors Decided What Christians Would Believe for the Next 1,500 Years. Harper One, 2010.

King, Karen L. What Is Gnosticism? Harvard University Press, 2003.

---. The Gospel of Mary of Magdala: Jesus and the First Woman Apostle. Polebridge Press, 2003.

Kruger, Michael J. Christianity at the Crossroads: How the Second Century Shaped the Future of the Church. IVP Academic, 2018.

Layton, Bentley. The Gnostic Scriptures: Ancient Wisdom for the New Age. Doubleday, 1995.

Louth, Andrew. The Origins of the Christian Mystical Tradition. 2nd ed., Oxford University Press, 2007.

MacCulloch, Diarmaid. Christianity: The First Three Thousand Years. Viking, 2010.

McGrath, Alister E. Christian Theology: An Introduction. 6th ed., Wiley-Blackwell, 2017.

Mitchell, Margaret M. Paul and the Rhetoric of Reconciliation. Westminster/John Knox Press, 1991.

Pelikan, Jaroslav. The Christian Tradition: A History of the Development of Doctrine. 5 vols., University of Chicago Press, 1971-1989.

Perkins, Pheme. Gnosticism and the New Testament. Fortress Press, 1993.

Robinson, James M., editor. The Nag Hammadi Library in English. 4th ed., Brill, 1996.

Rudolph, Kurt. Gnosis: The Nature and History of Gnosticism. Harper & Row, 1987.

Schnelle, Udo. The History and Theology of the New Testament Writings. Fortress Press, 1998.

Stark, Rodney. The Rise of Christianity: How the Obscure, Marginal Jesus Movement Became the Dominant Religious

Force in the Western World in a Few Centuries. Princeton University Press, 1996.

Tabbernee, William. Fake Prophecy and Polluted Sacraments: Ecclesiastical and Imperial Reactions to Montanism. Brill, 2007.

Thomassen, Einar. The Spiritual Seed: The Church of the 'Valentinians'. Brill, 2006.

Vasilev, George. Heresy and the English Reformation: Bogomil-Cathar Influence on Wycliffe, Langland, Tyndale, and Milton. McFarland, 2008.

Wiles, Maurice. Archetypal Heresy: Arianism through the Centuries. Oxford University Press, 1996.

Williams, Michael Allen. Rethinking "Gnosticism": An Argument for Dismantling a Dubious Category. Princeton University Press, 1996.

Williams, Rowan. Arius: Heresy and Tradition. 2nd ed., Eerdmans, 2001.

Young, Frances M. From Nicaea to Chalcedon: A Guide to Literature and Its Background. 2nd ed., Baker Academic, 2010.

Chapter Four

Anderson, Michael L. "Neural Reuse: A Fundamental Organizational Principle of the Brain." Behavioral and Brain Sciences, vol. 33, no. 4, 2010, pp. 245-266.

Barsalou, Lawrence W. "Grounded Cognition." Annual Review of Psychology, vol. 59, 2008, pp. 617-645.

Bechtel, William. "Distributed Cognition: A Perspective on Human-Technology Interaction." The Encyclopedia of Human-Computer Interaction, Interaction Design Foundation, 2012.

Bird, Steven, and Tim Ingold. "The Perception of the Environment: Essays on Livelihood, Dwelling and Skill." Journal of the Royal Anthropological Institute, vol. 7, no. 3, 2001, pp. 569-571.

Borghi, Anna M., and Ferdinand Binkofski. "Words as Social Tools: An Embodied View on Abstract Concepts." Springer, 2014.

Chalmers, David J. "Extended Mind." Oxford University Press, 2010.

---. "The Extended Mind." Analysis, vol. 58, no. 1, 1998, pp. 7-19.

Clark, Andy. "Being There: Putting Brain, Body and World Together Again." MIT Press, 1997.

---. "Extended Mind." Oxford University Press, 2008.

---. "Supersizing the Mind: Embodiment, Action, and Cognitive Extension." Oxford University Press, 2011.

Cole, Michael. "Cultural Psychology: A Once and Future Discipline." Harvard University Press, 1996.

Cowley, Stephen J., editor. "Distributed Language." John Benjamins, 2011.

Donald, Merlin. "A Mind So Rare: The Evolution of Human Consciousness." W.W. Norton, 2001.

Gallagher, Shaun. "Enactivist Interventions: Rethinking the Mind." Oxford University Press, 2017.

Gibson, James J. "The Ecological Approach to Visual Perception." Houghton Mifflin, 1979.

Gladwin, Thomas. "East Is a Big Bird: Navigation and Logic on Puluwat Atoll." Harvard University Press, 1970.

Goody, Jack. "The Interface Between the Written and the Oral." Cambridge University Press, 1987.

Hollan, James, et al. "Distributed Cognition: Toward a New Foundation for Human-Computer Interaction Research." ACM Transactions on Computer-Human Interaction, vol. 7, no. 2, 2000, pp. 174-196.

Hutchins, Edwin. "Cognition in the Wild." MIT Press, 1995.

---. "Distributed Cognition." International Encyclopedia of the Social and Behavioral Sciences, edited by Neil J. Smelser and Paul B. Baltes, Elsevier, 2001, pp. 2068-2072.

---. "Material Anchors for Conceptual Blends." Journal of Pragmatics, vol. 37, no. 10, 2005, pp. 1555-1577.

Ingold, Tim. "The Perception of the Environment: Essays on Livelihood, Dwelling and Skill." Routledge, 2000.

---. "Being Alive: Essays on Movement, Knowledge and Description." Routledge, 2011.

Johnson, Mark. "The Body in the Mind: The Bodily Basis of Meaning, Imagination, and Reason." University of Chicago Press, 1987.

Kirsh, David. "The Intelligent Use of Space." Artificial Intelligence, vol. 73, no. 1-2, 1995, pp. 31-68.

---. "Embodied Cognition and the Magical Future of Interaction Design." ACM Transactions on Computer-Human Interaction, vol. 20, no. 1, 2013, pp. 1-30.

Lave, Jean. "Cognition in Practice: Mind, Mathematics and Culture in Everyday Life." Cambridge University Press, 1988.

Lave, Jean, and Etienne Wenger. "Situated Learning: Legitimate Peripheral Participation." Cambridge University Press, 1991.

Lewis, David. "We, the Navigators: The Ancient Art of Landfinding in the Pacific." University Press of Hawaii, 1994.

Menary, Richard. "Cognitive Integration: Mind and Cognition Unbounded." Palgrave Macmillan, 2007.

---. "The Extended Mind." MIT Press, 2010.

Newen, Albert, et al., editors. "The Oxford Handbook of 4E Cognition." Oxford University Press, 2018.

Norman, Donald A. "Things That Make Us Smart: Defending Human Attributes in the Age of the Machine." Addison-Wesley, 1993.

Pea, Roy D. "Practices of Distributed Intelligence and Designs for Education." Distributed Cognitions: Psychological and Educational Considerations, edited by Gavriel Salomon, Cambridge University Press, 1993, pp. 47-87.

Robbins, Philip, and Murat Aydede, editors. "The Cambridge Handbook of Situated Cognition." Cambridge University Press, 2009.

Rogers, Yvonne. "HCI Theory: Classical, Modern, and Contemporary." Morgan & Claypool, 2012.

Rowlands, Mark. "The New Science of the Mind: From Extended Mind to Embodied Phenomenology." MIT Press, 2010.

Salomon, Gavriel, editor. "Distributed Cognitions: Psychological and Educational Considerations." Cambridge University Press, 1993.

Shapiro, Lawrence. "Embodied Cognition." Routledge, 2011.

Suchman, Lucy A. "Plans and Situated Actions: The Problem of Human-Machine Communication." Cambridge University Press, 1987.

---. "Human-Machine Reconfigurations: Plans and Situated Actions." 2nd ed., Cambridge University Press, 2007.

Thelen, Esther, and Linda B. Smith. "A Dynamic Systems Approach to the Development of Cognition and Action." MIT Press, 1994.

Thompson, Evan. "Mind in Life: Biology, Phenomenology, and the Sciences of Mind." Harvard University Press, 2007.

Varela, Francisco J., et al. "The Embodied Mind: Cognitive Science and Human Experience." MIT Press, 1991.

Vygotsky, Lev S. "Mind in Society: The Development of Higher Psychological Processes." Harvard University Press, 1978.

Wenger, Etienne. "Communities of Practice: Learning, Meaning, and Identity." Cambridge University Press, 1998.

Wilson, Margaret. "Six Views of Embodied Cognition." Psychonomic Bulletin & Review, vol. 9, no. 4, 2002, pp. 625-636.

Zhang, Jiajie, and Donald A. Norman. "Representations in Distributed Cognitive Tasks." Cognitive Science, vol. 18, no. 1, 1994, pp. 87-122.

Chapter Five

Abelard, Peter. Sic et Non. Translated by Blanche B. Boyer and Richard McKeon, University of Chicago Press, 1976.

Adams, Marilyn McCord. William Ockham. 2 vols., University of Notre Dame Press, 1987.

Alford, John A., editor. A Companion to Piers Plowman. University of California Press, 1988.

Anselm of Canterbury. Proslogion. Translated by M.J. Charlesworth, University of Notre Dame Press, 1979.

Aquinas, Thomas. Summa Theologiae. Translated by the Fathers of the English Dominican Province, Benziger Brothers, 1947.

---. Summa Contra Gentiles. Translated by Anton C. Pegis, University of Notre Dame Press, 1975.

Augustine of Hippo. City of God. Translated by Henry Bettenson, Penguin Classics, 1972.

---. Confessions. Translated by R.S. Pine-Coffin, Penguin Classics, 1961.

Baldwin, John W. The Scholastic Culture of the Middle Ages, 1000-1300. D.C. Heath, 1971.

Benson, Robert L., and Giles Constable, editors. Renaissance and Renewal in the Twelfth Century. Harvard University Press, 1982.

Boethius. The Consolation of Philosophy. Translated by V.E. Watts, Penguin Classics, 1969.

Bonner, Gerald. St. Augustine of Hippo: Life and Controversies. 3rd ed., Canterbury Press, 2002.

Brown, Peter. Augustine of Hippo: A Biography. Revised ed., University of California Press, 2000.

Burr, David. The Spiritual Franciscans: From Protest to Persecution in the Century after Saint Francis. Pennsylvania State University Press, 2001.

Bynum, Caroline Walker. Jesus as Mother: Studies in the Spirituality of the High Middle Ages. University of California Press, 1982.

Chadwick, Henry. Augustine: A Very Short Introduction. Oxford University Press, 2001.

---. The Early Church. Revised ed., Penguin Books, 1993.

Chenu, M.-D. Nature, Man, and Society in the Twelfth Century. Translated by Jerome Taylor and Lester K. Little, University of Chicago Press, 1968.

Clanchy, M.T. Abelard: A Medieval Life. Blackwell, 1997.

---. From Memory to Written Record: England 1066-1307. 3rd ed., Wiley-Blackwell, 2013.

Cobban, Alan B. The Medieval Universities: Their Development and Organization. Methuen, 1975.

Courtenay, William J. Schools and Scholars in Fourteenth-Century England. Princeton University Press, 1987.

d'Alverny, Marie-Thérèse. Avicenna en Occident au moyen âge. Vrin, 1993.

Davies, Brian. The Thought of Thomas Aquinas. Oxford University Press, 1992.

de Libera, Alain. Philosophy in the Middle Ages. Translated by E.C. Fryde, Cambridge University Press, 1998.

Dronke, Peter. Women Writers of the Middle Ages: A Critical Study of Texts from Perpetua to Marguerite Porete. Cambridge University Press, 1984.

Evans, G.R. Anselm and Talking about God. Oxford University Press, 1978.

---. Old Arts and New Theology: The Beginnings of Theology as an Academic Discipline. Oxford University Press, 1980.

Ferruolo, Stephen C. The Origins of the University: The Schools of Paris and Their Critics, 1100-1215. Stanford University Press, 1985.

Gilson, Étienne. History of Christian Philosophy in the Middle Ages. Random House, 1955.

---. Reason and Revelation in the Middle Ages. Charles Scribner's Sons, 1938.

---. The Christian Philosophy of St. Augustine. Translated by L.E.M. Lynch, Random House, 1960.

Grabmann, Martin. Die Geschichte der scholastischen Methode. 2 vols., Akademische Verlagsgesellschaft Athenaion, 1957.

Grant, Edward. God and Reason in the Middle Ages. Cambridge University Press, 2001.

Grellard, Christophe, and Aurélien Robert, editors. Atomism in Late Medieval Philosophy and Theology. Brill, 2009.

Haskins, Charles Homer. The Renaissance of the Twelfth Century. Harvard University Press, 1927.

---. The Rise of Universities. Henry Holt, 1923.

Hissette, Roland. Enquête sur les 219 articles condamnés à Paris le 7 mars 1277. Vrin, 1977.

Jolivet, Jean. Philosophy in the Middle Ages: From Eriugena to Ockham. SUNY Press, 1969.

Kenny, Anthony. Medieval Philosophy. Oxford University Press, 2005.

Klima, Gyula. John Buridan. Oxford University Press, 2009.

Knowles, David. The Evolution of Medieval Thought. 2nd ed., Longman, 1988.

Kretzmann, Norman, et al., editors. The Cambridge History of Later Medieval Philosophy. Cambridge University Press, 1982.

Lambert, Malcolm. Medieval Heresy: Popular Movements from the Gregorian Reform to the Reformation. 3rd ed., Blackwell, 2002.

Le Goff, Jacques. Intellectuals in the Middle Ages. Translated by Teresa Lavender Fagan, Blackwell, 1993.

---. Medieval Civilization. Translated by Julia Barrow, Basil Blackwell, 1988.

Leclercq, Jean. The Love of Learning and the Desire for God: A Study of Monastic Culture. 3rd ed., Fordham University Press, 1982.

Leff, Gordon. Paris and Oxford Universities in the Thirteenth and Fourteenth Centuries. John Wiley & Sons, 1968.

Marenbon, John. Early Medieval Philosophy (480-1150): An Introduction. 2nd ed., Routledge, 1988.

---. Later Medieval Philosophy (1150-1350): An Introduction. Routledge, 1987.

---. Medieval Philosophy: An Historical and Philosophical Introduction. Routledge, 2007.

McGrath, Alister E. Christian Theology: An Introduction. 6th ed., Wiley-Blackwell, 2017.

---. Theology: The Basics. 4th ed., Wiley-Blackwell, 2018.

McInerny, Ralph. A History of Western Philosophy: Medieval Philosophy. University of Notre Dame Press, 1970.

---. Aquinas. Polity Press, 2004.

Mews, Constant J. Abelard and Heloise. Oxford University Press, 2005.

Murdoch, John E. Album of Science: Antiquity and the Middle Ages. Charles Scribner's Sons, 1984.

Murray, Alexander. Reason and Society in the Middle Ages. Oxford University Press, 1978.

O'Donnell, James J. Augustine: A New Biography. HarperCollins, 2005.

Otten, Willemien. From Paradise to Paradigm: A Study of Twelfth-Century Humanism. Brill, 2004.

Pelikan, Jaroslav. The Growth of Medieval Theology (600-1300). University of Chicago Press, 1978.

Pieper, Josef. Philosophy in the Middle Ages. Translated by Richard Winston, Pantheon Books, 1960.

Radding, Charles M. A World Made by Men: Cognition and Society, 400-1200. University of North Carolina Press, 1985.

Rashdall, Hastings. The Universities of Europe in the Middle Ages. Edited by F.M. Powicke and A.B. Emden, 3 vols., Oxford University Press, 1936.

Riedl, John O. A Catalogue of Renaissance Philosophers (1350-1650). Marquette University Press, 1940.

Rorem, Paul. Hugh of St. Victor. Oxford University Press, 2009.

Southern, Richard W. Medieval Humanism and Other Studies. Basil Blackwell, 1970.

---. Robert Grosseteste: The Growth of an English Mind in Medieval Europe. Oxford University Press, 1986.

---. Saint Anselm: A Portrait in a Landscape. Cambridge University Press, 1990.

---. Scholastic Humanism and the Unification of Europe. 2 vols., Blackwell, 1995-2001.

Spade, Paul Vincent. Five Texts on the Mediaeval Problem of Universals. Hackett Publishing, 1994.

Swanson, R.N. The Twelfth-Century Renaissance. Manchester University Press, 1999.

TeSelle, Eugene. Augustine the Theologian. Herder and Herder, 1970.

Thijssen, J.M.M.H. Censure and Heresy at the University of Paris, 1200-1400. University of Pennsylvania Press, 1998.

Van Steenberghen, Fernand. Aristotle in the West: The Origins of Latin Aristotelianism. Translated by Leonard Johnston, Nauwelaerts, 1970.

Verger, Jacques. Men of Learning in Europe at the End of the Middle Ages. Translated by Lisa Neal and Steven Rendall, University of Notre Dame Press, 2000.

Walsh, James J. High Points of Medieval Culture. Books for Libraries Press, 1969.

Wei, Ian P. Intellectual Culture in Medieval Paris: Theologians and the University, c. 1100-1330. Cambridge University Press, 2012.

Weinberg, Julius R. A Short History of Medieval Philosophy. Princeton University Press, 1964.

Wippel, John F. Medieval Reactions to the Encounter between Faith and Reason. Marquette University Press, 1995.

---. The Metaphysical Thought of Thomas Aquinas. Catholic University of America Press, 2000.

Chapter Six

Annas, Julia, and Jonathan Barnes. The Modes of Scepticism: Ancient Texts and Modern Interpretations. Cambridge University Press, 1985.

Aquinas, Thomas. Summa Theologiae. Translated by the Fathers of the English Dominican Province, Benziger Brothers, 1947.

Ariew, Roger. Descartes and the Last Scholastics. Cornell University Press, 1999.

Bouwsma, William J. The Waning of the Renaissance, 1550-1640. Yale University Press, 2000.

Burke, Kenneth. The Rhetoric of Religion: Studies in Logology. University of California Press, 1970.

Burnyeat, Myles. "The Sceptic in His Place and Time." Philosophy in History, edited by Richard Rorty et al., Cambridge University Press, 1984, pp. 225-254.

Cassirer, Ernst. The Individual and the Cosmos in Renaissance Philosophy. Translated by Mario Domandi, University of Pennsylvania Press, 1972.

---. The Philosophy of the Enlightenment. Translated by Fritz C.A. Koelln and James P. Pettegrove, Princeton University Press, 1951.

Clarke, Desmond M. Descartes: A Biography. Cambridge University Press, 2006.

Cottingham, John. Descartes. Blackwell, 1986.

---. The Rationalists. Oxford University Press, 1988.

---. editor. The Cambridge Companion to Descartes. Cambridge University Press, 1992.

Dear, Peter. Revolutionizing the Sciences: European Knowledge and Its Ambitions, 1500-1700. Princeton University Press, 2001.

Descartes, René. Discourse on Method and Meditations on First Philosophy. Translated by Donald A. Cress, Hackett Publishing, 1998.

---. The Philosophical Writings of Descartes. Translated by John Cottingham et al., 3 vols., Cambridge University Press, 1984-1991.

Erasmus, Desiderius. The Praise of Folly. Translated by Betty Radice, Penguin Classics, 1971.

---. The Education of a Christian Prince. Translated by Neil M. Cheshire and Michael J. Heath, Cambridge University Press, 1997.

Ferguson, Wallace K. The Renaissance in Historical Thought. Houghton Mifflin, 1948.

Garber, Daniel. Descartes' Metaphysical Physics. University of Chicago Press, 1992.

---. Descartes Embodied: Reading Cartesian Philosophy through Cartesian Science. Cambridge University Press, 2001.

Garin, Eugenio. Italian Humanism: Philosophy and Civic Life in the Renaissance. Translated by Peter Munz, Harper & Row, 1965.

Gaukroger, Stephen. Descartes: An Intellectual Biography. Oxford University Press, 1995.

---. Francis Bacon and the Transformation of Early-Modern Philosophy. Cambridge University Press, 2001.

---. The Emergence of a Scientific Culture: Science and the Shaping of Modernity, 1210-1685. Oxford University Press, 2006.

Gilson, Étienne. Index Scolastico-Cartésien. 2nd ed., Vrin, 1979.

---. Studies on the Role of Medieval Philosophy in the Formation of the Cartesian System. Journal of the History of Ideas, 1979.

Grafton, Anthony. The Footnote: A Curious History. Harvard University Press, 1997.

---. What Was History? The Art of History in Early Modern Europe. Cambridge University Press, 2007.

Grafton, Anthony, and Lisa Jardine. From Humanism to the Humanities: Education and the Liberal Arts in Fifteenth- and Sixteenth-Century Europe. Harvard University Press, 1986.

Hale, John R. The Civilization of Europe in the Renaissance. Atheneum, 1994.

Hall, A. Rupert. The Revolution in Science, 1500-1750. 3rd ed., Longman, 1983.

Hankins, James. Plato in the Italian Renaissance. 2 vols., E.J. Brill, 1990.

---. editor. Renaissance Civic Humanism: Reappraisals and Reflections. Cambridge University Press, 2000.

Hatfield, Gary. Descartes and the Meditations. Routledge, 2003.

Henry, John. The Scientific Revolution and the Origins of Modern Science. 3rd ed., Palgrave Macmillan, 2008.

Huizinga, Johan. Erasmus and the Age of Reformation. Translated by F. Hopman, Harper Torchbooks, 1957.

Israel, Jonathan I. Radical Enlightenment: Philosophy and the Making of Modernity, 1650-1750. Oxford University Press, 2001.

Jardine, Lisa. *Erasmus, Man of Letters*. Princeton University Press, 1993.

Kenny, Anthony. *Descartes: A Study of His Philosophy*. Random House, 1968.

---. *Medieval Philosophy*. Oxford University Press, 2005.

Kristeller, Paul Oskar. *Renaissance Thought and Its Sources*. Edited by Michael Mooney, Columbia University Press, 1979.

---. *Renaissance Thought: The Classic, Scholastic, and Humanist Strains*. Harper Torchbooks, 1961.

Kuhn, Thomas S. *The Copernican Revolution: Planetary Astronomy in the Development of Western Thought*. Harvard University Press, 1957.

---. *The Structure of Scientific Revolutions*. 4th ed., University of Chicago Press, 2012.

Leibniz, Gottfried Wilhelm. *Philosophical Essays*. Translated by Roger Ariew and Daniel Garber, Hackett Publishing, 1989.

---. *New Essays on Human Understanding*. Translated by Peter Remnant and Jonathan Bennett, Cambridge University Press, 1996.

Lindberg, David C. *The Beginnings of Western Science: The European Scientific Tradition in Philosophical, Religious, and Institutional Context, Prehistory to A.D. 1450*. 2nd ed., University of Chicago Press, 2007.

Locke, John. *An Essay Concerning Human Understanding*. Edited by Peter H. Nidditch, Oxford University Press, 1975.

---. Two Treatises of Government. Edited by Peter Laslett, Cambridge University Press, 1988.

---. A Letter Concerning Toleration. Edited by James H. Tully, Hackett Publishing, 1983.

Marenbon, John. Medieval Philosophy: An Historical and Philosophical Introduction. Routledge, 2007.

Marshall, John. John Locke, Toleration and Early Enlightenment Culture. Cambridge University Press, 2006.

McConica, James Kelsey. Erasmus. Oxford University Press, 1991.

Nadler, Steven M. Spinoza: A Life. Cambridge University Press, 1999.

---. editor. The Cambridge Companion to Spinoza. Cambridge University Press, 1996.

---. editor. A Companion to Early Modern Philosophy. Blackwell, 2002.

Oberman, Heiko A. The Roots of Anti-Semitism in the Age of Renaissance and Reformation. Translated by James I. Porter, Fortress Press, 1984.

Ong, Walter J. Ramus, Method, and the Decay of Dialogue. Harvard University Press, 1958.

Pasnau, Robert. Metaphysical Themes, 1274-1671. Oxford University Press, 2011.

Popkin, Richard H. The History of Scepticism: From Savonarola to Bayle. Revised ed., Oxford University Press, 2003.

Rabil, Albert Jr., editor. Renaissance Humanism: Foundations, Forms, and Legacy. 3 vols., University of Pennsylvania Press, 1988.

Rodis-Lewis, Geneviève. Descartes: His Life and Thought. Translated by Jane Marie Todd, Cornell University Press, 1998.

Rosen, Edward. Copernicus and the Scientific Revolution. Krieger, 1984.

Rummel, Erika. Erasmus. Continuum, 2004.

---. Erasmus and His Catholic Critics. 2 vols., Nieuwkoop, 1989.

Schmaltz, Tad M. Descartes on Causation. Oxford University Press, 2008.

Shapin, Steven. The Scientific Revolution. University of Chicago Press, 1996.

Skinner, Quentin. The Foundations of Modern Political Thought. 2 vols., Cambridge University Press, 1978.

---. Renaissance Virtues. Cambridge University Press, 1990.

Spinoza, Baruch. Ethics. Translated by Edwin Curley, Penguin Classics, 1996.

---. A Spinoza Reader: The Ethics and Other Works. Edited and translated by Edwin Curley, Princeton University Press, 1994.

Stewart, M.A., editor. Studies in Seventeenth-Century European Philosophy. Oxford University Press, 1997.

Tracy, James D. Erasmus of the Low Countries. University of California Press, 1996.

---. Erasmus: The Growth of a Mind. Droz, 1972.

Tuck, Richard. Philosophy and Government, 1572-1651. Cambridge University Press, 1993.

Verbeek, Theo. Descartes and the Dutch: Early Reactions to Cartesian Philosophy, 1637-1650. Southern Illinois University Press, 1992.

Watson, Richard A. The Breakdown of Cartesian Metaphysics. Hackett Publishing, 1987.

Westman, Robert S. The Copernican Question: Prognostication, Skepticism, and Celestial Order. University of California Press, 2011.

Williams, Bernard. Descartes: The Project of Pure Enquiry. Penguin Books, 1978.

Wilson, Catherine. Descartes's Meditations: An Introduction. Cambridge University Press, 2003.

Wilson, Margaret Dauler. Descartes. Routledge, 1978.

Yolton, John W. John Locke and the Way of Ideas. Oxford University Press, 1956.

---. Locke and the Compass of Human Understanding. Cambridge University Press, 1970.

Chapter Seven

Aldridge, Alfred Owen. Voltaire and the Century of Light. Princeton University Press, 1975.

Baker, Keith Michael. Condorcet: From Natural Philosophy to Social Mathematics. University of Chicago Press, 1975.

---. Inventing the French Revolution: Essays on French Political Culture in the Eighteenth Century. Cambridge University Press, 1990.

Barker-Benfield, G.J. The Culture of Sensibility: Sex and Society in Eighteenth-Century Britain. University of Chicago Press, 1992.

Berlin, Isaiah. The Age of Enlightenment. Oxford University Press, 1956.

---. Against the Current: Essays in the History of Ideas. Hogarth Press, 1979.

Besterman, Theodore. Voltaire. 3rd ed., University of Chicago Press, 1976.

Blom, Philipp. Encyclopédie: The Triumph of Reason in an Unreasonable Age. Fourth Estate, 2004.

---. A Wicked Company: The Forgotten Raconteurs Who Made Modern France. Basic Books, 2010.

Broadie, Alexander. The Scottish Enlightenment: The Historical Age of the Historical Nation. Birlinn, 2001.

---. editor. The Cambridge Companion to the Scottish Enlightenment. Cambridge University Press, 2003.

Brown, Stewart J., editor. William Robertson and the Expansion of Empire. Cambridge University Press, 1997.

Burke, Edmund. Reflections on the Revolution in France. Edited by Conor Cruise O'Brien, Penguin Classics, 1968.

Campbell, R.H., and Andrew S. Skinner, editors. Adam Smith. Croom Helm, 1982.

Cassirer, Ernst. The Philosophy of the Enlightenment. Translated by Fritz C.A. Koelln and James P. Pettegrove, Princeton University Press, 1951.

---. Rousseau, Kant and Goethe. Translated by James Gutmann et al., Princeton University Press, 1945.

Chartier, Roger. The Cultural Origins of the French Revolution. Translated by Lydia G. Cochrane, Duke University Press, 1991.

Chitnis, Anand C. The Scottish Enlightenment: A Social History. Croom Helm, 1976.

Clark, J.C.D. English Society, 1660-1832. 2nd ed., Cambridge University Press, 2000.

Cranston, Maurice. The Noble Savage: Jean-Jacques Rousseau, 1754-1762. University of Chicago Press, 1991.

---. The Solitary Self: Jean-Jacques Rousseau in Exile and Adversity. University of Chicago Press, 1997.

Curran, Mark. Diderot and the Art of Thinking Freely. Other Press, 2019.

Darnton, Robert. The Business of Enlightenment: A Publishing History of the Encyclopédie, 1775-1800. Harvard University Press, 1979.

---. The Forbidden Best-Sellers of Pre-Revolutionary France. W.W. Norton, 1995.

---. The Great Cat Massacre and Other Episodes in French Cultural History. Basic Books, 1984.

De Gouges, Olympe. The Rights of Woman. Translated by Nupur Chaudhuri, in Women in World History, edited by Sarah Shaver Hughes and Brady Hughes, M.E. Sharpe, 1997.

Diderot, Denis. Encyclopedia: The Complete Illustrations, 1762-1777. Harry N. Abrams, 1978.

---. Rameau's Nephew and D'Alembert's Dream. Translated by Leonard Tancock, Penguin Classics, 1966.

---. Selected Writings on Art and Literature. Translated by Geoffrey Bremner, Penguin Classics, 1994.

Doyle, William. The Oxford History of the French Revolution. 2nd ed., Oxford University Press, 2002.

Duchet, Michèle. Diderot et l'Histoire des deux Indes ou l'écriture fragmentaire. Nizet, 1978.

Ferguson, Adam. An Essay on the History of Civil Society. Edited by Fania Oz-Salzberger, Cambridge University Press, 1995.

Fletcher, F.T.H. Montesquieu and English Politics, 1750-1800. Edward Arnold, 1939.

Forman-Barzilai, Fonna. Adam Smith and the Circles of Sympathy. Cambridge University Press, 2010.

Gay, Peter. The Enlightenment: An Interpretation. 2 vols., Knopf, 1966-1969.

---. Voltaire's Politics: The Poet as Realist. 2nd ed., Yale University Press, 1988.

Gordon, Daniel. Citizens without Sovereignty: Equality and Sociability in French Thought, 1670-1789. Princeton University Press, 1994.

Goodman, Dena. The Republic of Letters: A Cultural History of the French Enlightenment. Cornell University Press, 1994.

Habermas, Jürgen. The Structural Transformation of the Public Sphere. Translated by Thomas Burger, MIT Press, 1989.

Haakonssen, Knud. The Science of a Legislator: The Natural Jurisprudence of David Hume and Adam Smith. Cambridge University Press, 1981.

---. editor. The Cambridge Companion to Adam Smith. Cambridge University Press, 2006.

Herder, Johann Gottfried. Ideas for the Philosophy of History of Humanity. Translated by T.O. Churchill, University of Chicago Press, 1968.

---. Reflections on the Philosophy of the History of Mankind. Translated by T.O. Churchill, University of Chicago Press, 1968.

Himmelfarb, Gertrude. The Roads to Modernity: The British, French, and American Enlightenments. Knopf, 2004.

Hont, Istvan. Jealousy of Trade: International Competition and the Nation-State in Historical Perspective. Harvard University Press, 2005.

Hont, Istvan, and Michael Ignatieff, editors. Wealth and Virtue: The Shaping of Political Economy in the Scottish Enlightenment. Cambridge University Press, 1983.

Hume, David. A Treatise of Human Nature. Edited by L.A. Selby-Bigge and P.H. Nidditch, Oxford University Press, 1978.

---. An Enquiry Concerning Human Understanding. Edited by L.A. Selby-Bigge and P.H. Nidditch, Oxford University Press, 1975.

---. Essays Moral, Political and Literary. Edited by Eugene F. Miller, Liberty Fund, 1987.

Hunt, Lynn. The Family Romance of the French Revolution. University of California Press, 1992.

Israel, Jonathan I. Democratic Enlightenment: Philosophy, Revolution, and Human Rights, 1750-1790. Oxford University Press, 2011.

---. Enlightenment Contested: Philosophy, Modernity, and the Emancipation of Man, 1670-1752. Oxford University Press, 2006.

---. A Revolution of the Mind: Radical Enlightenment and the Intellectual Origins of Modern Democracy. Princeton University Press, 2010.

Kafka, Ben. The Demon of Writing: Powers and Failures of Paperwork. Zone Books, 2012.

Kant, Immanuel. Critique of Pure Reason. Translated by Norman Kemp Smith, St. Martin's Press, 1965.

---. Groundwork for the Metaphysics of Morals. Translated by Mary Gregor, Cambridge University Press, 1997.

---. Political Writings. Edited by Hans Reiss, Cambridge University Press, 1991.

Kelly, Christopher. Rousseau as Author: Consecrating One's Life to the Truth. University of Chicago Press, 2003.

Keohane, Nannerl O. Philosophy and the State in France: The Renaissance to the Enlightenment. Princeton University Press, 1980.

Kreimendahl, Lothar, editor. Aufklärung: Das deutsche 18. Jahrhundert. Rowohlt, 1995.

Landes, Joan B. Women and the Public Sphere in the Age of the French Revolution. Cornell University Press, 1988.

Lough, John. Essays on the Encyclopédie of Diderot and d'Alembert. Oxford University Press, 1968.

---. The Encyclopédie. Longman, 1971.

Mason, Haydn T. Voltaire: A Biography. Johns Hopkins University Press, 1981.

Masters, Roger D. The Political Philosophy of Rousseau. Princeton University Press, 1968.

McMahon, Darrin M. Enemies of the Enlightenment: The French Counter-Enlightenment and the Making of Modernity. Oxford University Press, 2001.

Melzer, Arthur M. The Natural Goodness of Man: On the System of Rousseau's Thought. University of Chicago Press, 1990.

Meek, Ronald L. Social Science and the Ignoble Savage. Cambridge University Press, 1976.

Miller, David. Philosophy and Ideology in Hume's Political Thought. Oxford University Press, 1981.

Mossner, Ernest Campbell. The Life of David Hume. 2nd ed., Oxford University Press, 1980.

Norton, David Fate. David Hume: Common-Sense Moralist, Sceptical Metaphysician. Princeton University Press, 1982.

---. editor. The Cambridge Companion to Hume. Cambridge University Press, 1993.

O'Brien, Karen. Narratives of Enlightenment: Cosmopolitan History from Voltaire to Gibbon. Cambridge University Press, 1997.

Outram, Dorinda. The Enlightenment. 3rd ed., Cambridge University Press, 2013.

Oz-Salzberger, Fania. Translating the Enlightenment: Scottish Civic Discourse in Eighteenth-Century Germany. Oxford University Press, 1995.

Palmer, R.R. Catholics and Unbelievers in Eighteenth Century France. Princeton University Press, 1939.

Phillipson, Nicholas. Adam Smith: An Enlightened Life. Yale University Press, 2010.

---. David Hume: The Philosopher as Historian. Yale University Press, 2012.

Pomeau, René. Voltaire. Flammarion, 1989.

Porter, Roy. The Enlightenment. 2nd ed., Palgrave, 2001.

---. Flesh in the Age of Reason. Allen Lane, 2003.

Raphael, D.D. Adam Smith. Oxford University Press, 1985.

Reid, Thomas. Essays on the Intellectual Powers of Man. Edited by Baruch A. Brody, MIT Press, 1969.

Riley, Patrick. The Cambridge Companion to Rousseau. Cambridge University Press, 2001.

Roche, Daniel. France in the Enlightenment. Translated by Arthur Goldhammer, Harvard University Press, 1998.

Rosanvallon, Pierre. The Demands of Liberty: Civil Society in France since the Revolution. Translated by Arthur Goldhammer, Harvard University Press, 2007.

Ross, Ian Simpson. The Life of Adam Smith. 2nd ed., Oxford University Press, 2010.

Rousseau, Jean-Jacques. The Social Contract and Other Later Political Writings. Edited by Victor Gourevitch, Cambridge University Press, 1997.

---. Discourse on the Origin of Inequality. Translated by Donald A. Cress, Hackett Publishing, 1992.

---. Emile, or On Education. Translated by Allan Bloom, Basic Books, 1979.

Sher, Richard B. Church and University in the Scottish Enlightenment. Princeton University Press, 1985.

---. The Enlightenment and the Book: Scottish Authors and Their Publishers in Eighteenth-Century Britain, Ireland, and America. University of Chicago Press, 2006.

Smith, Adam. The Theory of Moral Sentiments. Edited by D.D. Raphael and A.L. Macfie, Oxford University Press, 1976.

---. An Inquiry into the Nature and Causes of the Wealth of Nations. Edited by R.H. Campbell and A.S. Skinner, Oxford University Press, 1976.

Spector, Céline. Montesquieu et l'émergence de l'économie politique. Honoré Champion, 2006.

Stewart, Dugald. Account of the Life and Writings of Adam Smith. Edited by I.S. Ross, Oxford University Press, 1980.

Taylor, Charles. Sources of the Self: The Making of the Modern Identity. Harvard University Press, 1989.

Venturi, Franco. Utopia and Reform in the Enlightenment. Cambridge University Press, 1971.

Voltaire. Candide. Translated by Roger Pearson, Oxford University Press, 2006.

---. Letters on England. Translated by Leonard Tancock, Penguin Classics, 1980.

---. Treatise on Tolerance. Translated by Brian Masters, Cambridge University Press, 2000.

---. The Voltaire Anthology. Edited by F.C. Green, J.M. Dent & Sons, 1973.

Wade, Ira O. The Intellectual Development of Voltaire. Princeton University Press, 1969.

---. Voltaire and Candide. Princeton University Press, 1959.

Wilson, Arthur M. Diderot. Oxford University Press, 1972.

Wokler, Robert. Rousseau on Society, Politics, Music and Language. Garland Publishing, 1987.

---. Rousseau, the Age of Enlightenment, and Their Legacies. Princeton University Press, 2012.

Wollstonecraft, Mary. A Vindication of the Rights of Woman. Edited by Miriam Brody, Penguin Classics, 1992.

---. The Collected Letters of Mary Wollstonecraft. Edited by Janet Todd, Columbia University Press, 2003.

Yolton, John W. Perceptual Acquaintance from Descartes to Reid. University of Minnesota Press, 1984.

Chapter Eight

Austin, J.L. How to Do Things with Words. 2nd ed., Harvard University Press, 1975.

Ayer, A.J. Language, Truth and Logic. 2nd ed., Dover Publications, 1946.

Baker, G.P., and P.M.S. Hacker. Wittgenstein: Understanding and Meaning. University of Chicago Press, 1980.

Berlin, Brent, and Paul Kay. Basic Color Terms: Their Universality and Evolution. University of California Press, 1969.

Blackburn, Patrick, and Johan Bos. Representation and Inference for Natural Language: A First Course in Computational Semantics. CSLI Publications, 2005.

Bloom, Paul. How Children Learn the Meanings of Words. MIT Press, 2000.

Boole, George. An Investigation of the Laws of Thought. Walton and Maberly, 1854.

Brentano, Franz. Psychology from an Empirical Standpoint. Translated by Antos C. Rancurello et al., Routledge, 1973.

Carnap, Rudolf. The Logical Structure of the World. Translated by Rolf A. George, University of California Press, 1967.

---. Logical Syntax of Language. Translated by Amethe Smeaton, Routledge, 1937.

Chandler, Daniel. Semiotics: The Basics. 3rd ed., Routledge, 2017.

Chomsky, Noam. Aspects of the Theory of Syntax. MIT Press, 1965.

---. Knowledge of Language: Its Nature, Origin, and Use. Praeger, 1986.

---. Language and Mind. 3rd ed., Cambridge University Press, 2006.

---. Syntactic Structures. Mouton, 1957.

Clark, Andy. Being There: Putting Brain, Body, and World Together Again. MIT Press, 1997.

Davidson, Donald. Truth and Interpretation. Oxford University Press, 1984.

---. Truth, Language, and History. Oxford University Press, 2005.

Deacon, Terrence W. The Symbolic Species: The Co-evolution of Language and the Brain. W.W. Norton, 1997.

Eco, Umberto. A Theory of Semiotics. Indiana University Press, 1976.

---. The Role of the Reader: Explorations in the Semiotics of Texts. Indiana University Press, 1979.

Evans, Nicholas, and Stephen C. Levinson. "The Myth of Language Universals: Language Diversity and Its Importance for Cognitive Science." Behavioral and Brain Sciences, vol. 32, no. 5, 2009, pp. 429-448.

Everett, Daniel L. Don't Sleep, There Are Snakes: Life and Language in the Amazonian Jungle. Pantheon Books, 2008.

---. Language: The Cultural Tool. Pantheon Books, 2012.

Fauconnier, Gilles. Mappings in Thought and Language. Cambridge University Press, 1997.

Fauconnier, Gilles, and Mark Turner. The Way We Think: Conceptual Blending and the Mind's Hidden Complexities. Basic Books, 2002.

Fodor, Jerry A. The Language of Thought. Harvard University Press, 1975.

---. The Modularity of Mind. MIT Press, 1983.

Frege, Gottlob. The Foundations of Arithmetic. Translated by J.L. Austin, Northwestern University Press, 1980.

---. Philosophical and Mathematical Correspondence. University of Chicago Press, 1980.

Gentzen, Gerhard. The Collected Papers of Gerhard Gentzen. Edited by M.E. Szabo, North-Holland, 1969.

Gödel, Kurt. Collected Works. Edited by Solomon Feferman et al., 5 vols., Oxford University Press, 1986-2003.

Goodman, Nelson. Ways of Worldmaking. Hackett Publishing, 1978.

Grice, H.P. Studies in the Way of Words. Harvard University Press, 1989.

Haack, Susan. Deviant Logic, Fuzzy Logic: Beyond the Formalism. University of Chicago Press, 1996.

---. Philosophy of Logics. Cambridge University Press, 1978.

Harris, Roy. The Language Myth. Duckworth, 1981.

---. The Semantics of Science. Continuum, 2005.

Hjelmslev, Louis. Prolegomena to a Theory of Language. Translated by Francis J. Whitfield, University of Wisconsin Press, 1961.

Hofstadter, Douglas R. Gödel, Escher, Bach: An Eternal Golden Braid. Basic Books, 1979.

Jackendoff, Ray. Foundations of Language: Brain, Meaning, Grammar, Evolution. Oxford University Press, 2002.

---. Languages of the Mind. MIT Press, 1992.

Jakobson, Roman. On Language. Harvard University Press, 1990.

Johnson, Mark. The Body in the Mind: The Bodily Basis of Meaning, Imagination, and Reason. University of Chicago Press, 1987.

Katz, Jerrold J., and Jerry A. Fodor. "The Structure of a Semantic Theory." Language, vol. 39, no. 2, 1963, pp. 170-210.

Kay, Paul, and Willett Kempton. "What Is the Sapir-Whorf Hypothesis?" American Anthropologist, vol. 86, no. 1, 1984, pp. 65-79.

Kleene, Stephen Cole. Introduction to Metamathematics. D. Van Nostrand, 1952.

Kripke, Saul A. Naming and Necessity. Harvard University Press, 1980.

---. Wittgenstein on Rules and Private Language. Harvard University Press, 1982.

Lakoff, George. Women, Fire, and Dangerous Things: What Categories Reveal about the Mind. University of Chicago Press, 1987.

Lakoff, George, and Mark Johnson. The Metaphors We Live By. University of Chicago Press, 1980.

---. Philosophy in the Flesh: The Embodied Mind and Its Challenge to Western Thought. Basic Books, 1999.

Levinson, Stephen C. Space in Language and Cognition. Cambridge University Press, 2003.

---. "Language and Mind: Let's Get the Issues Straight!" Language in Mind: Advances in the Study of Language and Thought, edited by Dedre Gentner and Susan Goldin-Meadow, MIT Press, 2003, pp. 25-46.

Lewis, David K. Convention: A Philosophical Study. Harvard University Press, 1969.

---. On the Plurality of Worlds. Blackwell, 1986.

Lucy, John A. Grammatical Categories and Cognition: A Case Study of the Linguistic Relativity Hypothesis. Cambridge University Press, 1992.

---. Language Diversity and Thought: A Reformulation of the Linguistic Relativity Hypothesis. Cambridge University Press, 1992.

Lyons, John. Language and Linguistics: An Introduction. Cambridge University Press, 1981.

---. Semantics. 2 vols., Cambridge University Press, 1977.

Majid, Asifa, et al. "Can Language Restructure Cognition? The Case for Space." Trends in Cognitive Sciences, vol. 8, no. 3, 2004, pp. 108-114.

McGinn, Colin. Wittgenstein on Meaning. Blackwell, 1984.

Miller, George A. Language and Communication. McGraw-Hill, 1951.

---. The Science of Words. Scientific American Library, 1991.

Nagel, Ernest, and James R. Newman. Gödel's Proof. New York University Press, 1958.

Palmer, F.R. Semantics. 2nd ed., Cambridge University Press, 1981.

Peirce, Charles Sanders. Collected Papers. Edited by Charles Hartshorne and Paul Weiss, 8 vols., Harvard University Press, 1931-1958.

---. The Essential Peirce. Edited by Nathan Houser and Christian Kloesel, 2 vols., Indiana University Press, 1992-1998.

Pinker, Steven. The Language Instinct. William Morrow, 1994.

---. The Stuff of Thought: Language as a Window into Human Nature. Viking, 2007.

---. Words and Rules: The Ingredients of Language. Basic Books, 1999.

Priest, Graham. Beyond the Limits of Thought. 2nd ed., Oxford University Press, 2002.

---. In Contradiction: A Study of the Transconsistent. 2nd ed., Oxford University Press, 2006.

Putnam, Hilary. Mind, Language and Reality. Cambridge University Press, 1975.

---. Reason, Truth and History. Cambridge University Press, 1981.

Quine, W.V.O. From a Logical Point of View. 2nd ed., Harvard University Press, 1980.

---. Ontological Relativity and Other Essays. Columbia University Press, 1969.

---. Word and Object. MIT Press, 1960.

Read, Stephen. Thinking About Logic: An Introduction to the Philosophy of Logic. Oxford University Press, 1995.

Russell, Bertrand. Introduction to Mathematical Philosophy. George Allen and Unwin, 1919.

---. The Principles of Mathematics. 2nd ed., George Allen and Unwin, 1937.

Russell, Bertrand, and Alfred North Whitehead. Principia Mathematica. 2nd ed., 3 vols., Cambridge University Press, 1925-1927.

Sapir, Edward. Language: An Introduction to the Study of Speech. Harcourt, Brace & World, 1921.

---. Selected Writings in Language, Culture, and Personality. University of California Press, 1949.

Saussure, Ferdinand de. Course in General Linguistics. Translated by Wade Baskin, Philosophical Library, 1959.

Searle, John R. Expression and Meaning. Cambridge University Press, 1979.

---. Speech Acts. Cambridge University Press, 1969.

Sebeok, Thomas A. Signs: An Introduction to Semiotics. 2nd ed., University of Toronto Press, 2001.

Shopen, Timothy, editor. Language Typology and Syntactic Description. 2nd ed., 5 vols., Cambridge University Press, 2007.

Slobin, Dan I. "From 'Thought and Language' to 'Thinking for Speaking.'" Rethinking Linguistic Relativity, edited by John J. Gumperz and Stephen C. Levinson, Cambridge University Press, 1996, pp. 70-96.

Smullyan, Raymond M. Forever Undecided: A Puzzle Guide to Gödel. Knopf, 1987.

---. Gödel's Incompleteness Theorems. Oxford University Press, 1992.

Strawson, P.F. Logico-Linguistic Papers. Methuen, 1971.

---. Subject and Predicate in Logic and Grammar. Methuen, 1974.

Tarski, Alfred. Logic, Semantics, Metamathematics. 2nd ed., Hackett Publishing, 1983.

Tomasello, Michael. Constructing a Language: A Usage-Based Theory of Language Acquisition. Harvard University Press, 2003.

---. The Cultural Origins of Human Cognition. Harvard University Press, 1999.

Turing, Alan M. "Computing Machinery and Intelligence." Mind, vol. 59, no. 236, 1950, pp. 433-460.

van Fraassen, Bas C. The Scientific Image. Oxford University Press, 1980.

Whorf, Benjamin Lee. Language, Thought, and Reality. Edited by John B. Carroll, MIT Press, 1956.

Wittgenstein, Ludwig. The Blue and Brown Books. Harper & Row, 1958.

---. On Certainty. Edited by G.E.M. Anscombe and G.H. von Wright, Harper & Row, 1969.

---. Philosophical Investigations. Translated by G.E.M. Anscombe, 3rd ed., Macmillan, 1958.

---. Remarks on the Foundations of Mathematics. Edited by G.H. von Wright et al., MIT Press, 1978.

---. Tractatus Logico-Philosophicus. Translated by D.F. Pears and B.F. McGuinness, Routledge, 1961.

Zadeh, Lotfi A. "Fuzzy Sets." Information and Control, vol. 8, no. 3, 1965, pp. 338-353.

Chapter Nine

Addams, Jane. Democracy and Social Ethics. Macmillan, 1902.

---. Twenty Years at Hull-House. Macmillan, 1910.

---. The Spirit of Youth and the City Streets. Macmillan, 1909.

---. Newer Ideals of Peace. Macmillan, 1907.

---. The Long Road of Woman's Memory. Macmillan, 1916.

Alexander, Thomas M. John Dewey's Theory of Art, Experience, and Nature. State University of New York Press, 1987.

Baldwin, James Mark. Mental Development in the Child and the Race. 3rd ed., Macmillan, 1906.

Bernstein, Richard J. The Pragmatic Turn. Polity Press, 2010.

---. Praxis and Action: Contemporary Philosophies of Human Activity. University of Pennsylvania Press, 1971.

Blumer, Herbert. Symbolic Interactionism: Perspective and Method. Prentice-Hall, 1969.

Boydston, Jo Ann, editor. The Collected Works of John Dewey. 37 vols., Southern Illinois University Press, 1967-1991.

Brandom, Robert B. Making It Explicit: Reasoning, Representing, and Discursive Commitment. Harvard University Press, 1994.

Brown, Hunter. William James on Radical Empiricism and Religion. University of Toronto Press, 2000.

Burke, Tom. Dewey's New Logic: A Reply to Russell. University of Chicago Press, 1994.

Campbell, James. The Community Reconstructs: The Meaning of Pragmatic Social Thought. University of Illinois Press, 1992.

---. Understanding John Dewey. Open Court, 1995.

Champlin, T.S. Reflexive Paradoxes. Routledge, 1988.

Colapietro, Vincent M. Peirce's Approach to the Self. State University of New York Press, 1989.

Cooley, Charles Horton. Human Nature and the Social Order. Charles Scribner's Sons, 1902.

---. Social Organization. Charles Scribner's Sons, 1909.

Cormier, Harvey. The Truth Is What Works: William James, Pragmatism, and the Seed of Death. Rowman & Littlefield, 2001.

Creighton, J.E. An Introductory Logic. Macmillan, 1898.

Dewey, John. Art as Experience. Minton, Balch & Company, 1934.

---. Democracy and Education. Macmillan, 1916.

---. Experience and Nature. Open Court, 1925.

---. How We Think. D.C. Heath, 1910.

---. The Public and Its Problems. Henry Holt, 1927.

---. Reconstruction in Philosophy. Henry Holt, 1920.

---. The Quest for Certainty. Minton, Balch & Company, 1929.

---. Logic: The Theory of Inquiry. Henry Holt, 1938.

---. The School and Society. University of Chicago Press, 1899.

---. The Child and the Curriculum. University of Chicago Press, 1902.

Dickstein, Morris. The Revival of Pragmatism: New Essays on Social Thought, Law, and Culture. Duke University Press, 1998.

Diggins, John Patrick. The Promise of Pragmatism: Modernism and the Crisis of Knowledge and Authority. University of Chicago Press, 1994.

Elshtain, Jean Bethke. Jane Addams and the Dream of American Democracy. Basic Books, 2002.

Feinstein, Howard M. Becoming William James. Cornell University Press, 1984.

Fisch, Max H. Peirce, Semiotic, and Pragmatism. Indiana University Press, 1986.

Flower, Elizabeth, and Murray G. Murphey. A History of Philosophy in America. 2 vols., G.P. Putnam's Sons, 1977.

Garrison, Jim. Dewey and Eros: Wisdom and Desire in the Art of Teaching. Teachers College Press, 1997.

Goodman, Russell B. American Philosophy and the Romantic Tradition. Cambridge University Press, 1990.

Green, Judith M. Deep Democracy: Community, Diversity, and Transformation. Rowman & Littlefield, 1999.

Haack, Susan. Evidence and Inquiry: Towards Reconstruction in Epistemology. Blackwell, 1993.

---. Manifesto of a Passionate Moderate. University of Chicago Press, 1998.

Haddock, Bruce A. A History of Political Thought: From Ancient Greece to Early Christianity. Polity Press, 2005.

Hall, David L. Richard Rorty: Prophet and Poet of the New Pragmatism. State University of New York Press, 1994.

Hickman, Larry A. John Dewey's Pragmatic Technology. Indiana University Press, 1990.

---. editor. Reading Dewey: Interpretations for a Postmodern Generation. Indiana University Press, 1998.

Hildebrand, David L. Beyond Realism and Antirealism: John Dewey and the Neopragmatists. Vanderbilt University Press, 2003.

Holmes, Oliver Wendell Jr. The Common Law. Little, Brown, 1881.

---. Collected Legal Papers. Harcourt, Brace and Howe, 1920.

---. The Mind and Faith of Justice Holmes. Edited by Max Lerner, Little, Brown, 1943.

Hook, Sidney. John Dewey: An Intellectual Portrait. John Day Company, 1939.

---. Pragmatism and the Tragic Sense of Life. Basic Books, 1974.

Hookway, Christopher. Peirce. Routledge, 1985.

---. Truth, Rationality, and Pragmatism. Oxford University Press, 2000.

Howe, Daniel Walker. Making the American Self: Jonathan Edwards to Abraham Lincoln. Harvard University Press, 1997.

James, William. The Principles of Psychology. 2 vols., Henry Holt, 1890.

---. The Will to Believe and Other Essays in Popular Philosophy. Longmans, Green, 1897.

---. The Varieties of Religious Experience. Longmans, Green, 1902.

---. Pragmatism: A New Name for Some Old Ways of Thinking. Longmans, Green, 1907.

---. A Pluralistic Universe. Longmans, Green, 1909.

---. The Meaning of Truth. Longmans, Green, 1909.

---. Essays in Radical Empiricism. Longmans, Green, 1912.

---. Writings 1902-1910. Library of America, 1987.

Joas, Hans. G.H. Mead: A Contemporary Re-examination of His Thought. MIT Press, 1985.

---. Pragmatism and Social Theory. University of Chicago Press, 1993.

---. The Creativity of Action. University of Chicago Press, 1996.

Kloppenberg, James T. Uncertain Victory: Social Democracy and Progressivism in European and American Thought, 1870-1920. Oxford University Press, 1986.

Knight, Louise W. Citizen: Jane Addams and the Struggle for Democracy. University of Chicago Press, 2005.

Kuklick, Bruce. A History of Philosophy in America, 1720-2000. Oxford University Press, 2001.

---. The Rise of American Philosophy: Cambridge, Massachusetts, 1860-1930. Yale University Press, 1977.

Lamont, Corliss. Dialogue on John Dewey. Horizon Press, 1959.

Levine, Barbara. Works of Love: Women's Philosophy and the Experience of the World. Continuum, 1999.

Lewis, C.I. Mind and the World Order. Charles Scribner's Sons, 1929.

---. An Analysis of Knowledge and Valuation. Open Court, 1946.

Livingston, James. Pragmatism and the Political Economy of Cultural Revolution, 1850-1940. University of North Carolina Press, 1994.

Loewen, James W. Lies My Teacher Told Me: Everything Your American History Textbook Got Wrong. New Press, 1995.

MacGilvray, Eric A. Reconstructing Public Reason. Harvard University Press, 2004.

Margolis, Joseph. Reinventing Pragmatism: American Philosophy at the End of the Twentieth Century. Cornell University Press, 2002.

Mead, George Herbert. Mind, Self, and Society. Edited by Charles W. Morris, University of Chicago Press, 1934.

---. The Philosophy of the Act. Edited by Charles W. Morris, University of Chicago Press, 1938.

---. The Philosophy of the Present. Edited by Arthur E. Murphy, Open Court, 1932.

---. Movements of Thought in the Nineteenth Century. Edited by Merritt H. Moore, University of Chicago Press, 1936.

---. Selected Writings. Edited by Andrew J. Reck, Bobbs-Merrill, 1964.

Menand, Louis. The Metaphysical Club. Farrar, Straus and Giroux, 2001.

---. Pragmatism: A Reader. Vintage Books, 1997.

Miller, David L. George Herbert Mead: Self, Language, and the World. University of Chicago Press, 1973.

Mills, C. Wright. Sociology and Pragmatism. Oxford University Press, 1964.

Morris, Charles W. The Pragmatic Movement in American Philosophy. George Braziller, 1970.

Murphy, John P. Pragmatism: From Peirce to Davidson. Westview Press, 1990.

Myers, Gerald E. William James: His Life and Thought. Yale University Press, 1986.

Nagl, Ludwig. Pragmatism vs. Europe. Rodopi, 1999.

Pappas, Gregory Fernando. John Dewey's Ethics: Democracy as Experience. Indiana University Press, 2008.

Peirce, Charles Sanders. Collected Papers. Edited by Charles Hartshorne and Paul Weiss, 8 vols., Harvard University Press, 1931-1958.

---. Writings of Charles S. Peirce: A Chronological Edition. Indiana University Press, 1982-.

---. The Essential Peirce. Edited by Nathan Houser and Christian Kloesel, 2 vols., Indiana University Press, 1992-1998.

Perry, Ralph Barton. The Thought and Character of William James. 2 vols., Little, Brown, 1935.

Posnock, Ross. The Trial of Curiosity: Henry James, William James, and the Challenge of Modernity. Oxford University Press, 1991.

Posner, Richard A. The Problems of Jurisprudence. Harvard University Press, 1990.

---. Law, Pragmatism, and Democracy. Harvard University Press, 2003.

Putnam, Hilary. Pragmatism: An Open Question. Blackwell, 1995.

---. Realism with a Human Face. Harvard University Press, 1990.

---. The Many Faces of Realism. Open Court, 1987.

---. Words and Life. Harvard University Press, 1994.

Putnam, Ruth Anna. The Cambridge Companion to William James. Cambridge University Press, 1997.

Richardson, Alan. Carnap's Construction of the World. Cambridge University Press, 1998.

Rockefeller, Steven C. John Dewey: Religious Faith and Democratic Humanism. Columbia University Press, 1991.

Rorty, Richard. Philosophy and the Mirror of Nature. Princeton University Press, 1979.

---. Consequences of Pragmatism. University of Minnesota Press, 1982.

---. Contingency, Irony, and Solidarity. Cambridge University Press, 1989.

---. Objectivity, Relativism, and Truth. Cambridge University Press, 1991.

---. Truth and Progress. Cambridge University Press, 1998.

---. Philosophy and Social Hope. Penguin Books, 1999.

Ryan, Alan. John Dewey and the High Tide of American Liberalism. W.W. Norton, 1995.

Scheffler, Israel. Four Pragmatists: A Critical Introduction to Peirce, James, Mead, and Dewey. Routledge, 1974.

Schneider, Herbert W. A History of American Philosophy. 2nd ed., Columbia University Press, 1963.

Seigfried, Charlene Haddock. Pragmatism and Feminism: Reweaving the Social Fabric. University of Chicago Press, 1996.

---. editor. Feminist Interpretations of John Dewey. Pennsylvania State University Press, 2002.

Shook, John R. Dewey's Empirical Theory of Knowledge and Reality. Vanderbilt University Press, 2000.

---. The Chicago School of Pragmatism. Thoemmes Press, 2000.

Shusterman, Richard. Practicing Philosophy: Pragmatism and the Philosophical Life. Routledge, 1997.

Simon, Linda. Genuine Reality: A Life of William James. Harcourt Brace, 1998.

Sleeper, Ralph W. The Necessity of Pragmatism: John Dewey's Conception of Philosophy. Yale University Press, 1986.

Smith, John E. Purpose and Thought: The Meaning of Pragmatism. Yale University Press, 1978.

---. The Spirit of American Philosophy. Oxford University Press, 1963.

Stuhr, John J. Classical American Philosophy. Oxford University Press, 1987.

---. Pragmatism and Classical American Philosophy. 2nd ed., Oxford University Press, 2000.

---. Genealogical Pragmatism: Philosophy, Experience, and Community. State University of New York Press, 1997.

Taylor, Eugene. William James on Consciousness beyond the Margin. Princeton University Press, 1996.

Thayer, H.S. Meaning and Action: A Critical History of Pragmatism. 2nd ed., Hackett Publishing, 1981.

Tiles, J.E. Dewey. Routledge, 1988.

Welchman, Jennifer. Dewey's Ethical Thought. Cornell University Press, 1995.

West, Cornel. The American Evasion of Philosophy: A Genealogy of Pragmatism. University of Wisconsin Press, 1989.

---. Prophetic Pragmatism: A Reader. Westminster John Knox Press, 1991.

---. Prophetic Thought in Postmodern Times. Common Courage Press, 1993.

White, Morton G. Social Thought in America: The Revolt Against Formalism. Viking Press, 1949.

---. Science and Sentiment in America. Oxford University Press, 1972.

---. Pragmatism and the American Mind. Oxford University Press, 1973.

Wiener, Philip P. Evolution and the Founders of Pragmatism. University of Pennsylvania Press, 1949.

Wilson, Daniel J. Science, Community, and the Transformation of American Philosophy, 1860-1930. University of Chicago Press, 1990.

Chapter Ten

Adolphs, Ralph. The Social Brain: Neural Basis of Social Knowledge. Annual Reviews, 2009.

Allen, Colin. Species of Mind: The Philosophy and Biology of Cognitive Ethology. MIT Press, 1997.

Andrews, Kristin. The Animal Mind: An Introduction to the Philosophy of Animal Cognition. Routledge, 2015.

---. Do Apes Read Minds? Toward a New Folk Psychology. MIT Press, 2012.

Balda, Russell P., et al., editors. Animal Cognition in Nature. Academic Press, 1998.

Bekoff, Marc. Animal Emotions: Exploring Passionate Natures. New World Library, 2007.

---. The Cognitive Animal: Empirical and Theoretical Perspectives on Animal Cognition. MIT Press, 2002.

---. Wild Justice: The Moral Lives of Animals. University of Chicago Press, 2009.

Boesch, Christophe. Wild Cultures: A Comparison Between Chimpanzee and Human Cultures. Cambridge University Press, 2012.

Bostrom, Nick. Superintelligence: Paths, Dangers, Strategies. Oxford University Press, 2014.

Bradshaw, Gay A. Elephants on the Edge: What Animals Teach Us about Humanity. Yale University Press, 2009.

Brooks, Rodney A. Cambrian Intelligence: The Early History of the New AI. MIT Press, 1999.

---. Flesh and Machines: How Robots Will Change Us. Pantheon Books, 2002.

Bugnyar, Thomas, et al. "Ravens Judge Competitors Through Experience with Play Caching." Current Biology, vol. 17, no. 20, 2007, pp. 1804-1808.

Byrne, Richard W. The Thinking Ape: Evolutionary Origins of Intelligence. Oxford University Press, 1995.

Call, Josep, and Michael Tomasello. The Gestural Communication of Apes and Monkeys. Lawrence Erlbaum Associates, 2007.

Chalmers, David J. The Character of Consciousness. Oxford University Press, 2010.

---. The Conscious Mind: In Search of a Fundamental Theory. Oxford University Press, 1996.

Cheney, Dorothy L., and Robert M. Seyfarth. Baboon Metaphysics: The Evolution of a Social Mind. University of Chicago Press, 2007.

---. How Monkeys See the World. University of Chicago Press, 1990.

Chomsky, Noam. Language and Problems of Knowledge. MIT Press, 1988.

Clark, Andy. Being There: Putting Brain, Body, and World Together Again. MIT Press, 1997.

---. Extended Mind. Oxford University Press, 2008.

---. Natural-Born Cyborgs: Minds, Technologies, and the Future of Human Intelligence. Oxford University Press, 2003.

Clayton, Nicola S., and Anthony Dickinson. "Episodic-like Memory During Cache Recovery by Scrub Jays." Nature, vol. 395, 1998, pp. 272-274.

Connor, Richard C. "Dolphin Social Intelligence: Complex Alliance Relationships in Bottlenose Dolphins and a Consideration of Selective Environments for Extreme Brain Size Evolution in Mammals." Philosophical Transactions of the Royal Society B, vol. 362, 2007, pp. 587-602.

Corballis, Michael C. The Recursive Mind: The Origins of Human Language, Thought, and Civilization. Princeton University Press, 2011.

Darwin, Charles. The Descent of Man and Selection in Relation to Sex. John Murray, 1871.

---. The Expression of the Emotions in Man and Animals. John Murray, 1872.

de Waal, Frans B.M. Are We Smart Enough to Know How Smart Animals Are?. W.W. Norton, 2016.

---. Chimpanzee Politics: Power and Sex Among Apes. Johns Hopkins University Press, 1982.

---. The Ape and the Sushi Master: Cultural Reflections by a Primatologist. Basic Books, 2001.

Dennett, Daniel C. Consciousness Explained. Little, Brown and Company, 1991.

---. Darwin's Dangerous Idea: Evolution and the Meanings of Life. Simon & Schuster, 1995.

---. From Bacteria to Bach and Back: The Evolution of Minds. W.W. Norton, 2017.

Dreyfus, Hubert L. What Computers Can't Do: The Limits of Artificial Intelligence. Harper & Row, 1972.

---. What Computers Still Can't Do: A Critique of Artificial Reason. MIT Press, 1992.

Emery, Nathan J. Bird Brain: An Exploration of Avian Intelligence. Princeton University Press, 2016.

Emery, Nathan J., and Nicola S. Clayton. "The Mentality of Crows: Convergent Evolution of Intelligence in Corvids and Apes." Science, vol. 306, 2004, pp. 1903-1907.

Fodor, Jerry A. The Modularity of Mind. MIT Press, 1983.

Gardner, Howard. Frames of Mind: The Theory of Multiple Intelligences. Basic Books, 1983.

Gibson, James J. The Ecological Approach to Visual Perception. Houghton Mifflin, 1979.

Goodall, Jane. In the Shadow of Man. Houghton Mifflin, 1971.

---. The Chimpanzees of Gombe: Patterns of Behavior. Harvard University Press, 1986.

---. Through a Window: My Thirty Years with the Chimpanzees of Gombe. Houghton Mifflin, 1990.

Griffin, Donald R. Animal Thinking. Harvard University Press, 1984.

---. The Question of Animal Awareness. Rockefeller University Press, 1976.

Hare, Brian, and Vanessa Woods. The Genius of Dogs. Dutton, 2013.

Heinrich, Bernd. Mind of the Raven. HarperCollins, 1999.

---. Ravens in Winter. Summit Books, 1989.

Herman, Louis M. "Intelligence and Rational Behaviour in the Bottlenosed Dolphin." Rational Animals?, edited by Susan Hurley and Matthew Nudds, Oxford University Press, 2006, pp. 439-467.

Heyes, Cecilia M. Cognitive Gadgets: The Cultural Evolution of Thinking. Harvard University Press, 2018.

Hunt, Gavin R. "Manufacture and Use of Hook-Tools by New Caledonian Crows." Nature, vol. 379, 1996, pp. 249-251.

Hurley, Susan, and Matthew Nudds, editors. Rational Animals?. Oxford University Press, 2006.

Hutchins, Edwin. Cognition in the Wild. MIT Press, 1995.

Kahneman, Daniel. Thinking, Fast and Slow. Farrar, Straus and Giroux, 2011.

Kawai, Masao. "Newly-Acquired Pre-Cultural Behavior of the Natural Troop of Japanese Monkeys on Koshima Islet." Primates, vol. 6, no. 1, 1965, pp. 1-30.

Kellogg, Winthrop N., and Luella A. Kellogg. The Ape and the Child. McGraw-Hill, 1933.

King, Barbara J. How Animals Grieve. University of Chicago Press, 2013.

Köhler, Wolfgang. The Mentality of Apes. Kegan Paul, Trench, Trubner & Co., 1925.

Krützen, Michael, et al. "Cultural Transmission of Tool Use in Bottlenose Dolphins." Proceedings of the National Academy of Sciences, vol. 102, no. 25, 2005, pp. 8939-8943.

Kurzweil, Ray. The Age of Spiritual Machines. Viking, 1999.

---. The Singularity Is Near. Viking, 2005.

LeCun, Yann, et al. "Deep Learning." Nature, vol. 521, 2015, pp. 436-444.

Marino, Lori. "Convergence of Complex Cognitive Abilities in Cetaceans and Primates." Brain, Behavior and Evolution, vol. 59, 2002, pp. 21-32.

McCarthy, John, et al. "A Proposal for the Dartmouth Summer Research Project on Artificial Intelligence." AI Magazine, vol. 27, no. 4, 2006, pp. 12-14.

McGrew, William C. Chimpanzee Material Culture: Implications for Human Evolution. Cambridge University Press, 1992.

---. The Cultured Chimpanzee: Reflections on Cultural Primatology. Cambridge University Press, 2004.

Mitchell, Melanie. Artificial Intelligence: A Guide for Thinking Humans. Farrar, Straus and Giroux, 2019.

Mitchell, Robert W., et al., editors. Self-Awareness in Animals and Humans. Cambridge University Press, 1994.

Moss, Cynthia. Elephant Memories: Thirteen Years in the Life of an Elephant Family. William Morrow, 1988.

Nagel, Thomas. "What Is It Like to Be a Bat?" The Philosophical Review, vol. 83, no. 4, 1974, pp. 435-450.

O'Connell, Caitjan, et al. "The Elephant's Secret Sense: The Hidden Life of the Wild Herds of Africa*. Free Press, 2007.

Pepperberg, Irene M. Alex & Me. Harper, 2008.

---. The Alex Studies: Cognitive and Communicative Abilities of Grey Parrots. Harvard University Press, 1999.

Plotnik, Joshua M., et al. "Self-Recognition in an Asian Elephant." Proceedings of the National Academy of Sciences, vol. 103, no. 45, 2006, pp. 17053-17057.

Poole, Joyce H. Coming of Age with Elephants. Hyperion, 1996.

Premack, David. "Human and Animal Cognition: Continuity and Discontinuity." Proceedings of the National Academy of Sciences, vol. 104, no. 35, 2007, pp. 13861-13867.

---. Intelligence in Ape and Man. Lawrence Erlbaum Associates, 1976.

Premack, David, and Guy Woodruff. "Does the Chimpanzee Have a Theory of Mind?" Behavioral and Brain Sciences, vol. 1, no. 4, 1978, pp. 515-526.

Reiss, Diana, and Lori Marino. "Mirror Self-Recognition in the Bottlenose Dolphin: A Case of Cognitive Convergence." Proceedings of the National Academy of Sciences, vol. 98, no. 10, 2001, pp. 5937-5942.

Russell, Stuart J. Human Compatible: Artificial Intelligence and the Problem of Control. Viking, 2019.

Russell, Stuart J., and Peter Norvig. Artificial Intelligence: A Modern Approach. 4th ed., Pearson, 2020.

Savage-Rumbaugh, Sue, et al. Apes, Language, and the Human Mind. Oxford University Press, 1998.

Searle, John R. "Minds, Brains, and Programs." Behavioral and Brain Sciences, vol. 3, no. 3, 1980, pp. 417-424.

---. The Rediscovery of the Mind. MIT Press, 1992.

Seyfarth, Robert M., et al. "Monkey Responses to Three Different Alarm Calls: Evidence of Predator Classification and Semantic Communication." Science, vol. 210, 1980, pp. 801-803.

Shanahan, Murray. The Technological Singularity. MIT Press, 2015.

Shettleworth, Sara J. Cognition, Evolution, and Behavior. 2nd ed., Oxford University Press, 2010.

---. Fundamentals of Comparative Cognition. Oxford University Press, 1998.

Silver, David, et al. "Mastering the Game of Go with Deep Neural Networks and Tree Search." Nature, vol. 529, 2016, pp. 484-489.

Sober, Elliott. Evidence and Evolution: The Logic Behind the Science. Cambridge University Press, 2008.

Suddendorf, Thomas. The Gap: The Science of What Separates Us from Other Animals. Basic Books, 2013.

Tegmark, Max. Life 3.0: Being Human in the Age of Artificial Intelligence. Knopf, 2017.

Tomasello, Michael. The Cultural Origins of Human Cognition. Harvard University Press, 1999.

---. A Natural History of Human Thinking. Harvard University Press, 2014.

---. Becoming Human: A Theory of Ontogeny. Harvard University Press, 2019.

Tomasello, Michael, et al. "Understanding and Sharing Intentions: The Origins of Cultural Cognition." Behavioral and Brain Sciences, vol. 28, no. 5, 2005, pp. 675-691.

Turing, Alan M. "Computing Machinery and Intelligence." Mind, vol. 59, no. 236, 1950, pp. 433-460.

van Schaik, Carel P., et al. "Orangutan Cultures and the Evolution of Material Culture." Science, vol. 299, 2003, pp. 102-105.

Varela, Francisco J., et al. The Embodied Mind: Cognitive Science and Human Experience. MIT Press, 1991.

Wasserman, Edward A., and Thomas R. Zentall, editors. Comparative Cognition: Experimental Explorations of Animal Intelligence. Oxford University Press, 2006.

Whiten, Andrew, et al. "Cultures in Chimpanzees." Nature, vol. 399, 1999, pp. 682-685.

Wilson, Edward O. The Social Conquest of Earth. Liveright, 2012.

---. Sociobiology: The New Synthesis. Harvard University Press, 1975.

Yudkowsky, Eliezer. Rationality: From AI to Zombies. Machine Intelligence Research Institute, 2015.

Chapter Eleven

Adler, Alfred. Understanding Human Nature. Translated by Walter Béran Wolfe, Greenberg Publisher, 1927.

Allport, Gordon W. The Nature of Prejudice. Addison-Wesley, 1954.

---. Pattern and Growth in Personality. Holt, Rinehart and Winston, 1961.

American Psychiatric Association. Diagnostic and Statistical Manual of Mental Disorders. 5th ed., American Psychiatric Publishing, 2013.

Anderson, Michael L. After Phrenology: Neural Reuse and the Interactive Brain. MIT Press, 2014.

Ariely, Dan. Predictably Irrational: The Hidden Forces That Shape Our Decisions. HarperCollins, 2008.

Aronson, Elliot, et al. Social Psychology. 9th ed., Pearson, 2019.

Baars, Bernard J. A Cognitive Theory of Consciousness. Cambridge University Press, 1988.

---. The Conscious Access Hypothesis: Origins and Recent Evidence. Trends in Cognitive Sciences, 2002.

Bandura, Albert. Social Learning Theory. Prentice-Hall, 1977.

---. Self-Efficacy: The Exercise of Control. W.H. Freeman, 1997.

---. Social Foundations of Thought and Action: A Social Cognitive Theory. Prentice-Hall, 1986.

Baron-Cohen, Simon. The Essential Difference: Male and Female Brains and the Truth about Autism. Basic Books, 2003.

---. Mindblindness: An Essay on Autism and Theory of Mind. MIT Press, 1995.

Beck, Aaron T. Depression: Causes and Treatment. University of Pennsylvania Press, 1967.

---. Cognitive Therapy and the Emotional Disorders. International Universities Press, 1976.

Beck, Aaron T., et al. Cognitive Therapy of Depression. Guilford Press, 1979.

Bem, Daryl J. "Self-Perception Theory." Advances in Experimental Social Psychology, vol. 6, edited by Leonard Berkowitz, Academic Press, 1972, pp. 1-62.

Blackmore, Susan. Consciousness: An Introduction. 2nd ed., Oxford University Press, 2010.

Bowlby, John. Attachment and Loss. 3 vols., Basic Books, 1969-1980.

Brewer, Marilynn B. "In-Group Bias in the Minimal Intergroup Situation: A Cognitive-Motivational Analysis." Psychological Bulletin, vol. 86, no. 2, 1979, pp. 307-324.

Brown, Roger. Social Psychology. 2nd ed., Free Press, 1986.

Bruner, Jerome S. Acts of Meaning. Harvard University Press, 1990.

---. Actual Minds, Possible Worlds. Harvard University Press, 1986.

Burns, David D. Feeling Good: The New Mood Therapy. William Morrow, 1980.

Buss, David M. Evolutionary Psychology: The New Science of the Mind. 6th ed., Pearson, 2019.

Cacioppo, John T., and William Patrick. Loneliness: Human Nature and the Need for Social Connection. W.W. Norton, 2008.

Chalmers, David J. The Character of Consciousness. Oxford University Press, 2010.

---. The Conscious Mind: In Search of a Fundamental Theory. Oxford University Press, 1996.

Chomsky, Noam. Language and Mind. 3rd ed., Cambridge University Press, 2006.

Cialdini, Robert B. Influence: The Psychology of Persuasion. Rev. ed., Harper Business, 2006.

Clark, Andy. Being There: Putting Brain, Body, and World Together Again. MIT Press, 1997.

---. Supersizing the Mind: Embodiment, Action, and Cognitive Extension. Oxford University Press, 2011.

Cosmides, Leda, and John Tooby. "Evolutionary Psychology: A Primer." Center for Evolutionary Psychology, University of California, Santa Barbara, 1997.

Csikszentmihalyi, Mihaly. Flow: The Psychology of Optimal Experience. Harper & Row, 1990.

Damasio, Antonio R. Descartes' Error: Emotion, Reason, and the Human Brain. G.P. Putnam's Sons, 1994.

---. The Feeling of What Happens: Body and Emotion in the Making of Consciousness. Harcourt Brace, 1999.

---. Self Comes to Mind: Constructing the Conscious Brain. Pantheon Books, 2010.

Darwin, Charles. The Expression of the Emotions in Man and Animals. John Murray, 1872.

Dennett, Daniel C. Consciousness Explained. Little, Brown and Company, 1991.

---. From Bacteria to Bach and Back: The Evolution of Minds. W.W. Norton, 2017.

Doidge, Norman. The Brain That Changes Itself: Stories of Personal Triumph from the Frontiers of Brain Science. Viking, 2007.

---. The Brain's Way of Healing: Remarkable Discoveries and Recoveries from the Frontiers of Neuroplasticity. Viking, 2015.

Dunning, David, and Justin Kruger. "Unskilled and Unaware of It: How Difficulties in Recognizing One's Own Incompetence Lead to Inflated Self-Assessments." Journal of Personality and Social Psychology, vol. 77, no. 6, 1999, pp. 1121-1134.

Eagly, Alice H., and Shelly Chaiken. The Psychology of Attitudes. Harcourt Brace Jovanovich, 1993.

Ellis, Albert. Reason and Emotion in Psychotherapy. Lyle Stuart, 1962.

---. A New Guide to Rational Living. Wilshire Book Company, 1975.

Erikson, Erik H. Childhood and Society. 2nd ed., W.W. Norton, 1963.

---. Identity: Youth and Crisis. W.W. Norton, 1968.

---. The Life Cycle Completed. W.W. Norton, 1982.

Evans, Jonathan St. B.T. Thinking Twice: Two Minds in One Brain. Oxford University Press, 2010.

Festinger, Leon. A Theory of Cognitive Dissonance. Stanford University Press, 1957.

---. When Prophecy Fails. University of Minnesota Press, 1956.

Fiske, Susan T., and Shelley E. Taylor. Social Cognition: From Brains to Culture. 3rd ed., SAGE Publications, 2017.

Fodor, Jerry A. The Modularity of Mind. MIT Press, 1983.

Frankl, Viktor E. Man's Search for Meaning. Beacon Press, 1963.

Freud, Sigmund. The Interpretation of Dreams. Translated by James Strachey, Basic Books, 1955.

---. The Ego and the Id. Translated by Joan Riviere, Hogarth Press, 1927.

---. Civilization and Its Discontents. Translated by James Strachey, W.W. Norton, 1961.

Gazzaniga, Michael S. The Split Brain Revisited. Scientific American, 1998.

---. Who's in Charge? Free Will and the Science of the Brain. Ecco, 2011.

---. The Consciousness Instinct: Unraveling the Mystery of How the Brain Makes Mind. Farrar, Straus and Giroux, 2018.

Gilbert, Daniel T. Stumbling on Happiness. Knopf, 2006.

Gilovich, Thomas, et al. Social Psychology. 4th ed., W.W. Norton, 2019.

Goleman, Daniel. Emotional Intelligence. Bantam Books, 1995.

Grandin, Temple. Thinking in Pictures: My Life with Autism. Doubleday, 1995.

Greenwald, Anthony G., et al. "Measuring Individual Differences in Implicit Cognition: The Implicit Association Test."

Journal of Personality and Social Psychology, vol. 74, no. 6, 1998, pp. 1464-1480.

Haidt, Jonathan. The Happiness Hypothesis. Basic Books, 2006.

---. The Righteous Mind: Why Good People Are Divided by Politics and Religion. Pantheon Books, 2012.

Hamilton, William D. "The Genetical Evolution of Social Behaviour." Journal of Theoretical Biology, vol. 7, no. 1, 1964, pp. 1-16.

Harlow, Harry F. "The Nature of Love." American Psychologist, vol. 13, no. 12, 1958, pp. 673-685.

Heath, Chip, and Dan Heath. Made to Stick: Why Some Ideas Survive and Others Die. Random House, 2007.

Heider, Fritz. The Psychology of Interpersonal Relations. John Wiley & Sons, 1958.

Henrich, Joseph. The WEIRDest People in the World. Farrar, Straus and Giroux, 2020.

Henrich, Joseph, et al. "The Weirdest People in the World?" Behavioral and Brain Sciences, vol. 33, no. 2-3, 2010, pp. 61-83.

Hoff Sommers, Christina, and Sally Satel. One Nation Under Therapy. St. Martin's Press, 2005.

Hofmann, Stefan G., et al. "The Efficacy of Cognitive Behavioral Therapy: A Review of Meta-analyses." Cognitive Therapy and Research, vol. 36, no. 5, 2012, pp. 427-440.

Horney, Karen. Neurosis and Human Growth. W.W. Norton, 1950.

---. The Neurotic Personality of Our Time. W.W. Norton, 1937.

James, William. The Principles of Psychology. 2 vols., Henry Holt, 1890.

---. The Varieties of Religious Experience. Longmans, Green, 1902.

Janis, Irving L. Groupthink: Psychological Studies of Policy Decisions and Fiascoes. 2nd ed., Houghton Mifflin, 1982.

Johnson, Mark. The Body in the Mind: The Bodily Basis of Meaning, Imagination, and Reason. University of Chicago Press, 1987.

Jung, Carl Gustav. The Archetypes and the Collective Unconscious. Translated by R.F.C. Hull, Princeton University Press, 1959.

---. Man and His Symbols. Doubleday, 1964.

---. Memories, Dreams, Reflections. Translated by Richard and Clara Winston, Pantheon Books, 1961.

---. Psychological Types. Translated by H.G. Baynes, Princeton University Press, 1971.

Kahneman, Daniel. Thinking, Fast and Slow. Farrar, Straus and Giroux, 2011.

Kahneman, Daniel, and Amos Tversky. "Prospect Theory: An Analysis of Decision under Risk." Econometrica, vol. 47, no. 2, 1979, pp. 263-291.

---. "Judgment Under Uncertainty: Heuristics and Biases." Science, vol. 185, no. 4157, 1974, pp. 1124-1131.

Kandel, Eric R. In Search of Memory: The Emergence of a New Science of Mind. W.W. Norton, 2006.

---. The Age of Insight: The Quest to Understand the Unconscious in Art, Mind, and Brain. Random House, 2012.

Kelley, Harold H. "Attribution Theory in Social Psychology." Nebraska Symposium on Motivation, vol. 15, edited by David Levine, University of Nebraska Press, 1967, pp. 192-238.

Klein, Gary. Sources of Power: How People Make Decisions. MIT Press, 1998.

Kohlberg, Lawrence. The Philosophy of Moral Development. Harper & Row, 1981.

Lakoff, George. Women, Fire, and Dangerous Things: What Categories Reveal about the Mind. University of Chicago Press, 1987.

Lakoff, George, and Mark Johnson. The Embodied Mind: The Bodily Basis of Meaning, Imagination, and Reason. Basic Books, 1999.

---. Metaphors We Live By. University of Chicago Press, 1980.

LeDoux, Joseph. The Emotional Brain: The Mysterious Underpinnings of Emotional Life. Simon & Schuster, 1996.

---. The Synaptic Self: How Our Brains Become Who We Are. Viking, 2002.

Linehan, Marsha M. Cognitive-Behavioral Treatment of Borderline Personality Disorder. Guilford Press, 1993.

Loftus, Elizabeth F. Eyewitness Testimony. Harvard University Press, 1979.

Maslow, Abraham H. Toward a Psychology of Being. 3rd ed., John Wiley & Sons, 1999.

---. Motivation and Personality. 3rd ed., Harper & Row, 1987.

May, Rollo. Love and Will. W.W. Norton, 1969.

---. The Meaning of Anxiety. Rev. ed., W.W. Norton, 1977.

McCrae, Robert R., and Paul T. Costa Jr. Personality in Adulthood: A Five-Factor Theory Perspective. 2nd ed., Guilford Press, 2003.

Milgram, Stanley. Obedience to Authority: An Experimental View. Harper & Row, 1974.

Miller, George A. "The Magical Number Seven, Plus or Minus Two: Some Limits on Our Capacity for Processing Information." Psychological Review, vol. 63, no. 2, 1956, pp. 81-97.

Mischel, Walter. The Marshmallow Test: Mastering Self-Control. Little, Brown and Company, 2014.

Myers, David G. Social Psychology. 13th ed., McGraw-Hill Education, 2019.

---. Psychology. 12th ed., Worth Publishers, 2018.

Nisbett, Richard E. The Geography of Thought: How Asians and Westerners Think Differently... and Why. Free Press, 2003.

Nisbett, Richard E., and Lee Ross. Human Inference: Strategies and Shortcomings of Social Judgment. Prentice-Hall, 1980.

Pavlov, Ivan P. Conditioned Reflexes: An Investigation of the Physiological Activity of the Cerebral Cortex. Translated by G.V. Anrep, Oxford University Press, 1927.

Piaget, Jean. The Construction of Reality in the Child. Translated by Margaret Cook, Basic Books, 1954.

---. The Origins of Intelligence in Children. Translated by Margaret Cook, International Universities Press, 1952.

---. The Psychology of the Child. Basic Books, 1969.

Pinker, Steven. How the Mind Works. W.W. Norton, 1997.

---. The Better Angels of Our Nature: Why Violence Has Declined. Viking, 2011.

---. The Blank Slate: The Modern Denial of Human Nature. Viking, 2002.

Pollan, Michael. How to Change Your Mind: What the New Science of Psychedelics Teaches Us about Consciousness, Dying, Addiction, Depression, and Transcendence. Penguin Press, 2018.

Ramachandran, V.S. The Tell-Tale Brain: A Neuroscientist's Quest for What Makes Us Human. W.W. Norton, 2011.

---. Phantoms in the Brain: Probing the Mysteries of the Human Mind. William Morrow, 1998.

Rogers, Carl R. On Becoming a Person. Houghton Mifflin, 1961.

---. Client-Centered Therapy. Houghton Mifflin, 1951.

Ross, Lee. "The Intuitive Psychologist and His Shortcomings: Distortions in the Attribution Process." Advances in

Experimental Social Psychology, vol. 10, edited by Leonard Berkowitz, Academic Press, 1977, pp. 173-220.

Sacks, Oliver. The Man Who Mistook His Wife for a Hat. Summit Books, 1985.

---. Awakenings. Doubleday, 1973.

Sapolsky, Robert M. Behave: The Biology of Humans at Our Best and Worst. Penguin Press, 2017.

---. Why Zebras Don't Get Ulcers. 3rd ed., Times Books, 2004.

Seligman, Martin E.P. Authentic Happiness. Free Press, 2002.

---. Learned Optimism. Knopf, 1991.

---. The Optimistic Child. Houghton Mifflin, 1995.

Sherif, Muzafer, et al. The Robbers Cave Experiment: Intergroup Conflict and Cooperation. Wesleyan University Press, 1988.

Skinner, B.F. Beyond Freedom and Dignity. Knopf, 1971.

---. Science and Human Behavior. Macmillan, 1953.

---. Verbal Behavior. Appleton-Century-Crofts, 1957.

---. Walden Two. Macmillan, 1948.

Sperry, Roger W. "Hemisphere Deconnection and Unity in Conscious Awareness." American Psychologist, vol. 23, no. 10, 1968, pp. 723-733.

Steele, Claude M. Whistling Vivaldi: How Stereotypes Affect Us and What We Can Do. W.W. Norton, 2010.

Steele, Claude M., and Joshua Aronson. "Stereotype Threat and the Intellectual Test Performance of African Americans."

Journal of Personality and Social Psychology, vol. 69, no. 5, 1995, pp. 797-811.

Sternberg, Robert J. Cognitive Psychology. 7th ed., Cengage Learning, 2017.

Sue, Derald Wing, and David Sue. Counseling the Culturally Diverse: Theory and Practice. 8th ed., John Wiley & Sons, 2019.

Tajfel, Henri. Human Groups and Social Categories. Cambridge University Press, 1981.

Tajfel, Henri, and John C. Turner. "The Social Identity Theory of Intergroup Behavior." Psychology of Intergroup Relations, edited by Stephen Worchel and William G. Austin, Nelson-Hall, 1986, pp. 7-24.

Thaler, Richard H. Misbehaving: The Making of Behavioral Economics. W.W. Norton, 2015.

Thaler, Richard H., and Cass R. Sunstein. Nudge: Improving Decisions about Health, Wealth, and Happiness. Yale University Press, 2008.

Tononi, Giulio. "An Information Integration Theory of Consciousness." BMC Neuroscience, vol. 5, 2004, pp. 1-22.

Trivers, Robert L. "The Evolution of Reciprocal Altruism." The Quarterly Review of Biology, vol. 46, no. 1, 1971, pp. 35-57.

Tversky, Amos, and Daniel Kahneman. "Availability: A Heuristic for Judging Frequency and Probability." Cognitive Psychology, vol. 5, no. 2, 1973, pp. 207-232.

---. "The Framing of Decisions and the Psychology of Choice." Science, vol. 211, no. 4481, 1981, pp. 453-458.

Vygotsky, Lev S. Mind in Society: The Development of Higher Psychological Processes. Harvard University Press, 1978.

Watson, John B. Behaviorism. University of Chicago Press, 1930.

Wilson, Timothy D. Strangers to Ourselves: Discovering the Adaptive Unconscious. Harvard University Press, 2002.

Yalom, Irvin D. The Theory and Practice of Group Psychotherapy. 5th ed., Basic Books, 2005.

---. Existential Psychotherapy. Basic Books, 1980.

Zimbardo, Philip G. The Lucifer Effect: Understanding How Good People Turn Evil. Random House, 2007.

Chapter Twelve

Adorno, Theodor W., and Max Horkheimer. Dialectic of Enlightenment. Translated by John Cumming, Continuum, 1972.

Althusser, Louis. For Marx. Translated by Ben Brewster, Verso, 1969.

---. Lenin and Philosophy and Other Essays. Translated by Ben Brewster, Monthly Review Press, 1971.

Anderson, Benedict. Imagined Communities: Reflections on the Origin and Spread of Nationalism. Rev. ed., Verso, 1991.

Anderson, Perry. Considerations on Western Marxism. New Left Books, 1976.

Balibar, Étienne, and Immanuel Wallerstein. Race, Nation, Class: Ambiguous Identities. Verso, 1991.

Bellah, Robert N., et al. Habits of the Heart: Individualism and Commitment in American Life. University of California Press, 1985.

Benjamin, Walter. Illuminations. Edited by Hannah Arendt, Schocken Books, 1968.

Berman, Marshall. All That Is Solid Melts into Air: The Experience of Modernity. Simon & Schuster, 1982.

Boas, Franz. Anthropology and Modern Life. W.W. Norton, 1928.

---. The Mind of Primitive Man. Macmillan, 1911.

---. Race, Language and Culture. Macmillan, 1940.

Bourdieu, Pierre. Distinction: A Social Critique of the Judgement of Taste. Translated by Richard Nice, Harvard University Press, 1984.

---. Language and Symbolic Power. Edited by John B. Thompson, Harvard University Press, 1991.

---. The Logic of Practice. Translated by Richard Nice, Stanford University Press, 1990.

---. Outline of a Theory of Practice. Translated by Richard Nice, Cambridge University Press, 1977.

---. Reproduction in Education, Society and Culture. Translated by Richard Nice, SAGE Publications, 1977.

---. The State Nobility: Elite Schools in the Field of Power. Translated by Lauretta C. Clough, Stanford University Press, 1996.

Bourdieu, Pierre, and Jean-Claude Passeron. The Inheritors: French Students and Their Relations to Culture. Translated by Richard Nice, University of Chicago Press, 1979.

Bourdieu, Pierre, and Loïc J.D. Wacquant. An Invitation to Reflexive Sociology. University of Chicago Press, 1992.

Brown, Paula Glick. Gender and Ethnicity in the Bolivian Andes. University of New Mexico Press, 1987.

Buroway, Michael. Manufacturing Consent: Changes in the Labor Process under Monopoly Capitalism. University of Chicago Press, 1979.

Collins, Patricia Hill. Black Feminist Thought: Knowledge, Consciousness, and the Politics of Empowerment. 2nd ed., Routledge, 2000.

Crenshaw, Kimberlé. "Mapping the Margins: Intersectionality, Identity Politics, and Violence against Women of Color." Stanford Law Review, vol. 43, no. 6, 1991, pp. 1241-1299.

Durkheim, Émile. The Division of Labor in Society. Translated by Lewis A. Coser, Free Press, 1984.

---. The Elementary Forms of Religious Life. Translated by Karen E. Fields, Free Press, 1995.

---. The Rules of Sociological Method. Translated by Sarah A. Solovay and John H. Mueller, Free Press, 1964.

---. Suicide: A Study in Sociology. Translated by John A. Spaulding and George Simpson, Free Press, 1951.

Engels, Friedrich. The Origin of the Family, Private Property and the State. International Publishers, 1972.

Faron, Louis C. Hawks of the Sun: Mapuche Morality and Its Ritual Attributes. University of Pittsburgh Press, 1964.

---. The Mapuche Indians of Chile. Holt, Rinehart and Winston, 1968.

Foucault, Michel. Discipline and Punish: The Birth of the Prison. Translated by Alan Sheridan, Pantheon Books, 1977.

---. The History of Sexuality. 3 vols., Translated by Robert Hurley, Pantheon Books, 1978-1986.

---. Madness and Civilization: A History of Insanity in the Age of Reason. Translated by Richard Howard, Pantheon Books, 1965.

---. Power/Knowledge: Selected Interviews and Other Writings 1972-1977. Edited by Colin Gordon, Pantheon Books, 1980.

---. Security, Territory, Population: Lectures at the Collège de France 1977-78. Translated by Graham Burchell, Palgrave Macmillan, 2007.

---. The Birth of Biopolitics: Lectures at the Collège de France 1978-79. Translated by Graham Burchell, Palgrave Macmillan, 2008.

Geertz, Clifford. The Interpretation of Cultures. Basic Books, 1973.

---. Local Knowledge: Further Essays in Interpretive Anthropology. Basic Books, 1983.

Giddens, Anthony. The Constitution of Society: Outline of the Theory of Structuration. University of California Press, 1984.

---. Modernity and Self-Identity: Self and Society in the Late Modern Age. Stanford University Press, 1991.

Goffman, Erving. Asylums: Essays on the Social Situation of Mental Patients and Other Inmates. Doubleday, 1961.

---. The Presentation of Self in Everyday Life. University of Edinburgh Social Sciences Research Centre, 1956.

---. Stigma: Notes on the Management of Spoiled Identity. Prentice-Hall, 1963.

Gramsci, Antonio. Prison Notebooks. Edited by Quintin Hoare and Geoffrey Nowell Smith, 3 vols., International Publishers, 1971-2007.

---. Selections from Cultural Writings. Edited by David Forgacs and Geoffrey Nowell-Smith, Harvard University Press, 1985.

---. Selections from Political Writings 1910-1920. Edited by Quintin Hoare, International Publishers, 1977.

Habermas, Jürgen. Knowledge and Human Interests. Translated by Jeremy J. Shapiro, Beacon Press, 1971.

---. The Structural Transformation of the Public Sphere. Translated by Thomas Burger, MIT Press, 1989.

---. The Theory of Communicative Action. 2 vols., Translated by Thomas McCarthy, Beacon Press, 1984-1987.

Hall, Stuart. Questions of Cultural Identity. SAGE Publications, 1996.

---. Resistance Through Rituals: Youth Subcultures in Post-war Britain. Hutchinson, 1976.

Harris, Marvin. The Rise of Anthropological Theory. Thomas Y. Crowell, 1968.

---. Cultural Materialism: The Struggle for a Science of Culture. Random House, 1979.

---. Cannibals and Kings: The Origins of Cultures. Random House, 1977.

Hobsbawm, Eric. Nations and Nationalism since 1780. Cambridge University Press, 1990.

---. The Age of Revolution: Europe 1789-1848. Weidenfeld and Nicolson, 1962.

Kroeber, Alfred L. Anthropology. Harcourt, Brace and Company, 1923.

---. The Nature of Culture. University of Chicago Press, 1952.

Lévi-Strauss, Claude. The Elementary Structures of Kinship. Translated by James Harle Bell, Beacon Press, 1969.

---. Structural Anthropology. Translated by Claire Jacobson and Brooke Grundfest Schoepf, Basic Books, 1963.

---. The Savage Mind. University of Chicago Press, 1966.

---. Tristes Tropiques. Translated by John and Doreen Weightman, Atheneum, 1974.

Lowie, Robert H. Primitive Society. Boni and Liveright, 1920.

---. Social Organization. Rinehart, 1948.

Lukács, Georg. History and Class Consciousness. Translated by Rodney Livingstone, MIT Press, 1971.

Mannheim, Karl. Ideology and Utopia. Translated by Louis Wirth and Edward Shils, Harcourt, Brace & World, 1936.

Marx, Karl. Capital. 3 vols., Translated by Ben Fowkes, Vintage Books, 1977-1981.

---. The Eighteenth Brumaire of Louis Bonaparte. International Publishers, 1963.

---. The German Ideology. International Publishers, 1970.

---. Grundrisse: Foundations of the Critique of Political Economy. Translated by Martin Nicolaus, Penguin Books, 1973.

Marx, Karl, and Friedrich Engels. The Communist Manifesto. International Publishers, 1948.

---. The Marx-Engels Reader. Edited by Robert C. Tucker, 2nd ed., W.W. Norton, 1978.

Mead, George Herbert. Mind, Self, and Society. Edited by Charles W. Morris, University of Chicago Press, 1934.

---. The Philosophy of the Present. Edited by Arthur E. Murphy, Open Court, 1932.

Mills, C. Wright. The Power Elite. Oxford University Press, 1956.

---. The Sociological Imagination. Oxford University Press, 1959.

Nozick, Robert. Anarchy, State, and Utopia. Basic Books, 1974.

Parsons, Talcott. The Social System. Free Press, 1951.

---. The Structure of Social Action. McGraw-Hill, 1937.

Poulantzas, Nicos. Political Power and Social Classes. Translated by Timothy O'Hagan, New Left Books, 1973.

Radcliffe-Brown, A.R. Structure and Function in Primitive Society. Cohen & West, 1952.

---. The Andaman Islanders. Cambridge University Press, 1922.

Rawls, John. A Theory of Justice. Harvard University Press, 1971.

---. Political Liberalism. Columbia University Press, 1993.

Sahlins, Marshall. Culture and Practical Reason. University of Chicago Press, 1976.

---. Historical Metaphors and Mythical Realities. University of Michigan Press, 1981.

Scott, James C. Domination and the Arts of Resistance: Hidden Transcripts. Yale University Press, 1990.

---. Seeing Like a State: How Certain Schemes to Improve the Human Condition Have Failed. Yale University Press, 1998.

---. Weapons of the Weak: Everyday Forms of Peasant Resistance. Yale University Press, 1985.

Shaw, George Bernard. The Intelligent Woman's Guide to Socialism and Capitalism. Brentano's, 1928.

---. Man and Superman. Constable, 1903.

---. Major Barbara. Constable, 1905.

---. Plays Pleasant and Unpleasant. 2 vols., Grant Richards, 1898.

Thompson, E.P. The Making of the English Working Class. Pantheon Books, 1963.

---. Whigs and Hunters: The Origin of the Black Act. Pantheon Books, 1975.

Tilly, Charles. From Mobilization to Revolution. Addison-Wesley, 1978.

---. Social Movements, 1768-2004. Paradigm Publishers, 2004.

Turner, Victor. The Ritual Process: Structure and Anti-Structure. Aldine, 1969.

---. Dramas, Fields, and Metaphors: Symbolic Action in Human Society. Cornell University Press, 1974.

Weber, Max. Economy and Society. Edited by Guenther Roth and Claus Wittich, University of California Press, 1978.

---. The Protestant Ethic and the Spirit of Capitalism. Translated by Talcott Parsons, Charles Scribner's Sons, 1958.

---. The Theory of Social and Economic Organization. Translated by A.M. Henderson and Talcott Parsons, Oxford University Press, 1947.

Williams, Raymond. Culture and Society 1780-1950. Columbia University Press, 1958.

---. Keywords: A Vocabulary of Culture and Society. Oxford University Press, 1976.

---. Marxism and Literature. Oxford University Press, 1977.

Wolf, Eric R. Europe and the People Without History. University of California Press, 1982.

---. Peasant Wars of the Twentieth Century. Harper & Row, 1969.

Chapter Thirteen

Ash, Timothy Garton. "The apocalypse that wasn't: AI was everywhere in 2024's elections, but deepfakes and misinformation were only part of the picture." Ash Center for Democratic Governance and Innovation, Harvard Kennedy School, 6 Aug. 2025, ash.harvard.edu/articles/the-apocalypse-that-wasnt-ai-was-everywhere-in-2024s-elections-but-deepfakes-and-misinformation-were-only-part-of-the-picture/.

"Auditing Political Exposure Bias: Algorithmic Amplification on Twitter During US Presidential Elections." arXiv, 3 Nov. 2024, arxiv.org/abs/2411.01852.

Baum, Frank, et al. "The Constructionist Approach to Framing: Bringing Culture Back In." Journal of Communication, 2007, fbaum.unc.edu/teaching/articles/J-Communication-2007-4.pdf..

"Big Question: How Does Digital Privacy Matter for Democracy and Its Advocates?" National Endowment for Democracy, 30 Apr. 2024, www.ned.org/big-question-how-does-digital-privacy-matter-for-democracy-and-its-advocates/.

"Can the Bias in Algorithms Help Us See Our Own?" Boston University, 9 Apr. 2024, www.bu.edu/articles/2024/can-the-bias-in-algorithms-help-us-see-our-own/.

"Climate change is a matter of justice – here's why." UNDP Climate Promise, 29 June 2023, climatepromise.undp.org/news-and-stories/climate-change-matter-justice-heres-why.

"Climate Change in the American Mind: Politics and Policy, Spring 2025." George Mason University Center for Climate Change Communication, 16 June 2025, climatecommunication.gmu.edu/all/climate-change-in-the-american-mind-politics-and-policy-spring-2025/.

"Collective action is key for building climate resilience." World Economic Forum, 2 June 2025, www.weforum.org/stories/2025/01/collective-action-is-key-to-climate-resilience/.

"Connecting the conceptual dots in embodied cognition." PMC, 29 June 2015, pmc.ncbi.nlm.nih.gov/articles/PMC4484980/.

Daring Cities. "POWERING COLLECTIVE ACTION TO RESPOND TO THE CLIMATE CRISIS." Daring Cities 2024 Report, Jan. 2025, daringcities.org/wp-content/uploads/2025/01/Daring-Cities-2024-Report.pdf.

De Cruz, Helen, and Johan De Smedt. "The artful mind meets art history: Toward a psycho-historical framework for the evolution of aesthetic cognition." Behavioral and Brain Sciences, helendecruz.net/docs/DeSmedt_DeCruz_BBS.pdf.

"Digital Threats to Democracy - The Carter Center." The Carter Center, 31 Dec. 2019, www.cartercenter.org/peace/democracy/digital-threats-to-democracy.html.

"Digital Threat Modeling Under Authoritarianism." Lawfare, 21 Sept. 2025, www.lawfaremedia.org/article/digital-threat-modeling-under-authoritarianism.

"Does Postmodernism Really Entail a Disregard for the Truth? Postmodernism, Science, and the Four Pillars of Ignorance." PMC, 16 Sept. 2020, pmc.ncbi.nlm.nih.gov/articles/PMC7527490/.

"Embodied Cognition." Internet Encyclopedia of Philosophy, 14 July 2025, iep.utm.edu/embodied-cognition/.

"Embodied Cognition." Stanford Encyclopedia of Philosophy, 24 June 2021, plato.stanford.edu/entries/embodied-cognition/.

"Environmental Justice: Case Studies." Resource Guides, UMass Medical School, 13 Mar. 2024, libraryguides.umassmed.edu/c.php?g=1388223&p=10282537.

"Environmental racism in Canada." PMC, 15 Dec. 2021, pmc.ncbi.nlm.nih.gov/articles/PMC9374073/.

"Environmental Racism and the Fight for Clean, Just Communities." ACT Environmental, 18 June 2025, www.actenviro.com/environmental-racism/.

"Environmental Racism in Chicago." Lake Forest College, 31 Dec. 2023, www.lakeforest.edu/academics/student-honors-and-research/student-publications/eukaryon/environmental-racism-in-chicago.

"Epistemic hegemony: the Western straitjacket and post-colonial resistance." Scielo

Brazil, 26 July 2020, www.scielo.br/j/rbpi/a/sHQ9fVJb-dv3JKHMh48nQDpp/?lang=en..

Fertik, Ted. "The Anti-Climate Common Sense." Phenomenal World, 24 Sept. 2025, www.phenomenalworld.org/analysis/the-anti-climate-common-sense/. Accessed 25 Sept. 2025.

"Framing Public Issues." FrameWorks Institute, July 2020, www.frameworksinstitute.org/app/uploads/2020/07/FramingPublicIssuesfinal.pdf. Accessed 25 Sept. 2025.

"Framing Processes and Social Movements." Annual Review of Sociology, 2000, fbaum.unc.edu/teaching/articles/AnnRevSoc-2000-Benford.pdf. 2025.

"Greta Thunberg and Climate Activism." E-International Relations, 25 Nov. 2023, www.e-ir.info/2023/11/26/greta-thunberg-and-climate-activism/.

"Historical materialism - Wikipedia." Wikipedia, 7 Mar. 2001, en.wikipedia.org/wiki/Historical_materialism..

"How AI deepfakes polluted elections in 2024." NPR, 21 Dec. 2024, www.npr.org/2024/12/21/nx-s1-5220301/deepfakes-memes-artificial-intelligence-elections.

"How Marx made history: the development of historical materialism." In Defence of Marxism, 22 July 2022, university.marxist.com/en/development-of-historical-materialism.

"Identity Politics - Stanford Encyclopedia of Philosophy." Stanford Encyclopedia of Philosophy, 15 July 2002, plato.stanford.edu/entries/identity-politics/.

"Identity politics pluses and minuses and continuing impact." Inside Higher Ed, 29 May 2024, www.insidehighered.com/opinion/columns/higher-ed-gamma/2024/05/30/identity-politics-pluses-and-minuses-and-continuing.

"Identifying and mitigating algorithmic bias in the safety net." PMC, 4 June 2025, pmc.ncbi.nlm.nih.gov/articles/PMC 12141433/.

"Intergenerational Approaches to Climate Action." CIRCA, 8 Jan. 2020, climateaging.bctr.cornell.edu/annotated-bibliography/intergenerational-approaches-to-climate-action.

"Intergenerational Justice." German Institute for Global and Area Studies, 23 Mar. 2021, dgap.org/en/research/glossary/climate-foreign-policy/intergenerational-justice.

"Intergenerational fairness from a climate policy perspective." European Parliament, 2025, www.europarl.europa.eu/RegData/etudes/BRIE/2025/769558/EPRS_BRI(2025)769558_EN.pdf.

"International Court's Ruling Could Transform Climate Action." Think Global Health, 14 Aug. 2025, www.thinkglobalhealth.org/article/international-courts-ruling-could-transform-climate-action.

Lentin, Alana. "Decolonising epistemologies." Alana Lentin, 9 Feb. 2017, www.alanalentin.net/2017/02/10/decolonising-epistemologies/. Accessed 25 Sept. 2025.

"The Making of a Movement (Together): How Climate Activists Understand Their Collective Identity." Wiley Online Library, 17 Aug. 2025, onlinelibrary.wiley.com/doi/10.1002/casp.70167.

"The Malicious Exploitation of Deepfake Technology: Political Manipulation and Disinformation Campaigns." Global Taiwan Institute, 6 May 2025, globaltaiwan.org/2025/05/the-malicious-exploitation-of-deepfake-technology/.

"Marxist Interventions into Contemporary Debates." Historical Materialism, 21 Dec. 2023, www.historicalmaterialism.org/article/marxist-interventions-into-contemporary-debates/.

"New Research Points to Possible Algorithmic Bias on X." Tech Policy Press, 16 Nov. 2024, techpolicy.press/new-research-points-to-possible-algorithmic-bias-on-x.

"Overcoming digital threats to democracy." Lowy Institute, 19 Feb. 2024, www.lowyinstitute.org/publications/overcoming-digital-threats-democracy. Accessed 25 Sept. 2025.

"Pandemic Risk and Standpoint Epistemology: A Matter of Solidarity." PMC, 24 Oct. 2021, pmc.ncbi.nlm.nih.gov/articles/PMC8544913

"PHILOSOPHICAL ANTHROPOLOGY." EOLSS, www.eolss.net/sample-chapters/c04/E6-20D-68-15.pdf. A

"Philosophical anthropology - New World Encyclopedia." New World Encyclopedia, 22 Nov. 2022, www.newworldencyclopedia.org/entry/Philosophical_anthropology. Accessed 25 Sept. 2025.

"Political deepfake videos no more deceptive than other fake news, research finds." Washington University in St. Louis, 18 Aug. 2024, source.washu.edu/2024/08/political-deepfake-videos-no-more-deceptive-than-other-fake-news-research-finds/

"Political Machines: The Rise of Automated Governance and the Global Challenge to Citizens Rights." Global Observatory, 26 Mar. 2025, theglobalobservatory.org/2025/03/political-machines-the-rise-of-automated-governance-and-the-global-challenge-to-citizens-rights/. Accessed 25 Sept. 2025.

"Postmodernism - Relativism, Deconstruction, Critique." Britannica, 27 July 2025, www.britannica.com/topic/postmodernism-philosophy/Postmodernism-and-relativism.

"The Problems with 'Intersectional' White Feminism in Practice: A Case Study of NGOs in Gender and Development." Oxford Academic, 15 June 2023, academic.oup.com/sp/article/30/2/630/6965078."Reading Minds and Telling Tales in a Cultural Borderland." PMC, 29 Feb. 2008, pmc.ncbi.nlm.nih.gov/articles/PMC2919771/.

"Recent Work in Standpoint Epistemology." Oxford Academic Analysis, 3 Oct. 2021, academic.oup.com/analysis/article/81/2/338/6333475.

"Relativism - Stanford Encyclopedia of Philosophy." Stanford Encyclopedia of Philosophy, 10 Sept. 2015, plato.stanford.edu/entries/relativism/.

"6 Cases of Environmental Justice Issues Across America." Environment.co, 29 July 2025, environment.co/environmental-justice/.

"Social construction of target populations: A theoretical framework for understanding government responses to crises." PMC, 22 Dec. 2021, pmc.ncbi.nlm.nih.gov/articles/PMC9017642/.

"Standpoint Epistemology and Epistemic Peerhood: A Defense of Epistemic Privilege." Cambridge Core, 19 Sept. 2024, www.cambridge.org/core/journals/journal-of-the-american-philosophical-association/article/standpoint-epistemology-and-epistemic-peerhood-a-defense-of-epistemic-privilege/137C3ABD67E82523A409A1960A230790.

"Standpoint Epistemology." New Discourses, 23 Mar. 2021, newdiscourses.com/tftw-standpoint-epistemology/.

"Targets, Objectives, and Emerging Tactics of Political Deepfakes." Recorded Future, 23 Sept. 2024, www.recordedfuture.com/research/targets-objectives-emerging-tactics-political-deepfakes.

"The challenges of platform capitalism: understanding the logic of a new business model." Institute for Public Policy Research, 24 Sept. 2025, www.ippr.org/articles/the-challenges-of-platform-capitalism.

"The epistemological irony of post-colonialism." SciELO South Africa, 31

Dec. 2024, www.scielo.org.za/scielo.php?script=sci_arttext&pid=S2074-77052023000100072.

"The failure of identity politics: A Marxist analysis." Marxist Left Review, 19 Aug. 2021, marxistleftreview.org/articles/the-failure-of-identity-politics-a-marxist-analysis/. Accessed 25 Sept. 2025.

"The Greta Thunberg Effect." Yale Program on Climate Change Communication, 28 June 2024, climatecommunication.yale.edu/publications/the-greta-thunberg-effect/.

"The impact of intersectional racial and gender biases on minority students' academic outcomes." Nature, 1 Jan. 2024, www.nature.com/articles/s41598-023-50392-x.

"Theses on Platform Capitalism and Neoliberalism." triple-c, www.triple-c.at/index.php/tripleC/article/view/1553/1662.

"The Validity of Karl Marx's Theory of Historical Materialism." University of Northern Iowa, scholarworks.uni.edu/context/mtie/article/1073/viewcontent/5_The_validity_of_Karl_Marxs_theory_Shimp.pdf.

"Translating the feminist theory of intersectionality into gender and development practice: challenges, possibilities and realities." SAGE Journals, 26 Apr. 2025, journals.sagepub.com/doi/10.1177/14647001241276185.

"Two Narratives of Platform Capitalism." Yale Law & Policy Review, 31 Jan. 2004, yalelawandpolicy.org/two-narratives-platform-capitalism.

"11.2 Case Studies in Environmental Inequity." Fiveable, 22 July 2024, fiveable.me/environmental-history/unit-11/case-studies-environmental-inequity/study-guide/hjQETVO6hFW10pOP.

"12 Examples of Environmental Racism to Know." Robert F. Smith, 12 May 2024, robertsmith.com/blog/examples-of-environmental-racism/.

"Voters: Here's how to spot AI 'deepfakes' that spread election-related misinformation." Carnegie Mellon University Heinz College, 15 Sept. 2024, www.heinz.cmu.edu/media/2024/October/voters-heres-how-to-spot-ai-deepfakes-that-spread-election-related-misinformation1.

"We Looked at 78 Election Deepfakes. Political Misinformation Is Not an AI Problem." Knight First Amendment Institute, 31 Dec. 2024, knightcolumbia.org/blog/we-looked-at-78-election-deepfakes-political-misinformation-is-not-an-ai-problem.

"What is meant by intergenerational climate justice?" London School of Economics, 15 Aug. 2024, www.lse.ac.uk/granthaminstitute/explainers/what-is-meant-by-intergenerational-climate-justice/.

"Why Platform Capitalism is Not the Future of Work." University of Leeds, eprints.whiterose.ac.uk/id/eprint/192534/3/WITGE%20submission%20Azz%20et%20al%2026%20Oct.pdf.

"Why Relativism is the Worst Idea Ever." Blog of the American Philosophical Association, 28 July 2021, blog.apaonline.org/2021/07/29/why-relativism-is-the-worst-idea-ever/.

"Zetetic standpoint epistemology." Cardiff University Open for Debate, 2 Feb. 2024, blogs.cardiff.ac.uk/openfordebate/zetetic-standpoint-epistemology/.

Zuboff, Shoshana. The Age of Surveillance Capitalism: The Fight for a Human Future at the New Frontier of Power. PublicAffairs, 2019.

Chapter Fourteen

Bronfenbrenner, Urie. The Ecology of Human Development: Experiments by Nature and Design. Harvard University Press, 1979.

Clark, Andy, and David Chalmers. "The Extended Mind." Phenomenology and the Cognitive Sciences, vol. 1, no. 4, 2008, pp. 5–20.

Dewey, John. Democracy and Education: An Introduction to the Philosophy of Education. Macmillan, 1916.

Foglia, Lisa, and Robert A. Wilson. "Embodied Cognition." Stanford Encyclopedia of Philosophy, Spring 2021 ed., plato.stanford.edu/entries/embodied-cognition/.

Gibson, James J. The Ecological Approach to Visual Perception. Houghton Mifflin, 1979.

Hutchins, Edwin. Cognition in the Wild. MIT Press, 1995.

Kaplan, Stephen. "The Restorative Benefits of Nature: Toward an Integrative Framework." Journal of Environmental Psychology, vol. 15, no. 3, 1995, pp. 169–182.

Kolb, Bryan, and Ian Q. Whishaw. Fundamentals of Human Neuropsychology. 7th ed., Worth, 2015.

Lave, Jean, and Etienne Wenger. Situated Learning: Legitimate Peripheral Participation. Cambridge University Press, 1991.

Masten, Ann S. "Ordinary Magic: Resilience Processes in Development." American Psychologist, vol. 56, no. 3, 2001, pp. 227–238.

Merleau-Ponty, Maurice. Phenomenology of Perception. Translated by Colin Smith, Routledge & Kegan Paul, 1962.

Odling-Smee, John, Kevin N. Laland, and Marcus W. Feldman. Niche Construction: The Neglected Process in Evolution. Princeton University Press, 2003.

Roth, Wolff-Michael, and Adrià Jornet. "Situated Cognition." International Encyclopedia of the Social & Behavioral Sciences, 2nd ed., Elsevier, 2015, pp. 377–382.

Sanders, Laura, et al. "Environmental Enrichment and Myelination: Critical Periods for Sensory Experience." Developmental Neurobiology, vol. 78, no. 1, 2018, pp. 1–12.

Varela, Francisco J., Evan Thompson, and Eleanor Rosch. The Embodied Mind: Cognitive Science and Human Experience. MIT Press, 1991.

Vygotsky, Lev S. Mind in Society: The Development of Higher Psychological Processes. Translated by Michael Cole et al., Harvard University Press, 1978.

Wilson, Robert A., and Lucia Foglia, editors. Embodied Cognition. Oxford University Press, 2011.

Woolf, Beverly. "Scaffolding in Education: Vygotsky's Theory in Practice." Journal of Educational Psychology, vol. 92, no. 4, 2020, pp. 785–798.

Chapter Fifteen

Bien, David. "Bridging Phenomenology and Neuroscience: Toward a Neurophenomenology." Journal of Consciousness Studies, vol. 11, no. 1, 2004, pp. 23–50.

Chalmers, David J. "Facing Up to the Problem of Consciousness." Journal of Consciousness Studies, vol. 2, no. 3, 1995, pp. 200–19.

Gallagher, Shaun, and Dan Zahavi. The Phenomenological Mind. 3rd ed., Routledge, 2019.

Haraway, Donna J. Situated Knowledges: The Science Question in Feminism and the Privilege of Partial Perspective. Routledge, 1991.

Husserl, Edmund. Ideas Pertaining to a Pure Phenomenology and to a Phenomenological Philosophy. Translated by F. Kersten, Springer, 1983.

Merleau-Ponty, Maurice. Phenomenology of Perception. Translated by Colin Smith, Routledge & Kegan Paul, 1962.

Smith, David Woodruff. Husserl and Intentionality: A Study of Mind, Meaning, and Language. Kluwer Academic, 2001.

Sprenger, Florian, and Axel Cleeremans, editors. Learned Nonuse and Disuse: Theoretical and Clinical Implications. Elsevier, 2016.

Varela, Francisco J., Evan Thompson, and Eleanor Rosch. The Embodied Mind: Cognitive Science and Human Experience. MIT Press, 1991.

Zahavi, Dan. Subjectivity and Selfhood: Investigating the First-Person Perspective. MIT Press, 2005

Chapter Sixteen

Chalmers, David J. "Facing Up to the Problem of Consciousness." Journal of Consciousness Studies, vol. 2, no. 3, 1995, pp. 200–19.

Gallagher, Shaun, and Dan Zahavi. The Phenomenological Mind. 3rd ed., Routledge, 2019.

Haraway, Donna J. Situated Knowledges: The Science Question in Feminism and the Privilege of Partial Perspective. Routledge, 1991.

Husserl, Edmund. Ideas Pertaining to a Pure Phenomenology and to Phenomenological Philosophy. Translated by F. Kersten, Springer, 1983.

Lincoln, Yvonna S., and Egon G. Guba. Naturalistic Inquiry. SAGE Publications, 1985.

Merleau-Ponty, Maurice. Phenomenology of Perception. Translated by Colin Smith, Routledge & Kegan Paul, 1962.

Noddings, Nel. Caring: A Relational Approach to Ethics and Moral Education. University of California Press, 1984.

Smith, David Woodruff. Husserl and Intentionality: A Study of Mind, Meaning, and Language. Kluwer Academic, 2001.

Varela, Francisco J., Evan Thompson, and Eleanor Rosch. The Embodied Mind: Cognitive Science and Human Experience. MIT Press, 1991.

Chapter Seventeen

Bronfenbrenner, Urie. The Ecology of Human Development: Experiments by Nature and Design. Harvard University Press, 1979.

Chalmers, David J. "Facing Up to the Problem of Consciousness." Journal of Consciousness Studies, vol. 2, no. 3, 1995, pp. 200–19.

Clark, Andy, and David Chalmers. "The Extended Mind." Phenomenology and the Cognitive Sciences, vol. 1, no. 4, 2008, pp. 5–20.

Gibson, James J. The Ecological Approach to Visual Perception. Houghton-Mifflin, 1979.

Husserl, Edmund. Ideas Pertaining to a Pure Phenomenology and to a Phenomenological Philosophy. Translated by F. Kersten, Springer, 1983.

Kaplan, Stephen. "The Restorative Benefits of Nature: Toward an Integrative Framework." Journal of Environmental Psychology, vol. 15, no. 3, 1995, pp. 169–82.

Merleau-Ponty, Maurice. Phenomenology of Perception. Translated by Colin Smith, Routledge & Kegan Paul, 1962.

Roth, Wolff-Michael, and Adrià Jornet. "Situated Cognition." International Encyclopedia of the Social & Behavioral Sciences, 2nd ed., Elsevier, 2015, pp. 377–82.

Sanders, Laura, et al. "Environmental Enrichment and Myelination: Critical Periods for Sensory Experience." Developmental Neurobiology, vol. 78, no. 1, 2018, pp. 1–12.

Smith, David Woodruff. Husserl and Intentionality: A Study of Mind, Meaning, and Language. Kluwer Academic, 2001.

Varela, Francisco J., Evan Thompson, and Eleanor Rosch. The Embodied Mind: Cognitive Science and Human Experience. MIT Press, 1991.

Vygotsky, Lev S. Mind in Society: The Development of Higher Psychological Processes. Translated by Michael Cole et al., Harvard University Press, 1978.

Wilson, Robert A., and Lucia Foglia, editors. Embodied Cognition. Oxford University Press, 2011.

Chapter Eighteen

"A Brief History of Collective Intelligence, Democracy, and Governance." Lex Paulson, Taylor & Francis, 31 Oct. 2015.

"Algorithmic Amplification for Collective Intelligence." Knight First Amendment Institute, 17 Sept. 2023, knightcolumbia.org/content/algorithmic-amplification-for-collective-intelligence.

Ash, Timothy Garton. "The Apocalypse That Wasn't: AI Was everywhere in 2024's Elections, but Deepfakes and Misinformation Were Only Part of the Picture." Ash Center for Democratic Governance and Innovation, Harvard Kennedy School, 6 Aug. 2025, ash.harvard.edu/articles/the-apocalypse-that-wasnt-ai-was

-everywhere-in-2024s-elections-but-deepfakes-and-misinformation-were-only-part-of-the-picture/.

"China's Social Credit System: Mechanisms and Impacts." Tsinghua University Report, July 2025.

"Climate Change in the American Mind: Politics and Policy, Spring 2025." George Mason University Center for Climate Change Communication, 16 June 2025, climatecommunication.gmu.edu/all/climate-change-in-the-american-mind-politics-and-policy-spring-2025/.

"Collective action is key for building climate resilience." World Economic Forum, 2 June 2025, www.weforum.org/stories/2025/01/collective-action-is-key-to-climate-resilience/.

"Connecting the Conceptual Dots in Embodied Cognition." PubMed Central, 29 June 2015, pmc.ncbi.nlm.nih.gov/articles/PMC4484980/.

"Democratic Reason: The Mechanisms of Collective Intelligence in Deliberation." SSRN, 31 Mar. 2011, papers.ssrn.com/sol3/papers.cfm?abstract_id=1845709.

"Democracy, Epistemic Agency, and AI: Political Epistemology in Practice." PubMed Central, 21 Nov. 2022, pmc.ncbi.nlm.nih.gov/articles/PMC9685050/.

"Environmental Racism and the Fight for Clean, Just Communities." ACT Environmental, 18 June 2025, www.actenviro.com/environmental-racism/.

"Epistemic Democracy: Combining Diverse Perspectives for Better Decisions." Deliberative Democracy Journal, vol. 6, no. 2, 15 Apr. 2012, delibdemjournal.org/article/401/galley/4668/view/.

"Embodiment and Agency in a Digital World." Frontiers in Psychology, 5 Sept. 2024, www.frontiersin.org/articles/10.3389/fpsyg.2024.1392949/full.

"Environmental Credit Score Pilot and Behavioral Changes." Tsinghua University Report, July 2025.

"Exploring Epistemology from Different Cultural Perspectives." Aithor, 16 July 2024, aithor.com/essay-examples/exploring-epistemology-from-different-cultural-perspectives.

"Governance and Collaboration in the Wikimedia Development Process." Wikimedia Research Report No. 12, 31 July 2025, research.wikimedia.org/report.html.

Ham, Margaret. "The Constructionist Approach to Framing: Bringing Culture Back In." Journal of Communication, vol. 57, no. 4, 2007, fbaum.unc.edu/teaching/articles/J-Communication-2007-4.pdf.

"Linux Foundation Governance Model." Linux Foundation, 2025, linuxfoundation.org/governance.

"Media Literacy and Education in Finland." Finland Life & Society Toolkit, 11 Mar. 2024, toolbox.finland.fi/life-society/media-literacy-and-education-in-finland/.

Nussbaum, Martha. Creating Capabilities: The Human Development Approach. Belknap Press, 2011.

"Opportunities and Risks of LLMs for Scalable Deliberation with Polis." ArXiv, 25 Feb. 2021, arxiv.org/html/2306.11932.

Rawls, John. Political Liberalism. Columbia University Press, 1993.

"Recursive Patterns in Online Echo Chambers." Scientific Reports, vol. 9, 26 Dec. 2019, www.nature.com/articles/s41598-019-56191-7.

"Social Drivers and Algorithmic Mechanisms on Digital Media." PubMed Central, 18 July 2023, pmc.ncbi.nlm.nih.gov/articles/PMC11373151/.

"Social Media Polarization and Echo Chambers in the Context of Political Events." PubMed Central, 4 Aug. 2021, pmc.ncbi.nlm.nih.gov/articles/PMC8371575/.

Srnicek, Nick. Platform Capitalism. Polity, 2017.

"Tactics of News Literacy: How Young People Access, Evaluate, and Mobilize Information." Communication Research, vol. 50, no. 2, 13 Mar. 2023, journals.sagepub.com/doi/10.1177/14614448211011447.

"Toward Building Deliberative Digital Media: From Subversion to Collaboration." PubMed Central, 14 Oct. 2024, pmc.ncbi.nlm.nih.gov/articles/PMC11475399/.

"Ubuntu and Consensus in African Governance." Ubuntu Research Review, vol. 3, 2024, ubuntujournal.org/consensus-in-african-governance.

"Wikimedia Foundation Public Policy Initiatives." Wikimedia Foundation, 24 Aug. 2025, wikimediafoundation.org/public-policy/.

"What We Can Learn from Finland." UW Center for an Informed Public, 28 Feb. 2023, cip.uw.edu/2023/03/01/finland-media-literacy/.

"Will vs. Reason: The Populist and Technocratic Forms of Political Representation." American Political Science Review, vol. 111, no. 1, Feb. 2017, academic.oup.com/apsr/article/111/1/148/5489877.

Zuboff, Shoshana. The Age of Surveillance Capitalism: The Fight for a Human Future at the New Frontier of Power. PublicAffairs, 2019.

Chapter Nineteen

Chalmers, David J., and Andy Clark. "The Extended Mind." Mind, vol. 33, no. 121, 1998, pp. 77–100.

Clark, Andy. Supersizing the Mind: Embodiment, Action, and Cognitive Extension. Oxford University Press, 2008.

Gibson, James J. The Ecological Approach to Visual Perception. Houghton Mifflin, 1979.

Hutchins, Edwin. Cognition in the Wild. MIT Press, 1995.

Ingold, Tim. The Perception of the Environment: Essays on Livelihood, Dwelling and Skill. Routledge, 2000.

Lave, Jean, and Etienne Wenger. Situated Learning: Legitimate Peripheral Participation. Cambridge University Press, 1991.

Pea, Roy D. "Practices of Distributed Intelligence and Designs for Education." Distributed Cognitions: Psychological and Educational Considerations, edited by Gary Salomon, Cambridge University Press, 1993, pp. 47–87.

Suchman, Lucy A. Plans and Situated Actions: The Problem of Human-Machine Communication. Cambridge University Press, 1987.

Vygotsky, Lev S. Mind in Society: The Development of Higher Psychological Processes. Edited by Michael Cole et al., Harvard University Press, 1978.

Wild, Chris. "Event-Structure Analysis: Foundations and Examples." Journal of Behavioral Science Methods, vol. 45, no. 2, 2012, pp. 123–145.

Chapter Twenty

My Rambling Mind!

Index

Index

A
abstract concepts, 159, 254, 285, 290
achieving cognitive harmony, 307, 323, 388
adaptation, creative, 71, 113
algorithmic curation, 238
Algorithmic Mind Painting, 359, 371
algorithmic reforms, 378
algorithms, machine learning, 101
American pragmatism, 117, 142
analytical reasoning, 173, 177
archaeological record, 11, 23, 393
architecture
 human psychological, 185–86
 neural, 149, 255–56
 neurobiological, 2, 392
authoritarian systems, 138
authorities
 ecclesiastical, 31, 33

institutional, 28, 225
authority structures, 242
autonomous cultural, 160, 217
autonomy, 202, 219, 222, 307, 321
  rational, 210
availability, 256, 275

B
barriers, political, 362, 374
behavior
  consumer, 188
  ethical, 316
  reconciliation, 151
beliefs
  religious, 18, 85
  shared, 34, 221–22, 310
belief systems, 10, 186, 235
Biased Brush, 169
biases, negative, 206
Brain Architecture, 175
brain structure, 176, 203, 266

C
Canvas of Cosmic Order, 314
capitalism, 219–20, 230
capitalist mind paintings, 220
challenges, fundamental, 32, 142, 145

chaos, cognitive, 72, 97
Christian, 27, 29, 31, 33–34, 37
Christianity, 26–27, 32, 36
climate change, 245, 362, 374
climate coalitions, 247
climate mind paintings, 249
climate paralysis, 250
climate politics, 235, 244, 362, 374
climate politics emphasis, 249
cognition, collective, 53, 69, 73
cognitive architecture, 76, 106, 113, 119, 172, 204
 constrained, 169, 171, 215
cognitive biases, 170, 185–86, 211, 396
cognitive challenges, 255, 261
cognitive dissonance, 52, 73, 83, 200, 382
cognitive harmony, 10, 99, 306, 309–10, 312, 321, 323, 382
cognitive mind paintings, 253
cognitive ordering, social dimension of, 319, 323, 325
cognitive palettes, 107
cognitive patterns, 394
Cognitive Resilience, 265
cognitive science, 6, 139
cognitive strategies, 165, 200
cognitive structures, 14
cognitive surplus, 15
cognitive tools, 2, 64, 114, 263–65, 323
coherence

abstract metaphysical, 83
logical, 326
rational, 54
coherent self-concepts, 200
collective mind paintings, 79, 221
collective welfare, 82, 92
communities
 agricultural, 17–18
 linguistic, 106, 109
comparative analysis, 90, 164, 167
comprehensive mind painting, 90–91
computational processes, 154, 156–57, 160–62
consciousness, collective, 221–23
constructed character, 98–99, 106, 110, 116, 119, 140, 177, 180, 188, 238, 240–41, 245, 247, 251
constructed realities, 326, 363, 375, 383
construction, niche, 260, 273–74, 278
contemporary challenges, 22, 24, 141, 235, 273, 325, 389
contemporary political life, 358, 370
core Enlightenment assumptions, 88, 93
cosmic order, 19, 72
cosmologies, 72–73, 316, 392
creative expression, 257, 261, 264, 269–70, 272, 277
creative processes, 97, 115–16, 141, 399
creative reinterpretation, 22, 25–26, 33, 43
critical reasoning, 67, 70
cultural continuity, 221

cultural development, 10, 13-14, 111, 116, 142, 216
cultural disruption, 274
cultural diversity, 12, 73, 132, 213, 271-72
 local, 12
cultural drift, 11, 26-27, 29-37
 historical, 388
 linguistic, 104
cultural drift management, 30
cultural drift reveals, 22
cultural evolution, 10, 46, 98, 109, 161
 cumulative, 152
cultural mind paintings, 102, 115, 251, 398
Cultural Psychology, 200
cultural transmission, 21, 35, 146, 150, 165, 167, 178, 257-58, 393, 398
cultural values, 21, 23, 73, 201-2
cultural variations, 92, 107, 111-12

D
democratic mind paintings, 368, 379
determinism
 biological, 396
 ecological, 274
 technological, 163, 368
developmental niche construction, 259-61, 275
developmental niches, 261, 278-79
dialogue, creative, 22, 24

Digital Commons Governance, 368, 379
digital mind paintings, 248, 360, 372
digital technologies, 220, 262, 264, 269–70, 277, 398
distinctive mind painting, 33, 244
distortions, cognitive, 205, 208
Divergent Canvases, 306–7
domains, cognitive, 7
dominance, political, 227, 229
dual-process architecture, 172, 174

E
ecological niches, 146, 165
education
 ecological, 263
 humanistic, 68
 institutional, 268
 rational, 93
educational philosophy, 68
elements, cultural, 227, 231, 278
embodied cognition, 235, 281, 290, 302, 388
embodied engagement, 277, 284, 288, 290, 293–94, 302
Embodied Existence, 296, 301
embodied practices, 235, 241, 244, 285, 358, 370
emerging possibilities, 66, 144, 162, 164, 166–67
Emerging Technopolitical Trends, 368, 379
emotional responses, 87, 157, 199, 236
empirical analysis, 306

empiricism, 75, 82
Enlightenment, 67, 69, 71–72, 74–75, 80, 82, 84, 87, 89, 92–95
 collective, 384
Enlightenment approaches, 67
Enlightenment arguments, 93
Enlightenment assumptions, 88–89
Enlightenment ideals, 90
Enlightenment innovations, 71
Enlightenment methodology, 67
Enlightenment mind painting, 71, 88, 93–95
Enlightenment principles, 92
Enlightenment rationalism, 66, 70
Enlightenment Social Revolution, 82
environmental niches, 260
environmental stress, 266
environmental transitions, 6
environmental variables, 3
environments
 cultural, 27
 digital, 270
Erasmus, 67, 69
evolutionary foundations, 147, 398
evolutionary inheritances, 115, 396, 399
Evolutionary Mind Paintings, 145

G

Global Perspectives, 364, 376
grammatical structures, 111, 173
group coherence, 4

H
Hegemony, 363, 375
 cultural, 227–29
historical development, 14, 25, 27, 36–37, 88, 92, 99
historical evolution, 26
historical processes, 275
human agency, 12–13, 210, 215
human capacity, 91, 96–97, 114–15, 140–41, 280, 399
human cognitive variation, 204
human consciousness, 2, 14, 19, 36, 76, 126, 392, 396, 399
human creativity, 13, 23, 101, 115–16, 215
Humanist Bridge, 66
human languages, 105–6, 147–48, 151–52
human meaning-making, 107, 110, 397–99
human meaning-making processes, 394, 398–99
human minds, 7, 15, 121, 189, 265, 390, 400
human nature, 88, 93, 140, 226
human psychology, 78, 188, 202, 210
human rationality, 85, 95, 97

I
identity
 collective, 223, 232, 320

political, 231, 241, 247
Institutional Implications, 365, 377
institutional reform, 74, 84–85, 87, 139
intellectual engagement, 68, 84, 109
interdisciplinary, 273
Intersectional Mind Painting, 240, 361, 373

K
Karl Marx, 217

L
language processing, 6, 110–11
liberation theology, 33
limitations
  human cognitive and cultural, 34
  human psychological, 211
  institutional, 247
  neurobiological, 396
  temporal, 17
limitations 153
linguistic systems, 110, 114–16
logical reasoning, 98, 101, 115, 154
logical systems, 98–101

M
material conditions, 13–14, 23–24, 217, 220, 222, 241, 250, 398

material environments, 253–54, 256, 261, 275
medieval period, 21, 43
Medieval Philosophy, 51
mental mind paintings, 274
metacognition, 382
metacognitive practices, 383
metaphors, 6, 22, 85, 224, 237, 287, 362, 374, 387
 conceptual, 109
mind painting framework, 106, 115, 122, 235, 251–52, 358, 362, 370, 374
moral philosophy, 86–87, 91, 94

N
narrative coherence, 189
narrative construction, 260, 396
narratives, 178, 221, 238, 261, 308, 382, 387, 393, 397
 coherent, 180, 392
 cultural, 187, 395
 evolutionary, 12
 historical, 231
 shared, 244
 symbolic, 1, 4
narrative thinking, 392
national identity, 223, 230–31
natural laws, 84, 250
natural rights, 80, 92–93
natural variations, 203, 214

neo-cortex constraint, 387–88
neurological mechanisms, 178, 210, 214
neuroscience, 169, 212, 273, 396, 398
 cognitive, 14
Nicaea, 30
non-human mind paintings, 144, 152
Normative Criteria, 365, 377

P
paralysis, political, 247
Patriarchal Mind Paintings, 284
pattern recognition, 6, 14, 114, 145, 153–54, 165, 388, 396
pattern-recognition, 99
political analysis, 243
political arrangements, inevitable, 250
political epistemology, 358, 370, 381
political preferences, 359, 371
pragmatists, 132, 134, 137–38
primate cultures, 147
principles
 ecological, 274, 278
 fundamental structural, 105
 logical, 110
 rational, 84, 99, 102
processing, cognitive, 79, 111, 188, 199
progress
 linear, 311, 313, 323, 325

philosophical, 24
psychological coherence, 192, 325
psychological disorders, 180, 196, 206, 214, 324
psychological insights, 171, 205, 308

R
rational analysis, 74, 76, 321, 325
rational foundations, 87–88, 94
rational reconstruction, 93
religious orthodoxies, 83, 91
religious truth claims, 36
Renaissance humanism, 66, 71
Renaissance humanists, 71
revelation, divine, 52, 54, 61–62, 67

S
sedentary revolution, 15, 23–24, 388
social cognition, 3, 160, 178
social cohesion, 1, 19, 222
social conditioning, 311
social conformity, 213
social construction, 35, 126, 236, 389
social continuity, 10
social control, 213
social harmony, 85, 312–13, 325
social hierarchies, 8, 16, 91, 223
social identities, 191, 241, 319, 323, 361, 373

social organization, 9, 11, 14–15, 24, 82, 88, 140, 218, 226, 228, 321, 323
social reform, 68–69, 82, 87, 94, 128
Society's Canvas, 217
spatial relationships, 155, 194, 254
spiritual authenticity, 33–34
spiritual development, 315, 318–20
spiritual insights, 34, 36
standards
 moral, 91
 rational, 93
statistical analysis, 225
stereotypes, actively constructed, 237
stimulus-response patterns, 127
structural continuities, 11
survival applications, 6
survival function, 204
survival skills, master, 17
synthetic mind paintings, 31, 34, 155–56
systematic distortions, 190

T
Taoism, 306, 310, 324, 389
Taoist communities, 311, 319
Technocracy, 363, 375
Temporal Mind Painting, 362, 374
truth

divine, 61
mathematical, 101, 112
sacred, 34, 61

U
unconscious attitudes, 184
unconscious desires, 182
unconscious priming mechanisms, 188

V
Vective reality, 122
Vectivity, 131–32
vigilance, cognitive, 4

[Created with TExtract / www.TExtract.com]